Please contact authors for permission requests. Information about authors can be found at:

https://sites.google.com/view/manoj-thomas/books?authuser=0

Screenshots in the book are for educational and instructional purposes only.

Front cover: **20:50** by Richard Wilson

Contemporary art at The Museum of Old and New Art (MONA), Hobart, Tasmania, Australia.

Photo by Manoj A. Thomas

ISBN: 978-0-6489304-1-9

First edition Aug 2020.

About the authors

Manoj Abraham Thomas is an Associate Professor of Information Systems at The University of Sydney Business School, Australia. He has longstanding experience in engaged research and interdisciplinary studies that involve Information Systems. His research is driven by opportunities to address global challenges through the use of emerging technologies and data science. Manoj has led numerous projects including many global ICT4D initiatives. He actively collaborates with leading academic institutions in Europe and the United States, as well as government agencies and international Non-Profit Organizations.

Ammu Susanna Zachariah is a Data Analytics professional. Her primary interest lies in Big Data Visualization and Visual Analytics. She is passionate about creating insights through innovative dashboards and story boards. She is actively involved in the field of data visualization through her professional career and various consulting projects. Through this book she hopes to translate her knowledge to help beginners kick-start their analytics journey.

Preface

Data visualization has emerged as a popular topic within business intelligence and data science… so popular that many books have been published discussing different aspects of it. This book came about as the result of a recognized lack of guidance for a keen person to get started with Tableau.

Whether a small outfit (such as a local grocery store or a family owned restaurant) or a large corporation (such as a hospital or an e-commerce store), identifying trends and patterns from data are increasingly important to decision makers. Data visualization is a powerful way to gain insights from data, reflect on the trends and patterns, and decide future actions. This is where Tableau Desktop and Tableau Public have emerged as leaders.

Tableau is a flexible, and powerful platform to create effective data visualizations. It enables the creation of visually appealing and interactive worksheets, dashboards, infographics, and visual stories. Drill-down and roll-up capabilities allow the user to easily interact with data based on the user's desired objectives.

The focus of this book is to help you get started with Tableau Desktop. It aims to provide a sound foundation and introduction to Tableau using examples in an easy to follow manner. The dataset used in the examples and the solution file are available for free in case the reader of this book wishes to follow along or have a reference.

We would like to point out that the book is not an exhaustive guide on Tableau, but it covers all essentials required for you to explore more advanced Tableau capabilities. New features are added to Tableau software almost every quarter. Nevertheless, the fundamentals generally remain the same. Thus, we hope that users of this book will find it a useful guide to understand Tableau and be encouraged to take the next step towards discovering advanced Tableau capabilities in the future.

Manoj A. Thomas
Ammu S. Zachariah
Aug 2020

Contents

1 Introduction to Tableau

Three types of Tableau products are available:

- Tableau Desktop: Helps create visualizations and interactive workbooks and dashboards for individual use. It can be used to work with a variety of data formats, from excel to large databases such as Oracle or Microsoft SQL server.
- Tableau Public: Tableau online is a free software and functions as a host service in the cloud. Any Tableau visualization uploaded to Tableau online is available to the public, so there is no privacy or confidentiality in the visualization. It is also a great resource for new users to find new ways of building visualizations and learn from others.
- Tableau Server (and Tableau Online): Helps create visualizations and interactive workbooks and dashboards for enterprise application. It enables safe and secure sharing of visualizations, but it is not a free software. Tableau Server is a solution available for businesses to install on a server, whereas Tableau Online is a hosted service provided by Tableau.

1.1 Tableau File Types

The difference file types associated with Tableau are:

- Tableau Workbook (.twb): Stores visualization without source data.
- Tableau data source (.tds): Stores the server address, password and other information required to access a data source.
- Tableau bookmark (.tbm): Stores a connection to a worksheet in another Tableau workbook.
- Tableau data extract (.tde): Stores Tableau data as a filtered and aggregated extract
- Tableau packaged workbook (.twbx): Stores extracted data and visualizations for viewing in Tableau.

1.2 Getting started with Tableau

- Tableau opens to display the start page.

Connect Pane: Provides options to load a file or server or saved data source.

Open: Lists the recent files in the form of thumbnails.

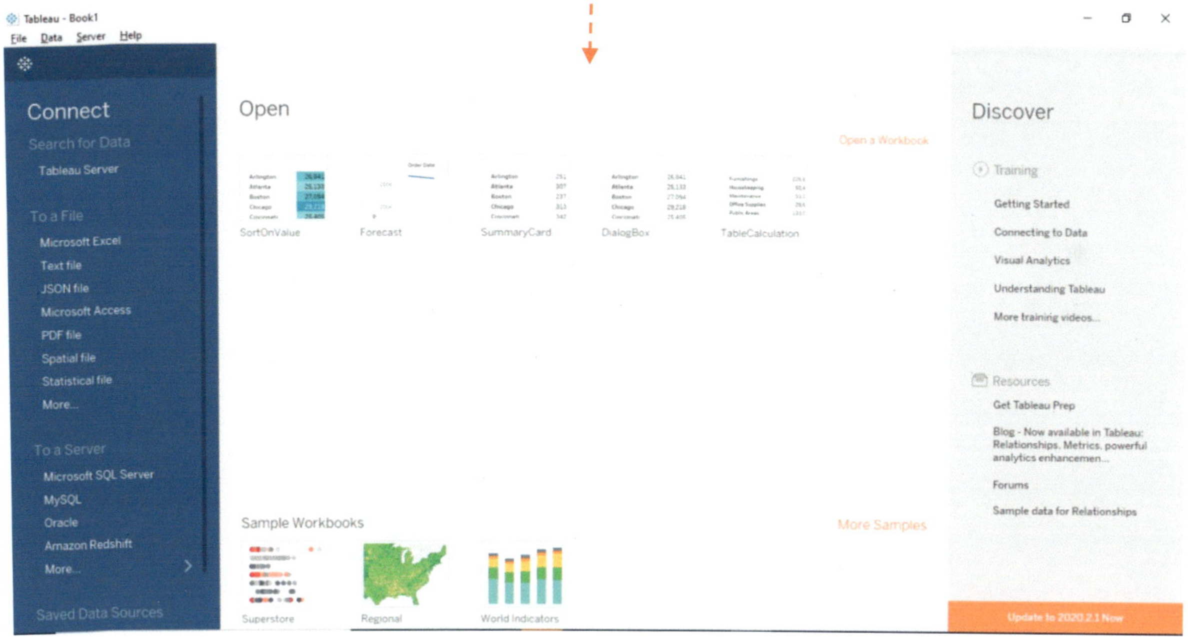

1.3 Resources used in this book

- Examples presented in the book uses an excel based dataset: **Dragon_Mart.xlsx**
- Tableau solution file is: **Solution.twb**

The dataset and the Tableau solution file are available for download from:

https://1drv.ms/u/s!As1YbuHG5fmKgZIerrmd6V524mnw6w?e=vzRZXn

- Examples presented in this book was developed using Tableau Professional (v.2020.2.0 64 bit).
    - Some differences might be there in the screenshots depending on whether you are using a Windows or a Mac computers, and depending on the version on the Tableau software.

> Just like any other good software, Tableau provides many ways to do an operation. The book shows some of the simpler and more common options to achieve an intended outcome.

2 Connecting to Data

- Involves locating data and using appropriate types of connections to read the data.
- Tableau can connect with various data sources such as text, excel file and databases to big data queries.
- In this tutorial data is used from an excel file.

2.1 Connecting to data source with excel

- Under "Connect" – Under Files click on Microsoft excel – Navigate and select the file "**Dragon_Mart.xlsx**" as shown below.

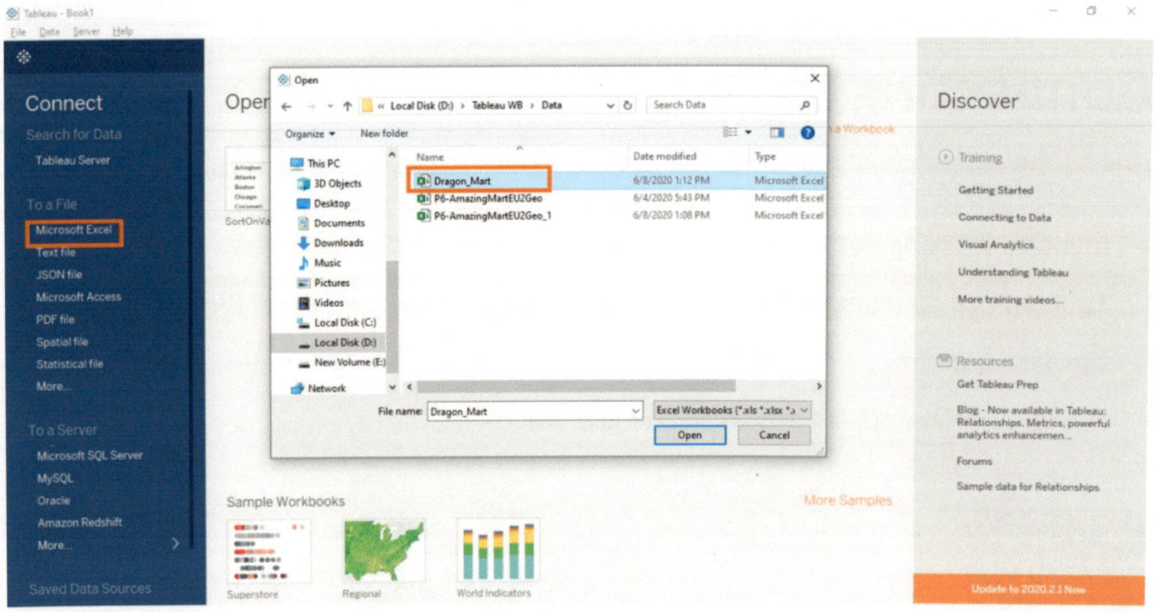

2.2 Importing data to workbook

- Data is imported via the Data Source page.
- Data Source page defines the data user wants to import into the Tableau workbook.
- Here, you can view the first few rows of data and make changes such as sort or hide fields, split fields into multiple columns, rename column headers, all without modifying the original data.

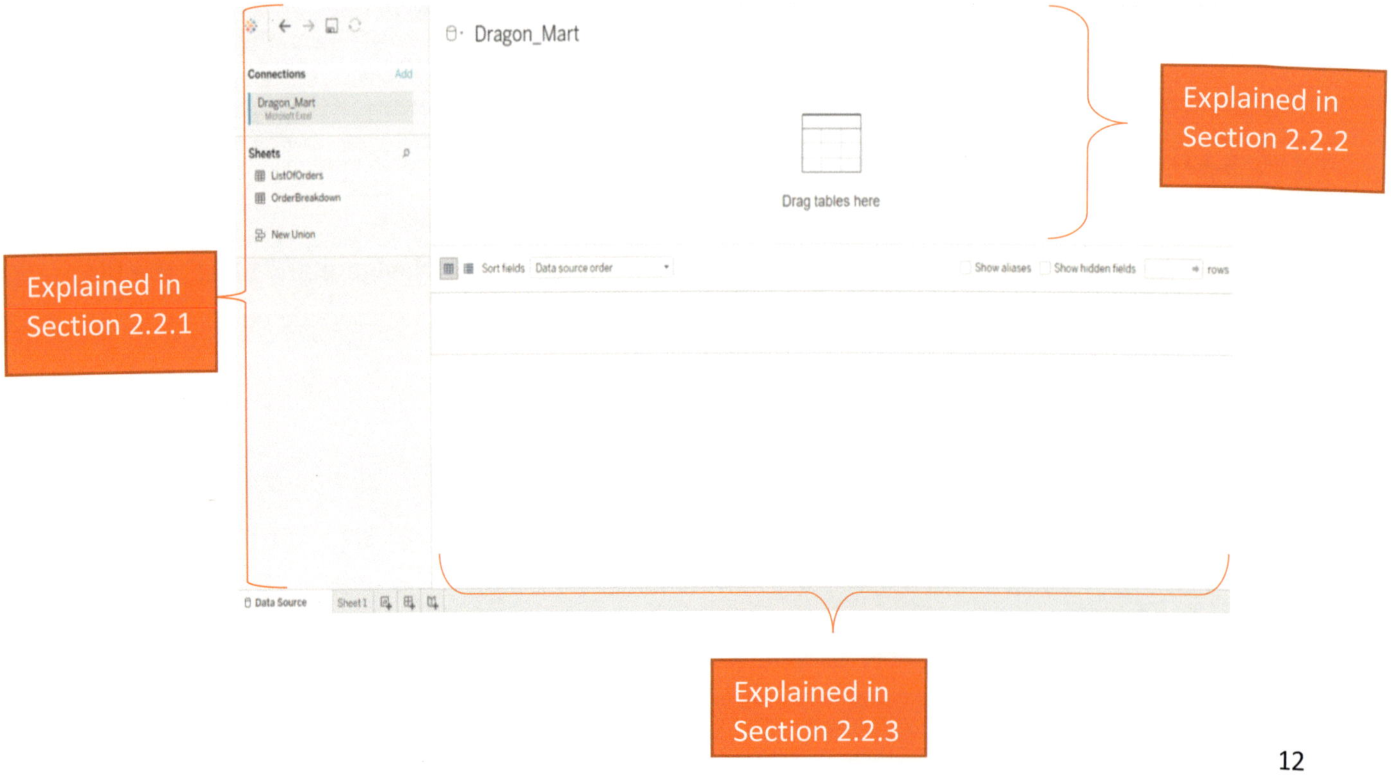

2.2.1 Creating Connections

Lists the data source files under *"Connections"* and sheets associated with the file under *"Sheets"*.

Under "Connections" we observe data source **"Dragon_Mart "**

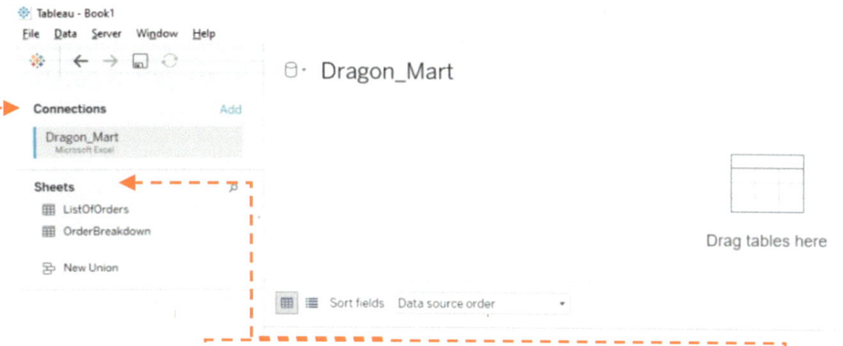

Under "Sheets" we observe two sheets: ListOfOrders & Orderbreakdown

Validation against Excel File: Data Source name: *"Dragon_Mart"*

Sheets*: "ListOfOrders"* and *"OrderBreakdown"*

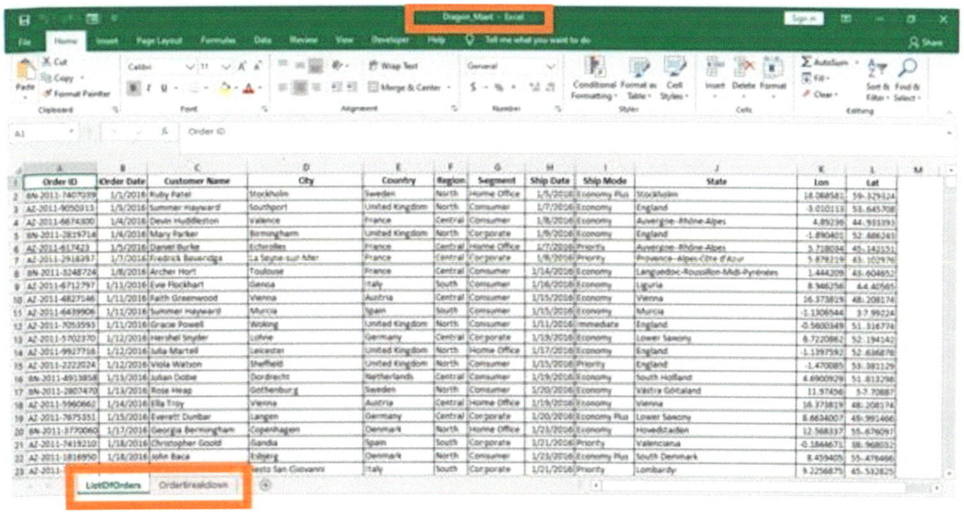

2.2.2 Importing Excel sheets to Tableau

Sheets to be imported to Tableau are dragged onto the pane shown in orange or by double clicking on the sheet name under the heading "Sheets".

Drag the sheet *"ListOfOrders"* onto the orange pane as shown below. All the data from *"ListofOrders"* is imported and can be observed at the lower half.

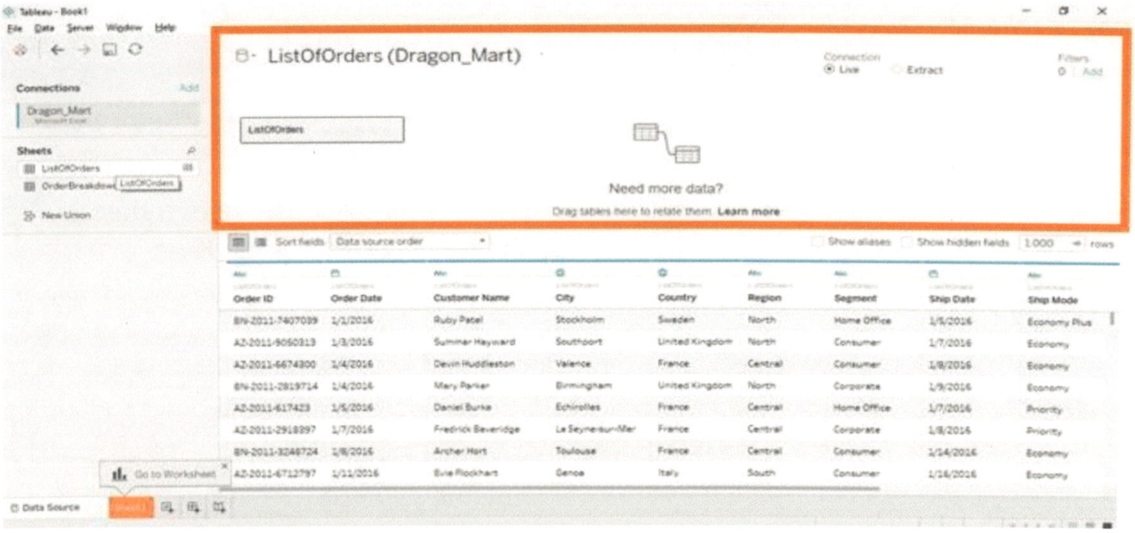

➢ If prompted you can specify the type of relationship to establish between the two table

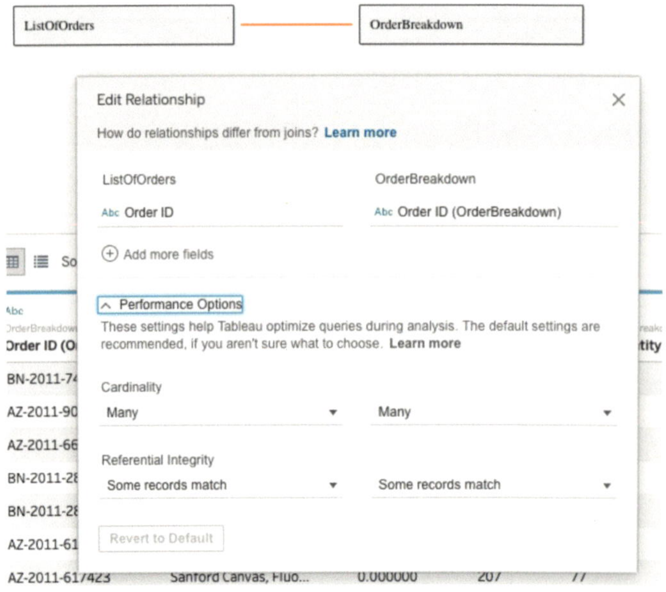

- ➢ Types of Connection: Once the sheet is imported, option to choose the type of connection appears on the top right corner as shown in the above screenshot.
- ➢ Two types of connections are *Extract* & *Live*
- ➢ *Extract*
  - Extract is a snapshot of the data; the extract needs to be refreshed to receive updates from the original data source.
  - Extracts tend to be much faster than live connections.
- ➢ *Live*
  - Offer the convenience of real-time updates, with any changes in the data source reflected in Tableau.

2.2.3 Preview of imported data

Displays a preview of the data imported in the form of rows and columns.

- ➢ Each column heading consists of icons.
  - ○ Icon represents the datatype of the respective columns.

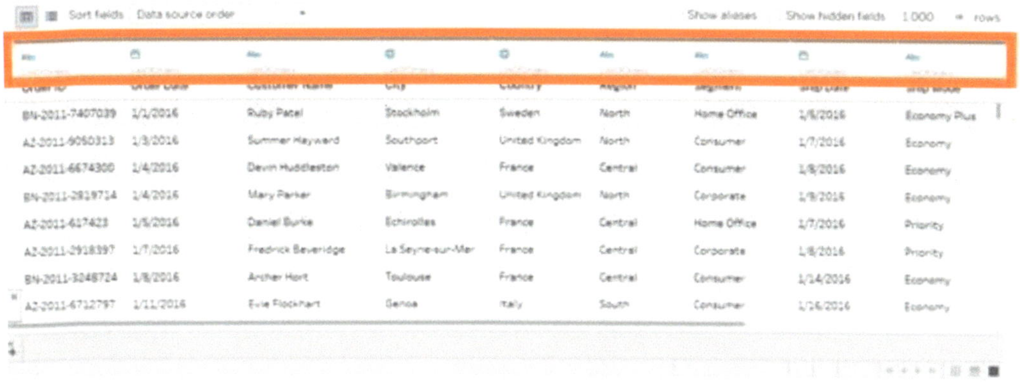

- ➢ Table below describes the different types of icons you will see in the preview header.

Icon	Data type
Abc	Text (string) values
	Date values
	Date & Time values
#	Numerical values
T|F	Boolean values (relational only)
	Geographic values (used with maps)
	Cluster Group (used with Find Clusters in Data)

Source: Tableau Desktop and Web Authoring Help

3 Creating Joins

- Joins are used to link multiple tables using similar fields.
- Create a join between *"ListOfOrders"* and *"OrderBreakdown"*
- Double click on the *"ListOf Orders"* to create joins or unions.

- Double click on *"OrdersBreakdown"* under Sheets to create a join.

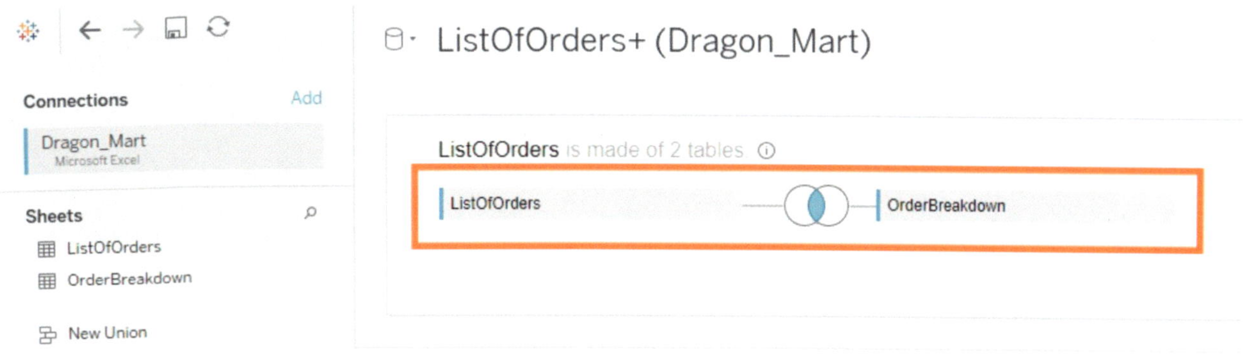

3.1 Types of Joins

- Click on the join symbol, a dialogue box appears, user can select the type of join and the fields used for the joins.

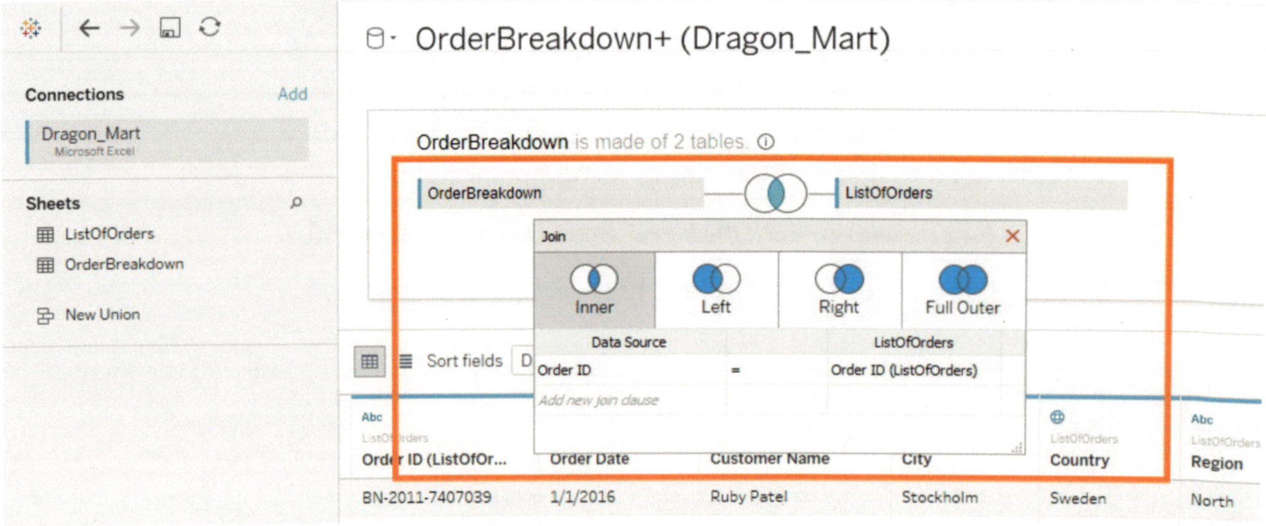

➢ Types of joins: Inner, Left, Right, and Full Outer join

3.2 Selecting fields for creating joins

➢ Automatic: Tableau by default creates a join between tables using similar fields (<u>matching the column headings & datatypes</u>)

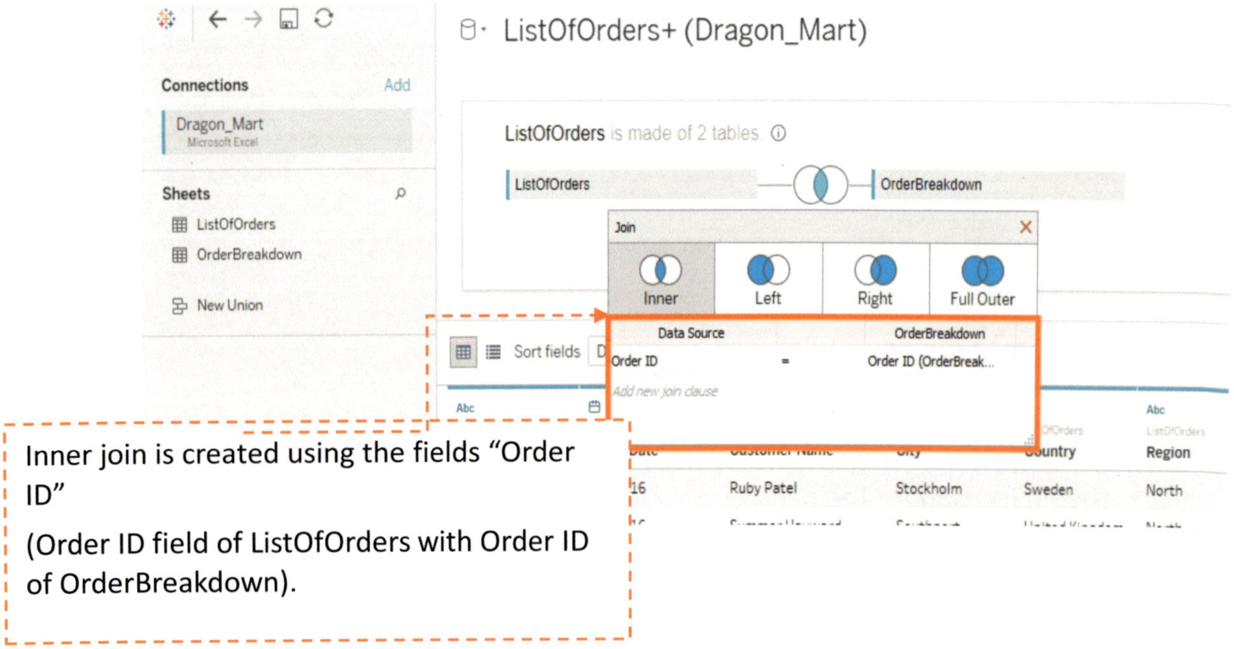

➢ Manual: Select the fields used for joins by clicking on the default field name and a drop down with the list of field names appears. Click on the required fields as shown below.

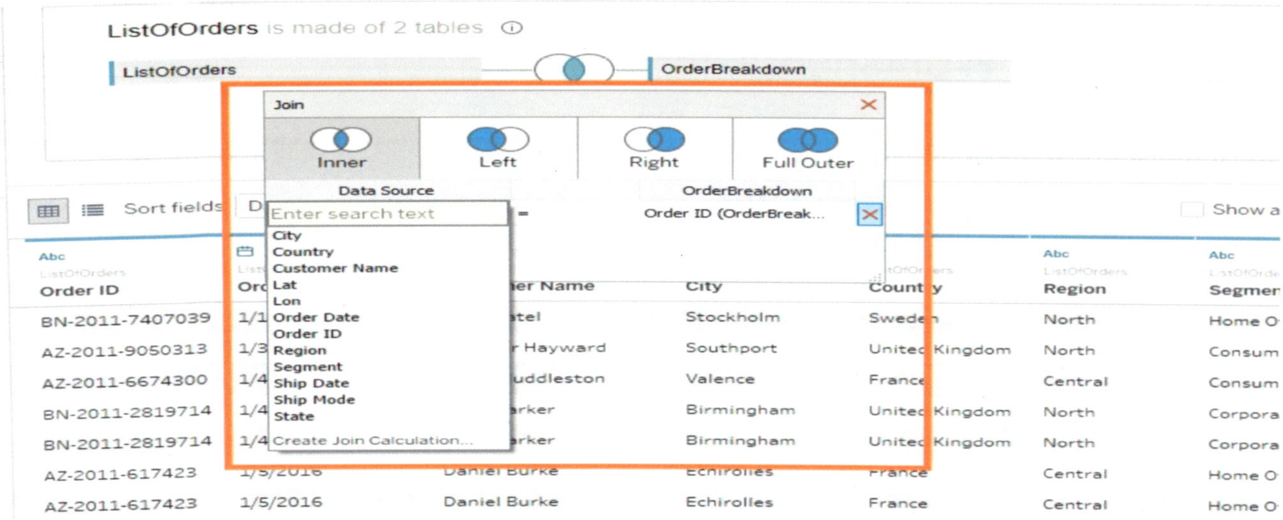

3.3 Errors while creating joins

➢ An error sign is displayed when Tableau is unable to create joins between the tables.

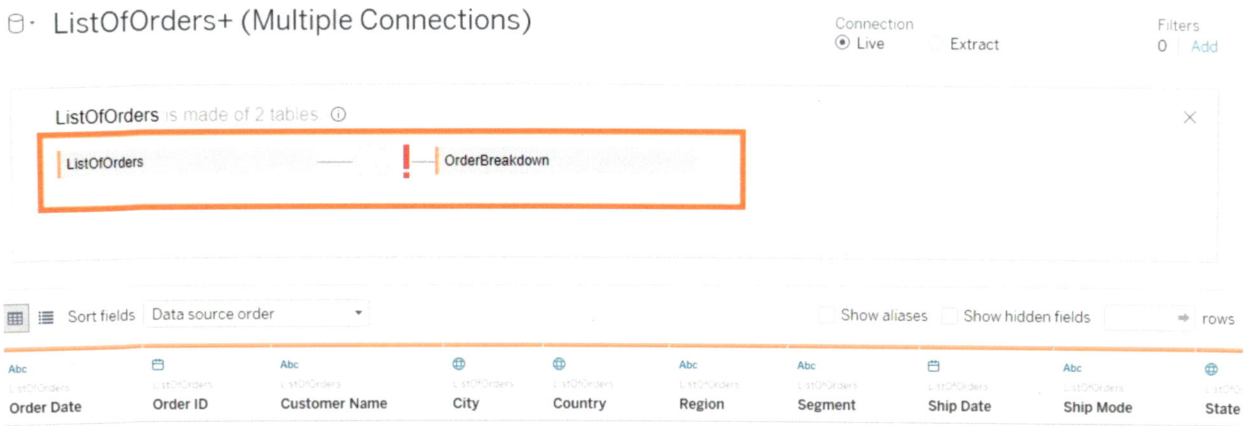

➢ Errors can be due to the following reasons:

- No similar fields between the joining tables
- Mismatch in the column headings of the fields joining the tables. This can be corrected by manually selecting the field names for the join.

4 Views and Analysis

4.1 Creating Worksheets

- Once data is imported into Tableau, user navigates to the worksheet where all the visualizations/views are created.
- As shown in the screenshot below, worksheet tab is at the bottom left corner next to the data source tab named "Sheet1".

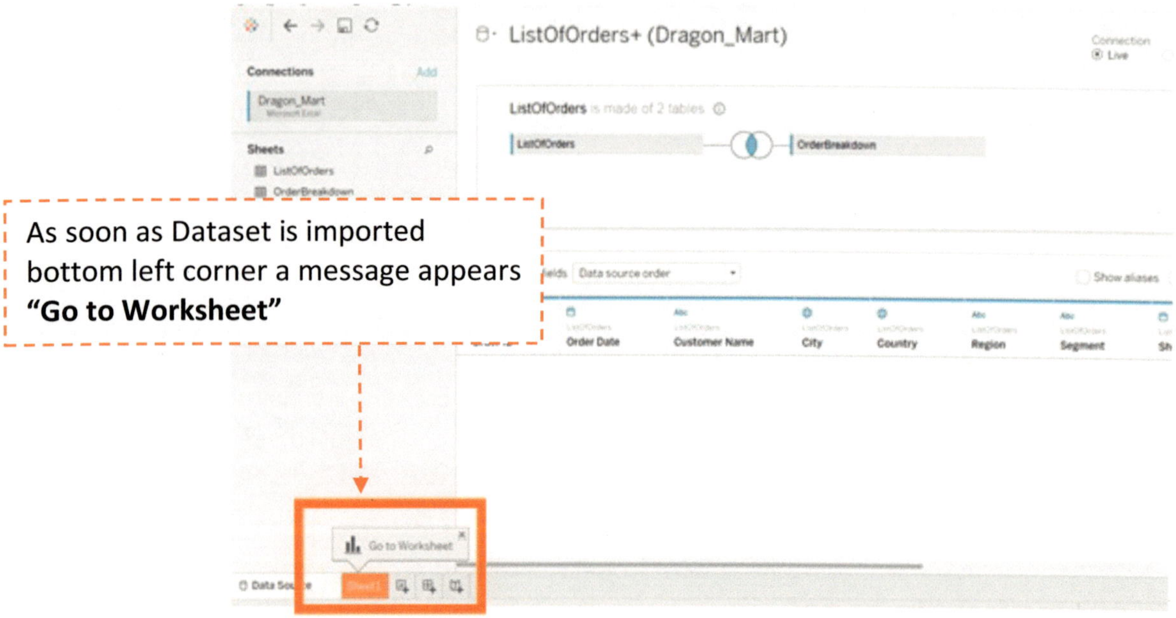

- Click on the "Sheet1"tab to reach the following screen.

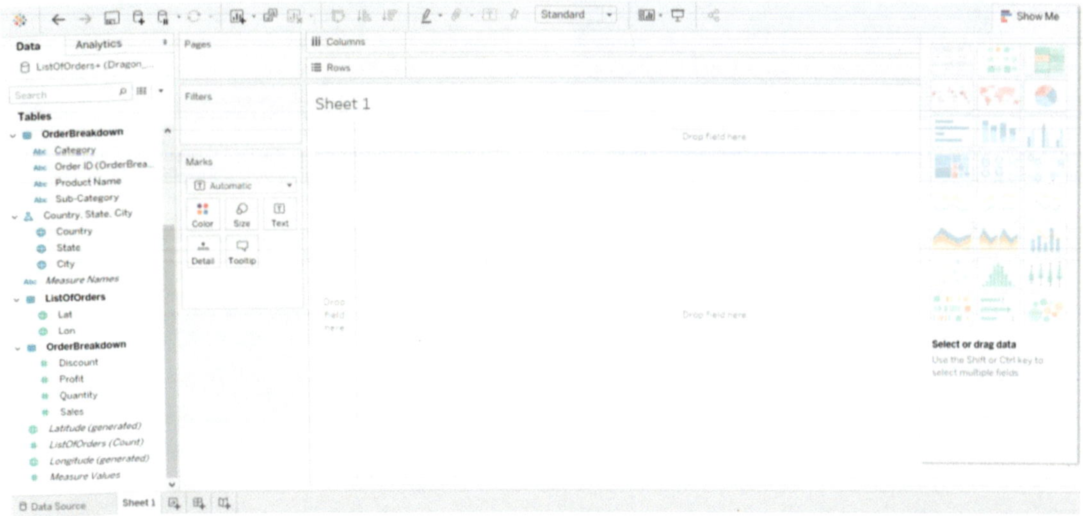

4.1.1 Data Pane

- Whenever user connects to a new data source, Tableau by default assigns each field in the data source as **Dimensions** or **Measures** in the data pane depending on the datatype as shown in the screenshot below.
- Fields under Dimensions are highlighted in blue and fields under Measures are highlighted in green.

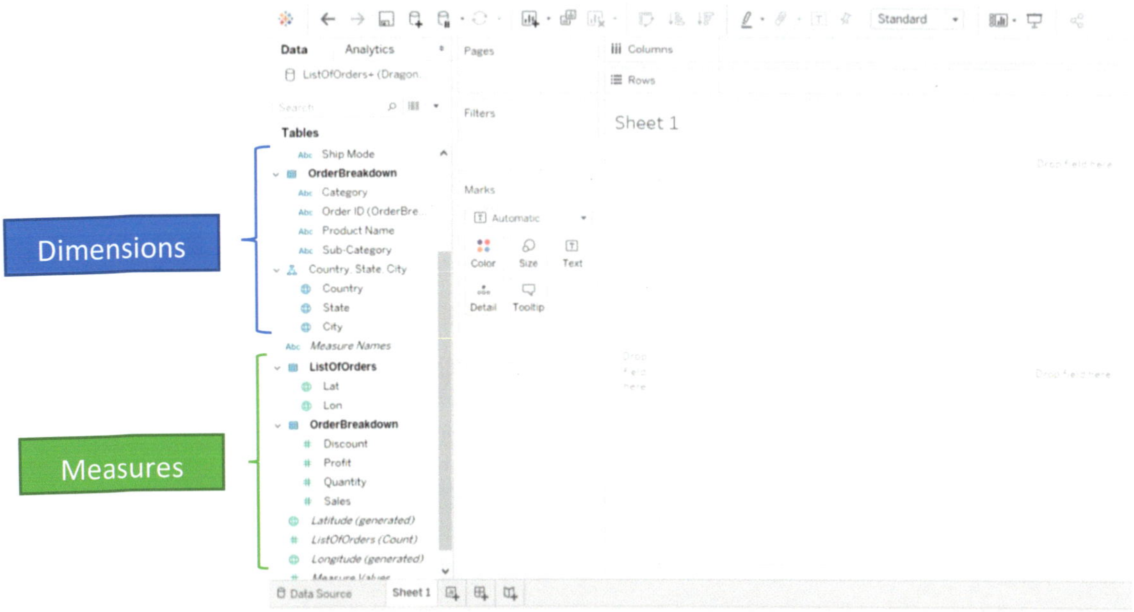

Dimensions

- Dimensions are fields that cannot be aggregated.
- The fields contain string or discreet or categorical or date values.
- These fields help create labels in the chart.
- Example of dimensions in "Dragon_mart": Order ID, Customer Name, Country, Category, Product Name, etc.

Measures

- Measures are fields which can be aggregated.
- Measures are numerical or continuous values.
- They create the axis in the chart
- Example of measures in "Dragon_mart": Latitude, Longitude, Discount, Profit, Quantity, Sales, etc.

PLEASE NOTE

In some cases, Tableau assigns data fields incorrectly to Dimensions or Measures. As seen in Dragon_Mart: "Sl No:" is incorrectly assigned to Measures. Tableau assumed the serial numbering as continuous type and considered the field as Measure. User needs to manually convert the field from Measures to Dimensions as shown below.

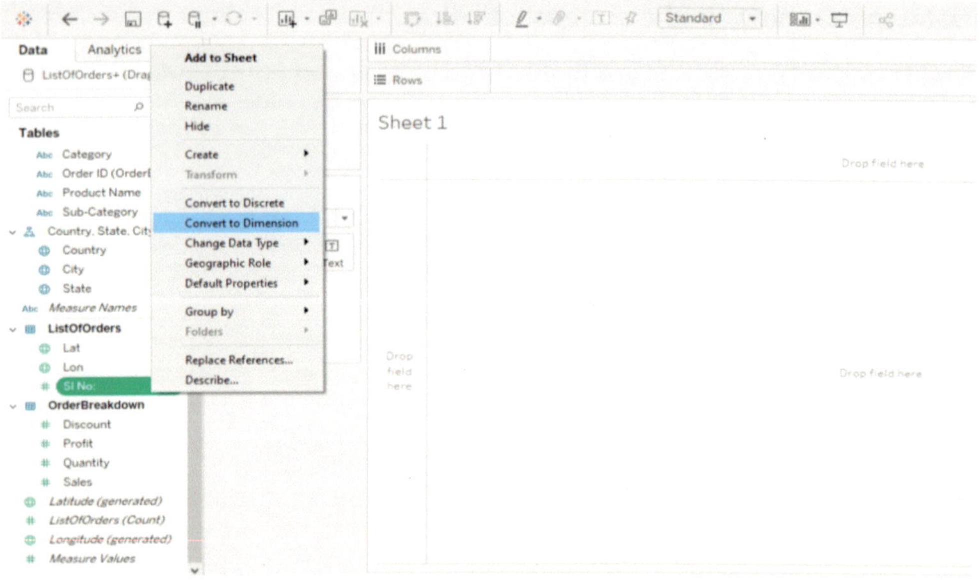

- "Sl No:" now appears under Dimensions in the Data pane.

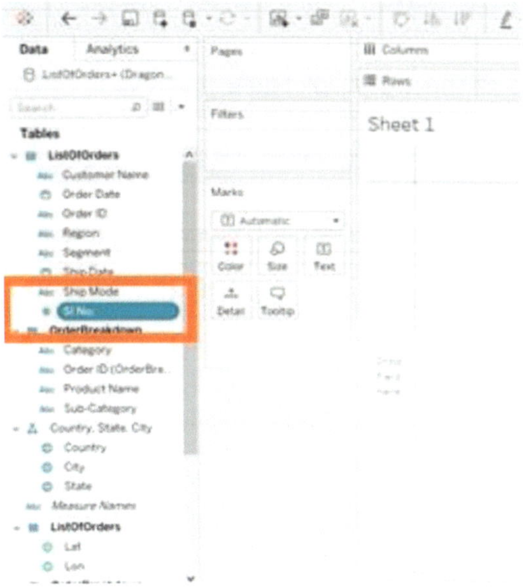

4.1.2 Shelves

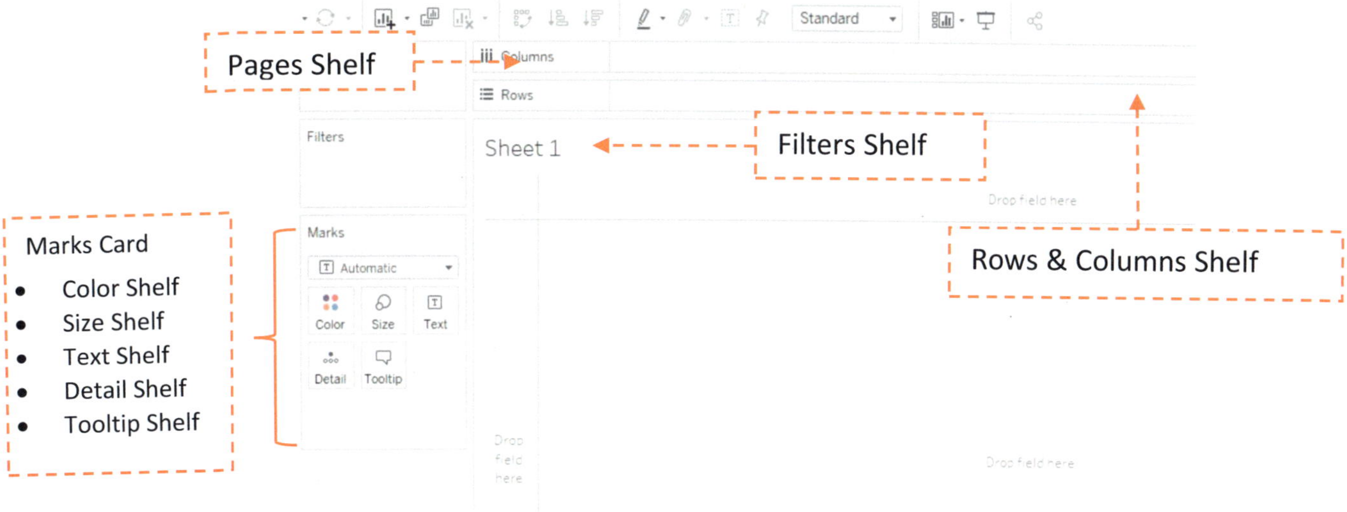

➢ Visualization in Tableau is done by dragging and dropping Measures and Dimensions onto these Shelves.

4.1.2.1 Rows and Columns Shelf

- Represent the rows or columns of the table, or the x and y axis of the charts. User can place any number of fields in these shelves.

- Double click/Drag the field "Quantity" under OrderBreakdown from Measures to the Rows shelf and repeat the same for the field "Regions" under ListOfOrders from Dimensions to the Columns Shelf.

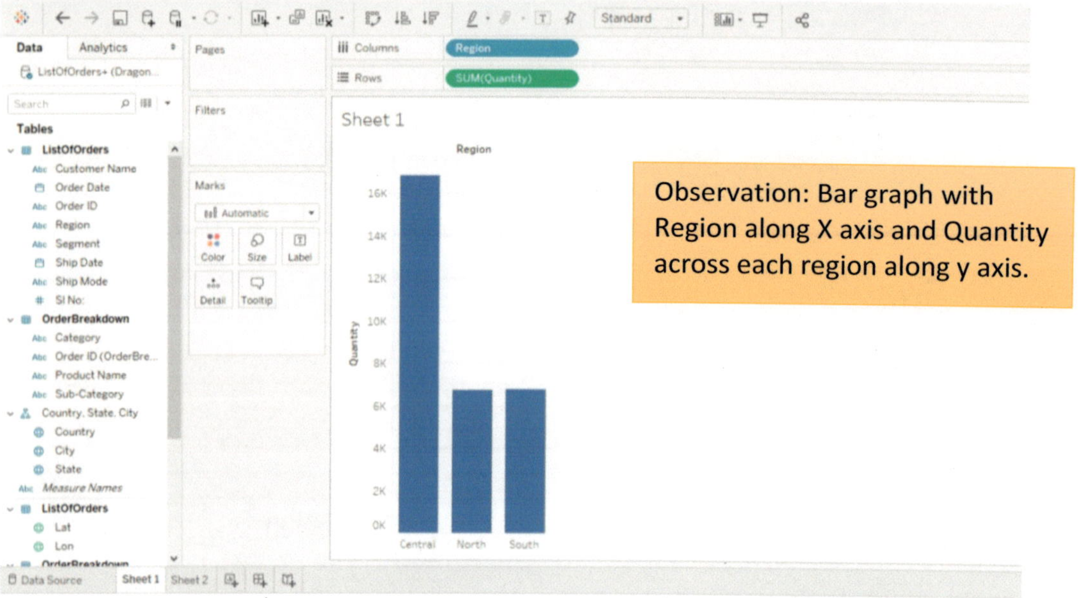

- Try adding one more field "Sub Category" under OrderBreakdown to the Column Shelf and observe the graph.

PLEASE NOTE

> To find a dimension or measure, use the search bar in the Data pane.

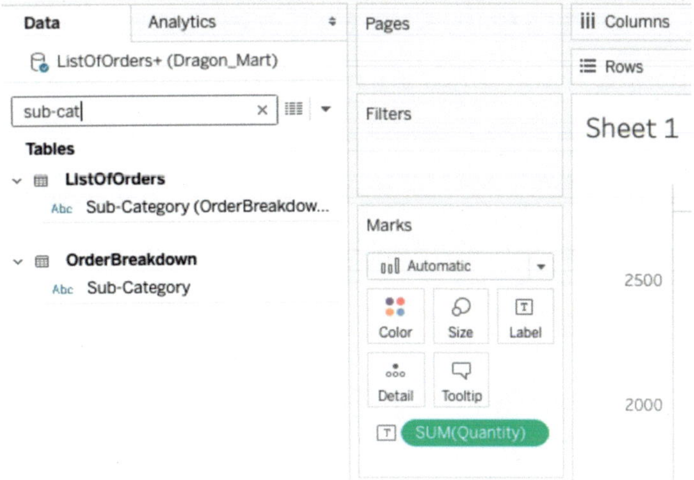

4.1.2.2 Marks Card

Marks card plays a key role in providing user with control over how data is displayed in view. The level of detail and context on the marks change based on the various fields dragged to the different shelfs of the Marks Card. User can choose to represent the data using shapes, size, text or color.

For example, create a view as shown below. Using Marks card, the view can be made more visual for analysis.

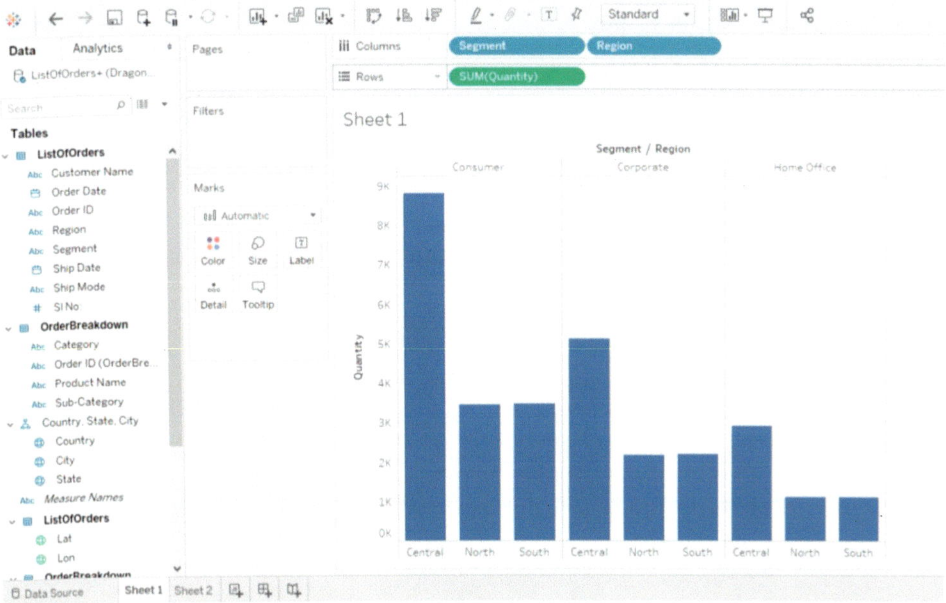

➤ Drag 'Segment' dimensions to the Color shelf in the Marks card. The three segments Consumer, Corporate, Home Office are now differentiated with three different colours as shown below.

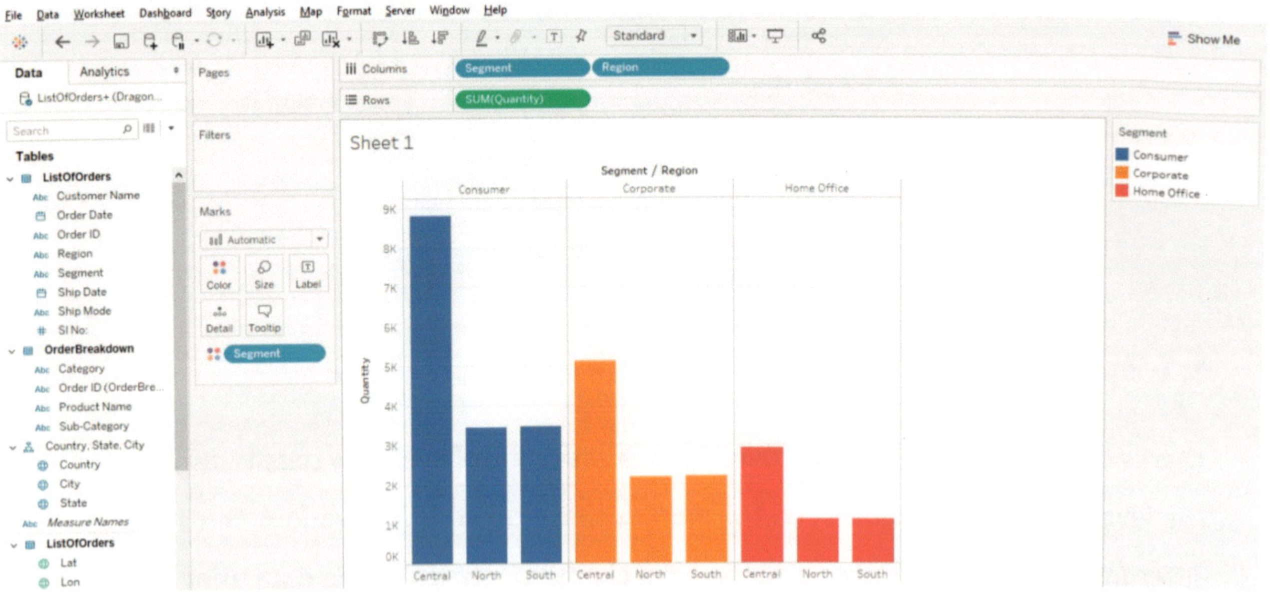

➤ User can change the graph from bar to shapes graph and give each region a unique shape. To do so, click on Marks drop down menu at top of the Marks card and click shapes. The graph changes from bars to circles, after that drag 'Region' onto the newly added shapes shelf as shown below.

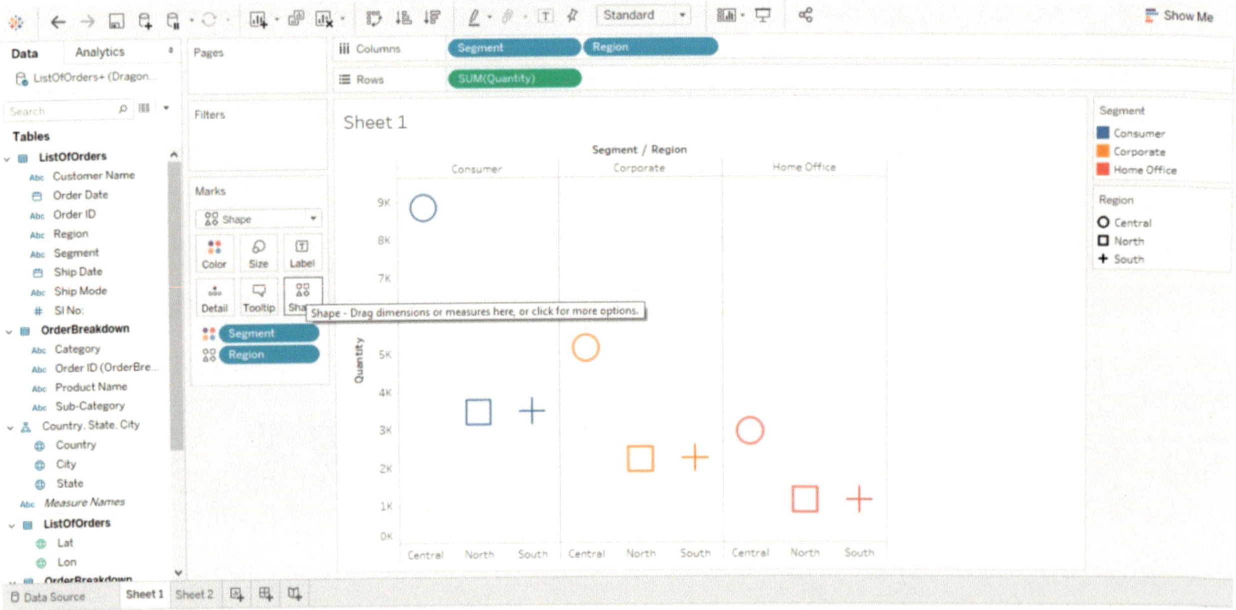

➢ User can visually represent the various sum of quantity in each region using different size. Based on the Total Sale the size varies as shown below. Drag Quantity measures onto Size shelf of Marks card.

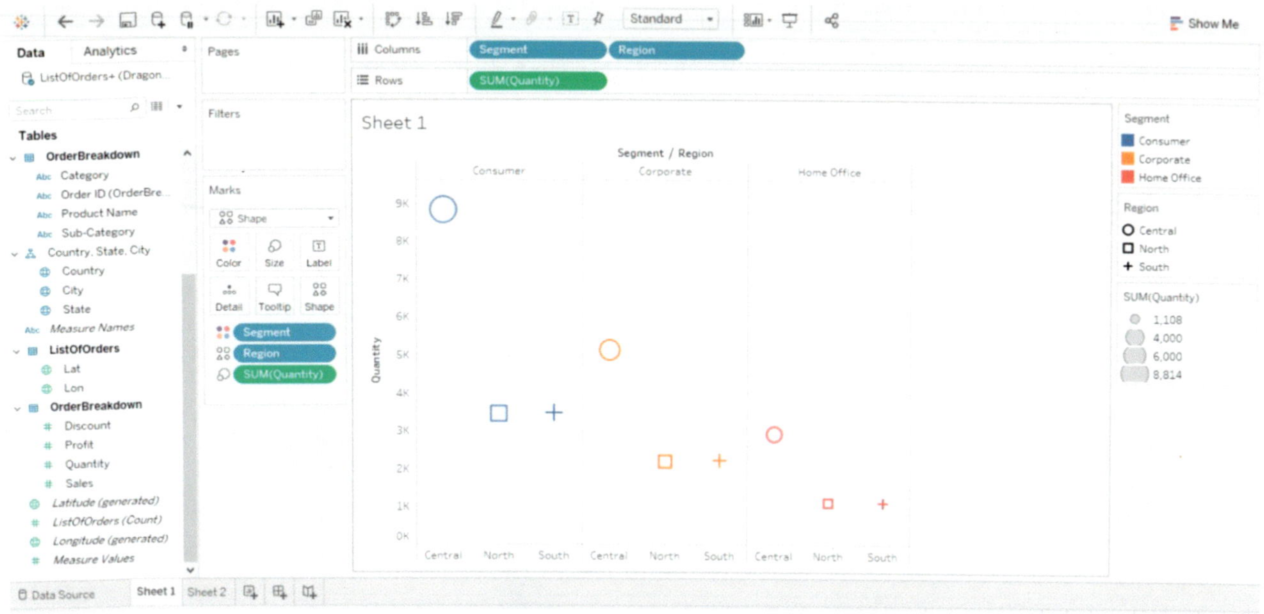

PLEASE NOTE

After a field is added to the Marks card, user can click the icon next to the field to change the property it is using.

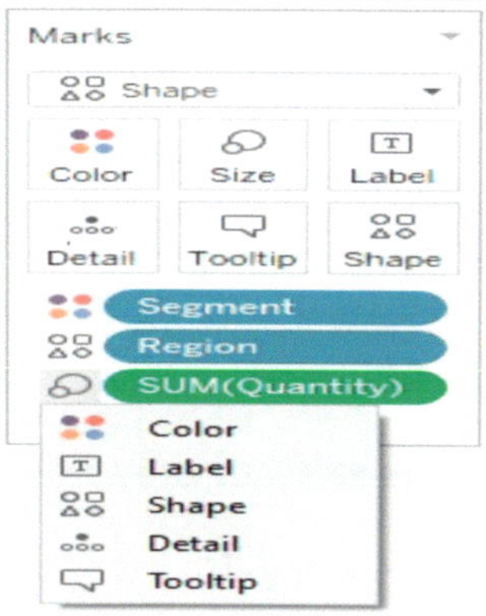

4.1.2.3 Filters Shelf

- Allows user to specify which data to include or exclude in the view. User can filter data using Measures or Dimensions or both at the same time.

User can filter data in two ways:

1. Internal Filter: Filter data using the fields that make up the column and rows of the table.

To illustrate the basic concepts of filtering create a view similar to the one shown below using Segment from ListOfOrders and Sales from OrderBreakdown.

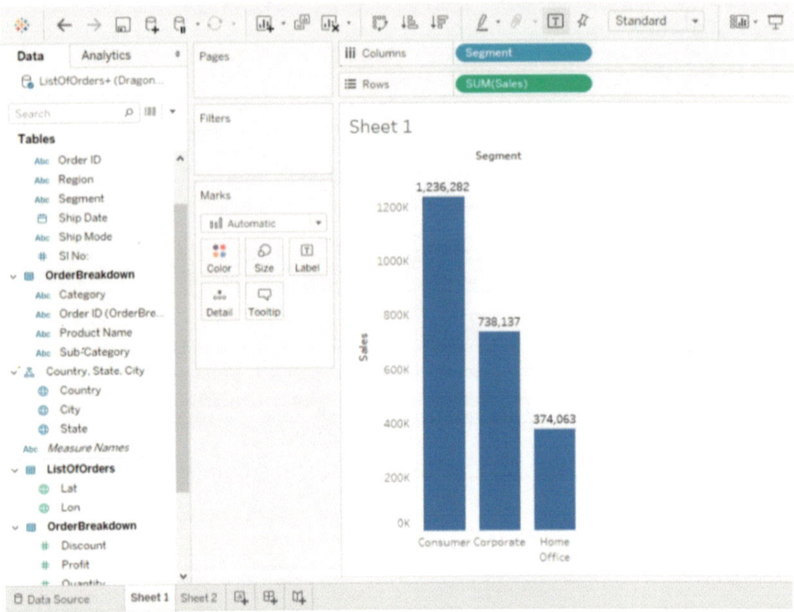

To display labels on the bar graph:

Click on the Label shelf from Mark cards – a pop up box appears – Click on the 'Show mark labels' at the top of the box.

- Suppose user wants to display the sales of only Home Office and Corporate in the view. User can remove Consumer column by filtering the segment dimension.
  - Note: Since segment makes up the axes of the chart this filtering is internal.

➢ In order to do so, Drag the segment dimension to the Filter shelf or Place the cursor on the Segment Dimension in the Columns shelf - Click on the down arrow that appears at the right corner- select Filter as shown below.

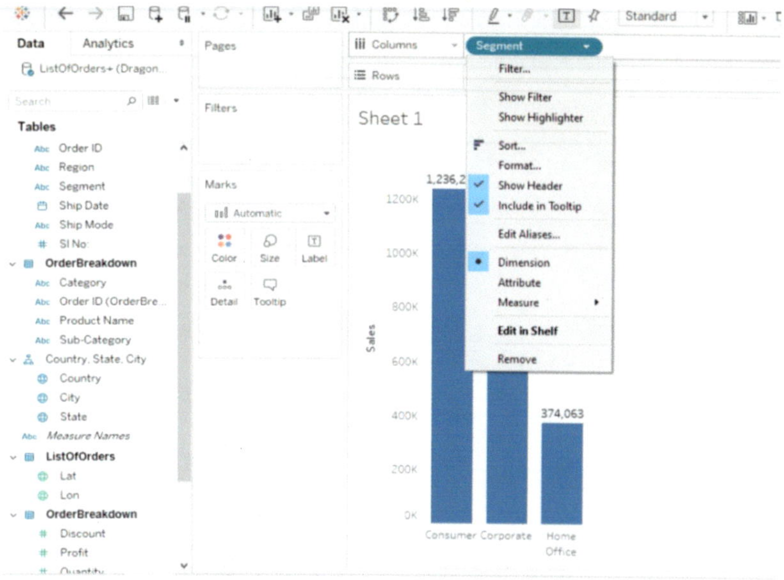

➢ Once filter is selected the Filter dialogue box appears as shown below. By default, all members are included.

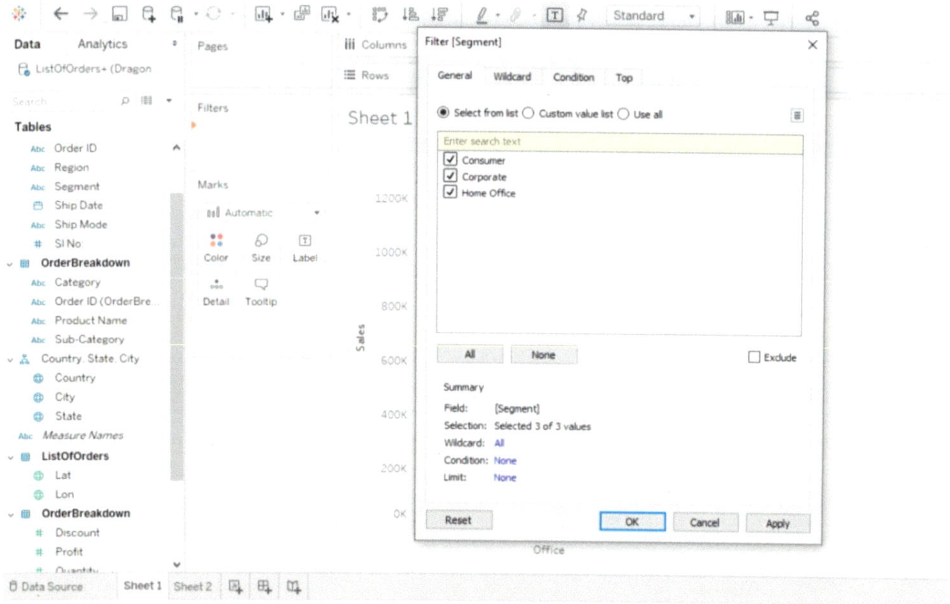

➢ Uncheck consumer and click okay. Only Home office and Corporate is included in the view.

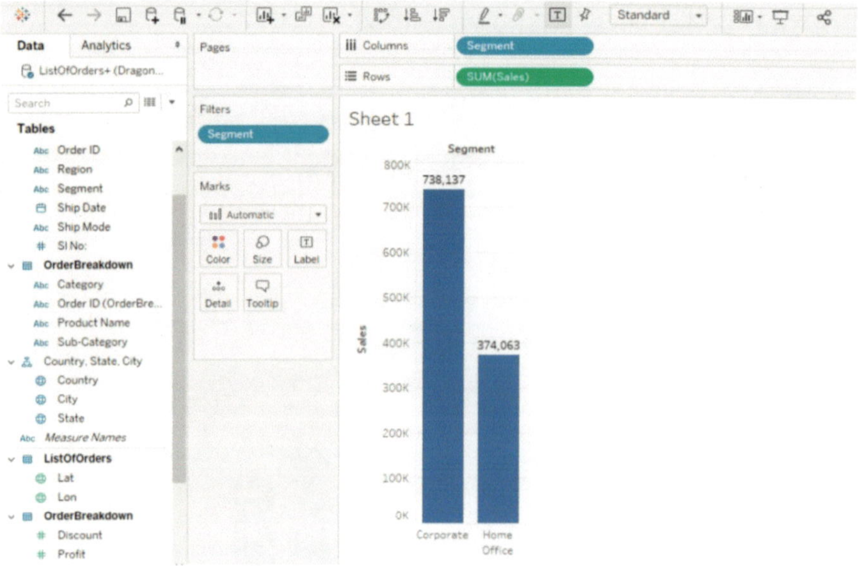

2. External Filter: Filter data using fields that do not contribute to headers or axes of table.

Continuing with the above example: Suppose user wants to know the sales based on 'Office Supplies' Category in the Corporate and Home office segment. Even though the Category field is not used in the rows and columns shelves, user can filter using external filtering.

To do so, drag Category dimension to the Filter shelf. The Filter dialogue box appears. By default, all the members are not selected as shown below.

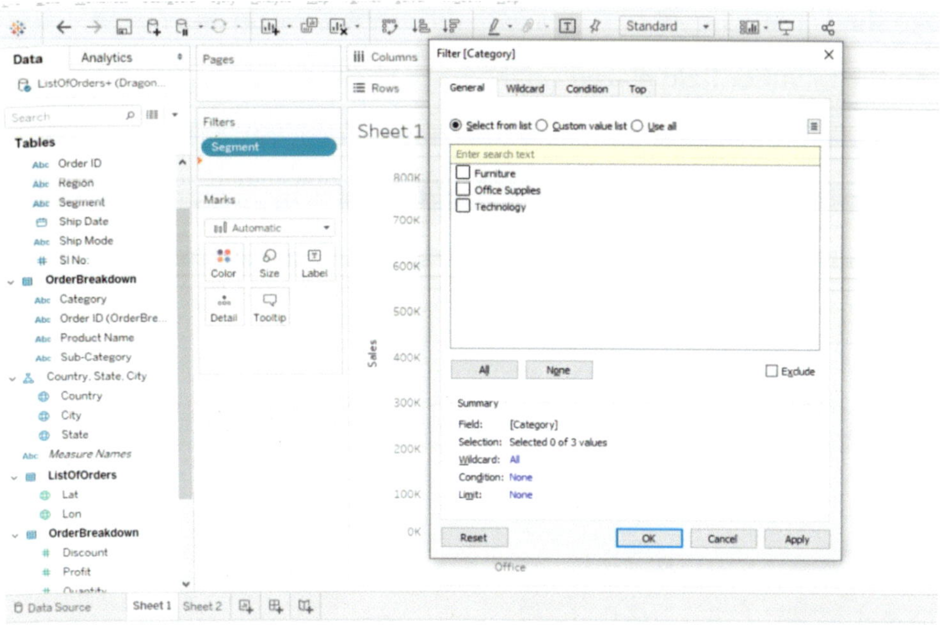

➢ Select Office Supplies and click okay. The changes are reflected in the view as show below.

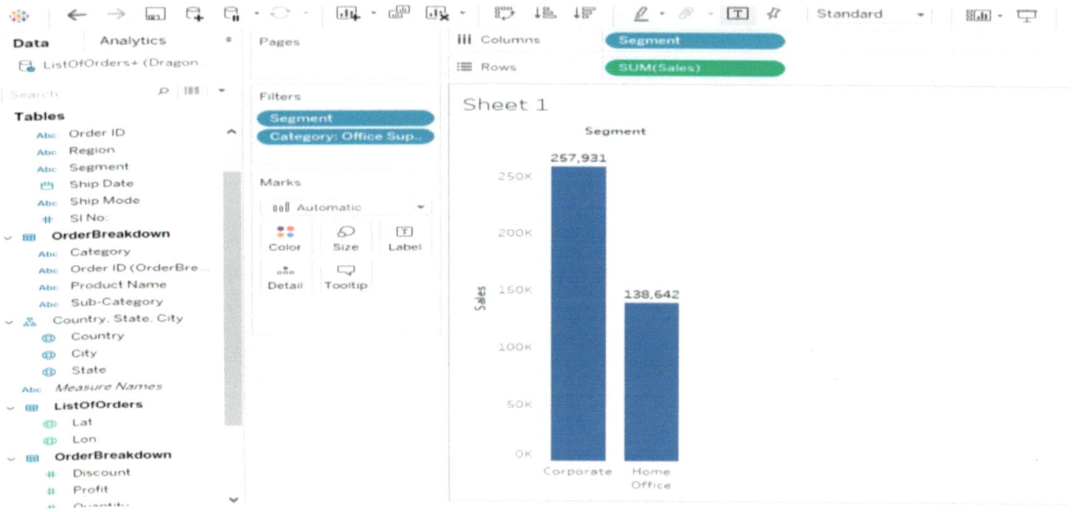

PLEASE NOTE

If Category is added as a filter and no values are selected, it will result in a blank sheet.

4.1.2.4 Pages Shelf

➢ Pages are used when any of the fields require a detailed visualization than a simple aggregated visualization.

- The Page shelf creates a set of pages with different view on each page. Each view is based on the member field placed on the page shelf. Controls get added when user moves a field on the page shelf. Using the controls user can flip through views.
- For example, the view below shows the Profit vs Sales by Region for each day throughout the month. User needs to scroll down to see other days of the month.

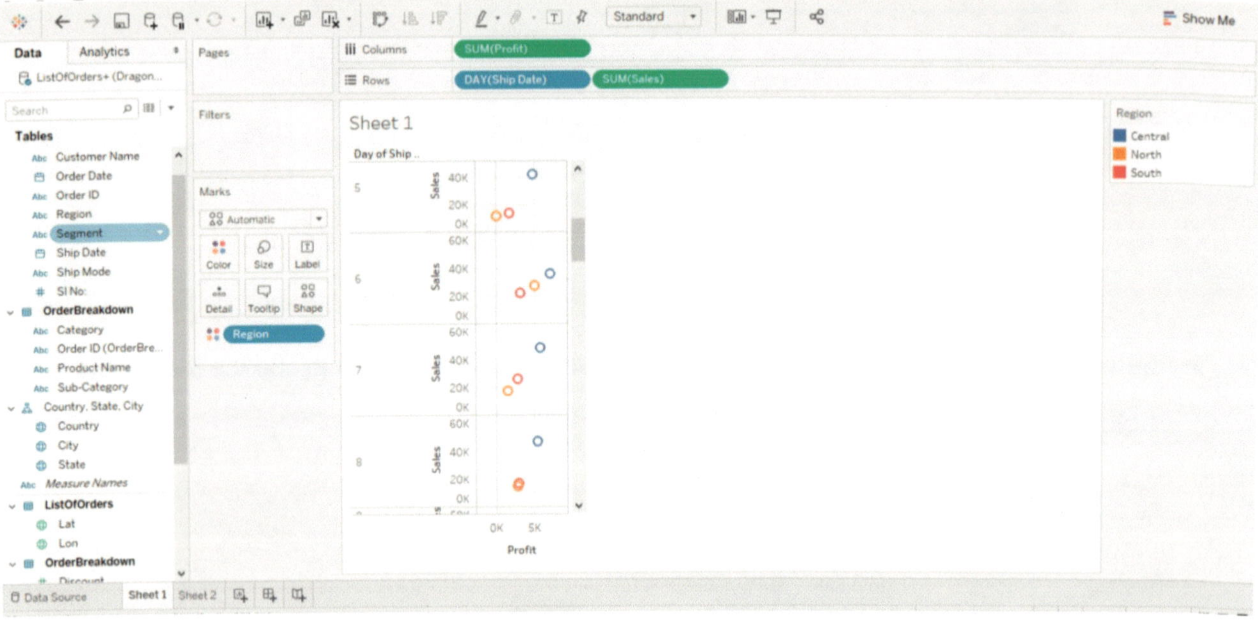

In order for the user to analyze and get insights from the view, move DAY(Ship Date) to Pages Shelf and use the associated control to flip through the pages (one for each day).

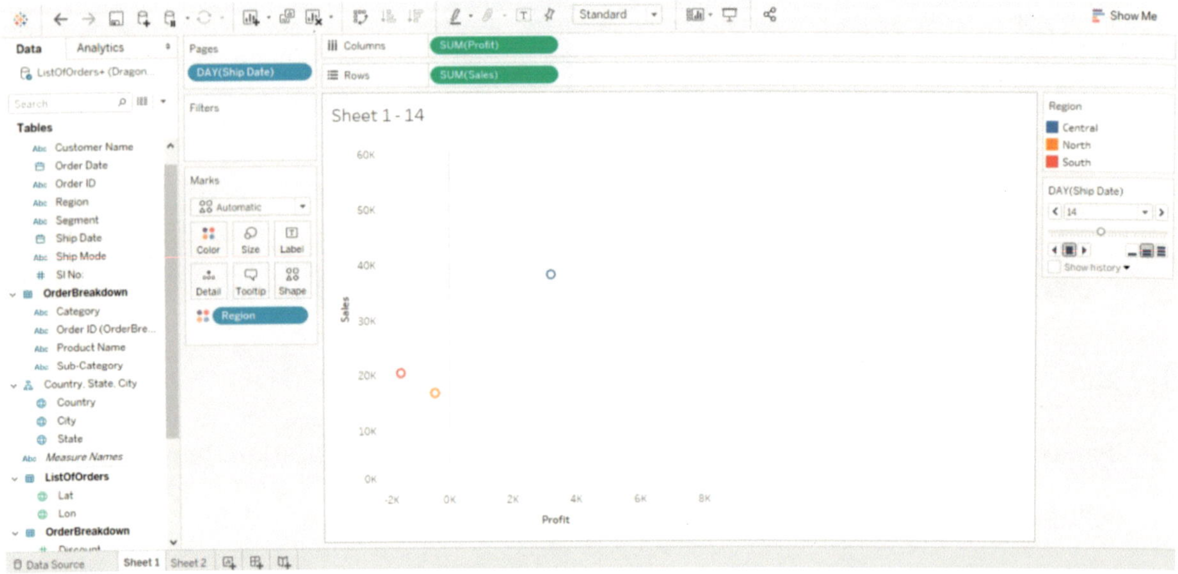

4.1.3 Show Me Pane

➢ Tableau creates default graphs when user drags and drops fields onto the visualization area. These graphs can be changed by referring to **Show me** option as shown in the below screenshot.

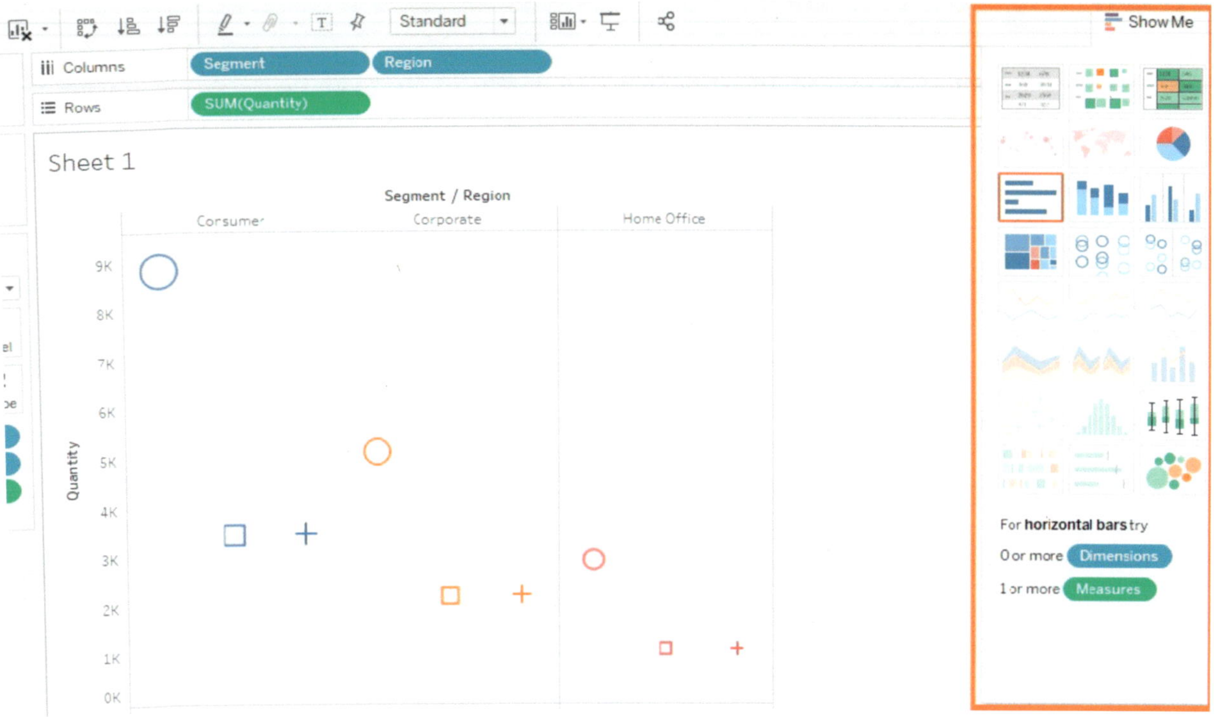

All the graphs can be made with a combination of Dimensions or Measures. Each graph has its own conditions for the number and type of fields that can used.

5 Working with Data

5.1 Sorting

- Tableau provides basic and advanced sorting methods that can be accessed easily through icons or menus.

PLEASE NOTE

> Sorting is not limited to the fields present in the view, any field in the data source can be used for sorting.

- Create a view of the total sales across different countries as shown below, with Country Dimension in the Rows shelf and Sales Measures in the Text shelf of the Marks card. Highlight the sales value by clicking on the **Highlight tables** in the **Show Me pane.**

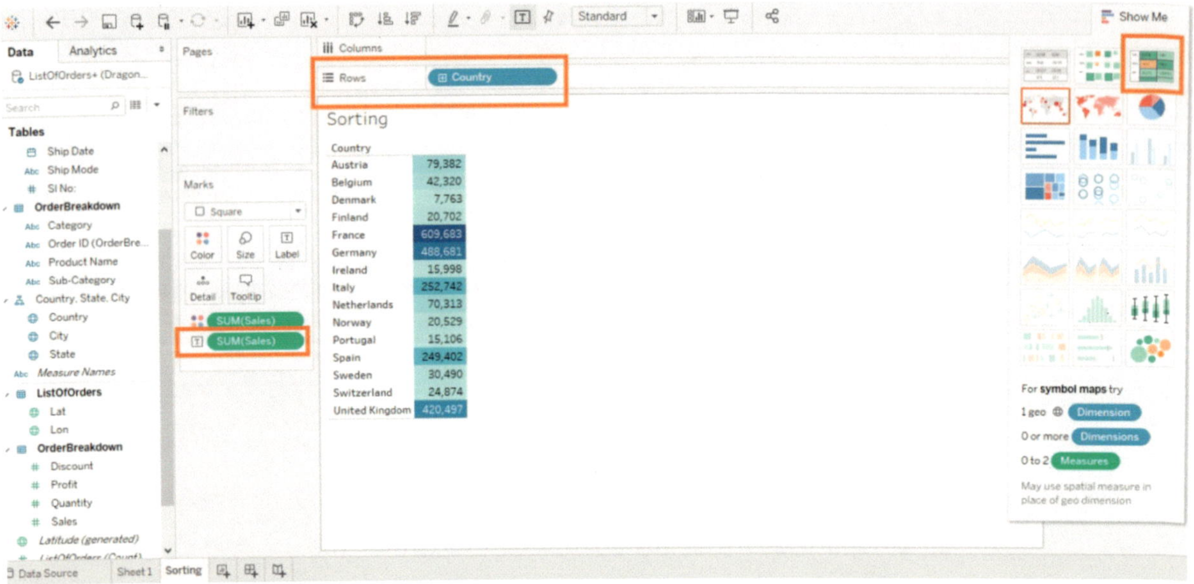

5.1.1 Sorting based on Icons/Basic Sorting

- Basic sorting is done via the icons that appear on the toolbar menu. Sorting based on values of the table can be done via the ascending or descending icon.

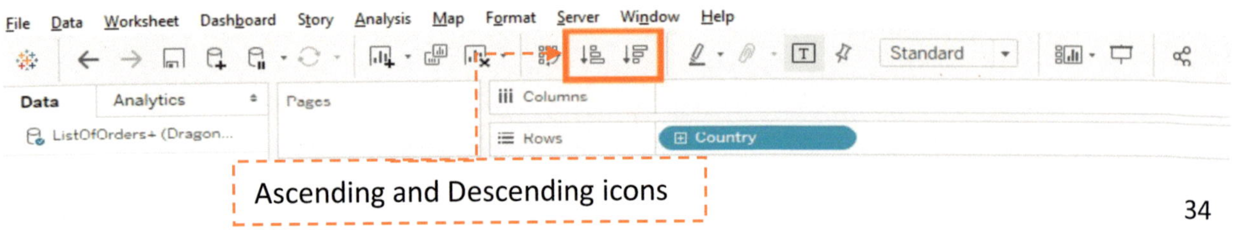

➢ In the view created let's sort the Sum of sales within Country in ascending order. To do so, click on the **Ascending icon** present on the toolbar.

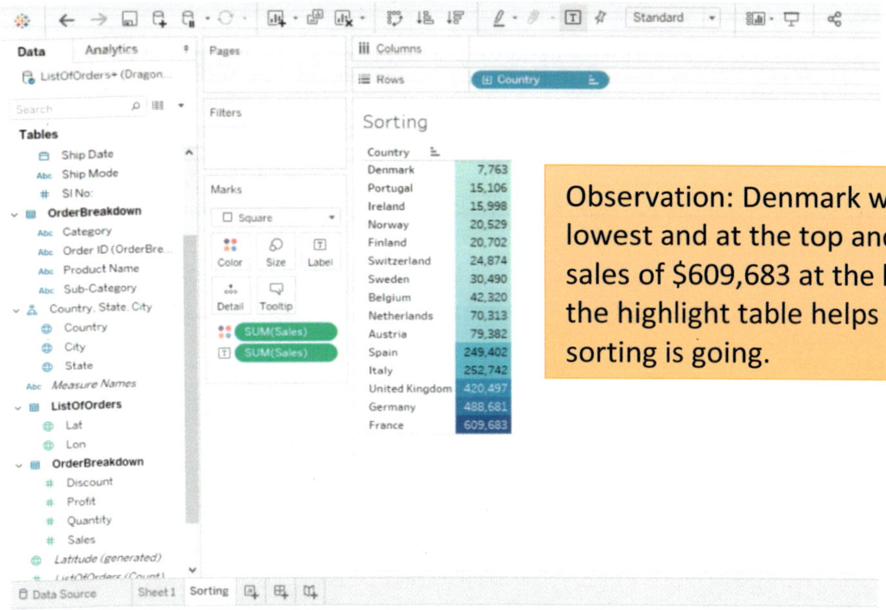

Observation: Denmark with sales of $7,763 is the lowest and at the top and France with the highest sales of $609,683 at the bottom. The colour coding of the highlight table helps to emphasize the way sorting is going.

5.1.2 Sorting based on sort menu/ Advanced Sorting

➢ Tableau allows data to be sorted by different dimensions using the sort menu.

➢ In the current view, user can sort values by country instead of value. To do so, hover the mouse pointer over Country and Click on the down arrow, a dialogue box appears and select sort.

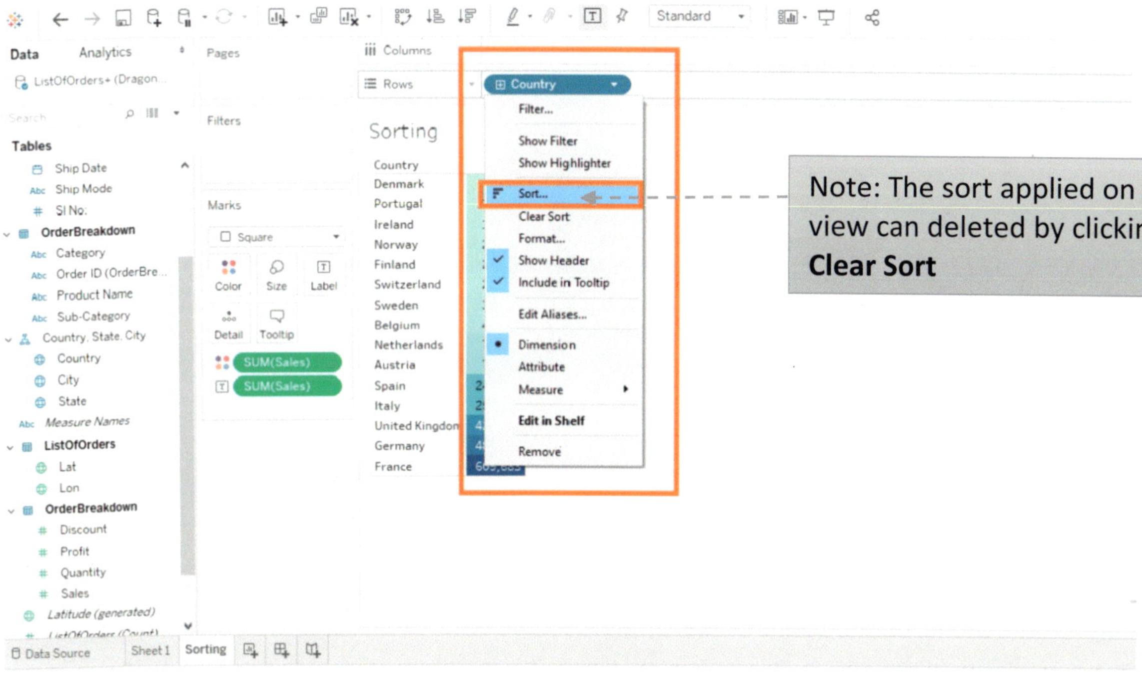

Note: The sort applied on the view can deleted by clicking **Clear Sort**

➢ A sort dialogue box appears with two options "Sort By" and "Sort Order". Users can select which fields to use for sorting as seen below. There are quite a few sorting options available.

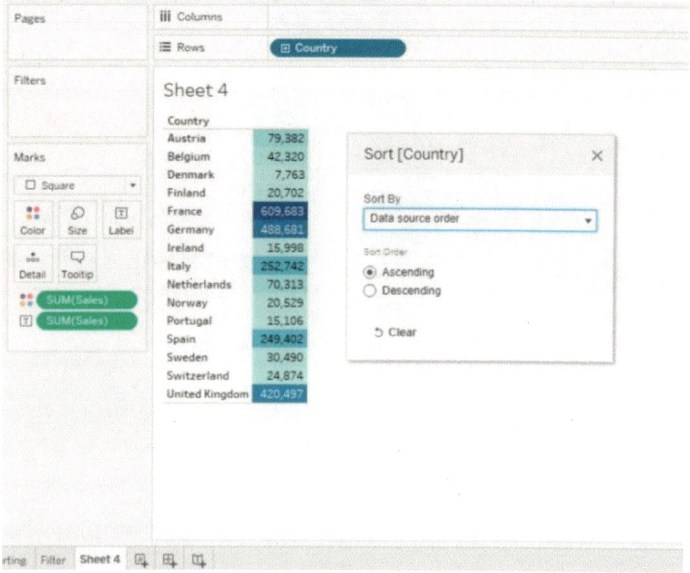

5.1.2.1 Alphabetic Order

➢ Select **Alphabetic** from the drop-down list of Sort By and click on Ascending from the sort order. The below view is obtained.

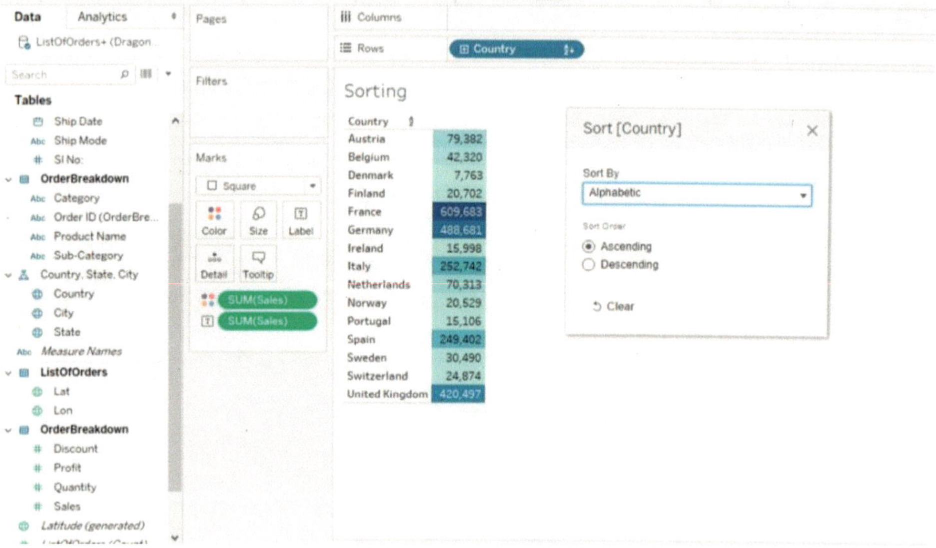

5.1.2.2 Data Source Order

- In the sort menu, the default **Sort By** is "Data Source Order". The order is used if the user wants to replicate the order of data in the data source. This order is basically the alphabetical order as shown below.

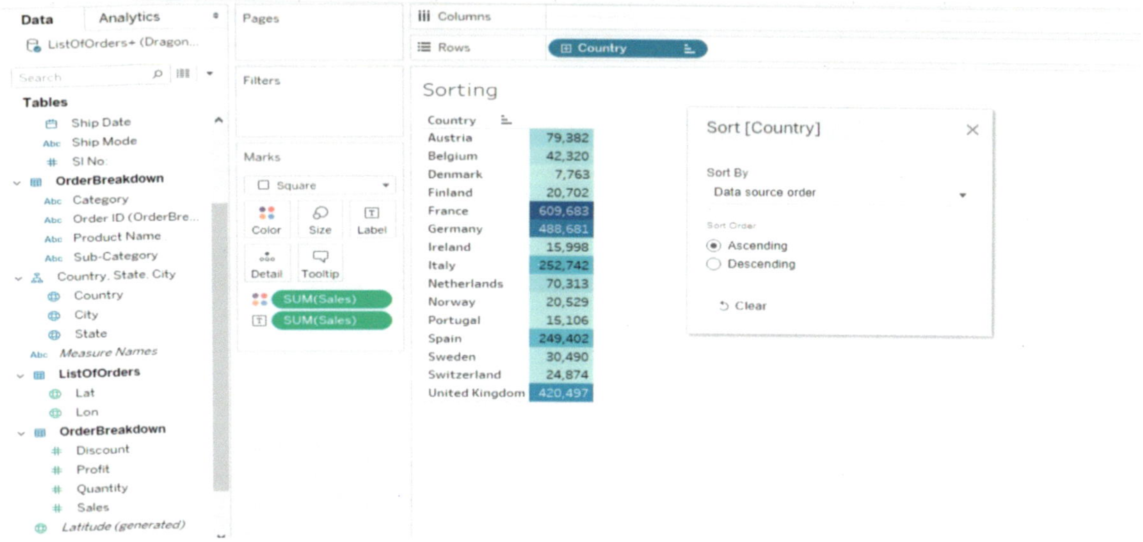

5.1.2.3 Field Order

- Data can be sorted by any field in the data source. It is not necessary for the field to be present in the current visualization.
- When user selects **Fields**, two more sections appear in the dialogue box: "Field Name" and "Aggregation". "Field Name" indicates which field user intends to apply for sorting. In "Aggregation", user can select the aggregation function to be applied on the selected field.
- In the current example, select "Field" in Sort By – Select "Ascending" in Sort Order- Select "Quantity" in Field name- Select sum in "Aggregation". The below view is created.

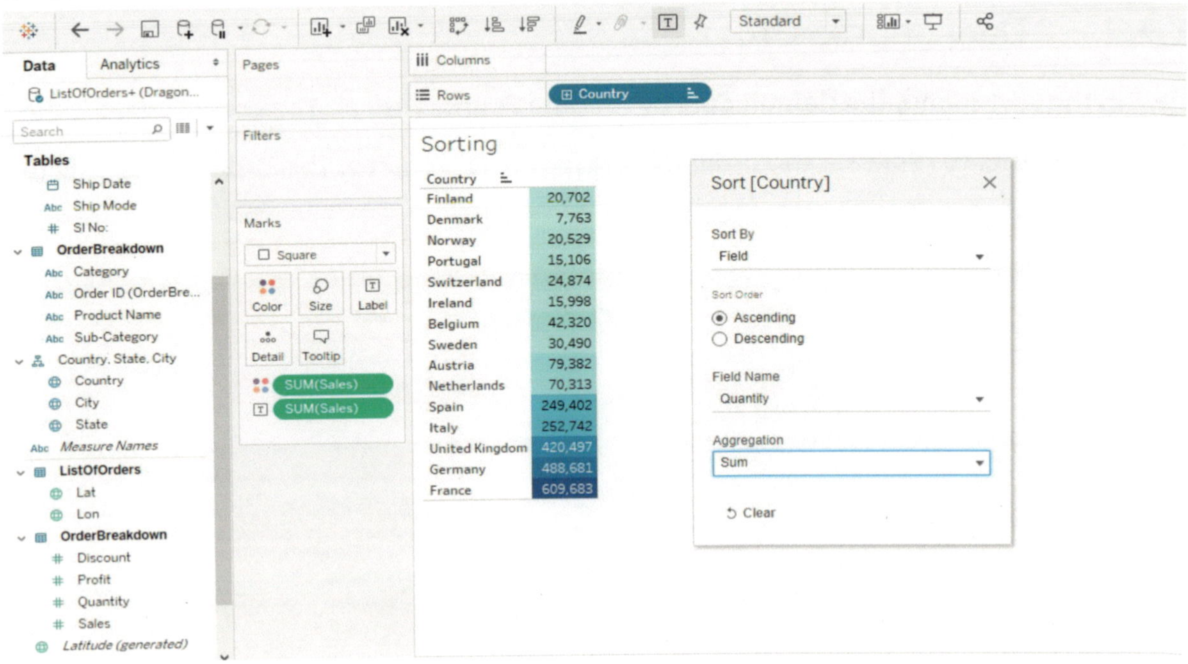

Observation: Current visualization is still displaying the sum of sales and not displaying the sum of quantity. From the view, we observe that Denmark with the least sales ordered more items than Finland. Sum of quantity is not part of the visualization, but sorting has been done in the ascending order of quantity.

5.1.2.4 Manual Order

- Using manual order, user can move a value upward or downward based on the position.
- User can sort the result by moving the dimension value. Manual may not be a feasible sorting option when there are several values for a dimension.
- In the current example, move the position of France to the top by Selecting Manual in Sort By – Select France – Click the Move up/ Move to top arrow key. Similarly move the position of Finland below Denmark by, Selecting Finland and Clicking on the Move down arrow.

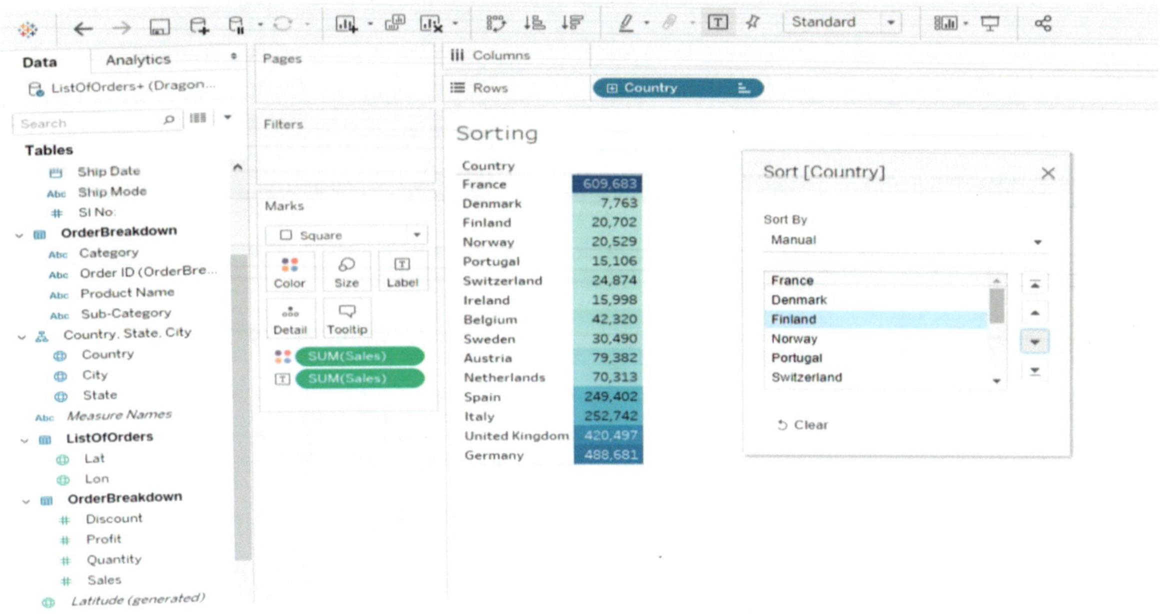

5.1.2.5 Nested Order

- Nested order is used when user sorts a dimension within another dimension over a measure.
- In the current example, drag dimensions Category into the Rows Shelf as shown below.

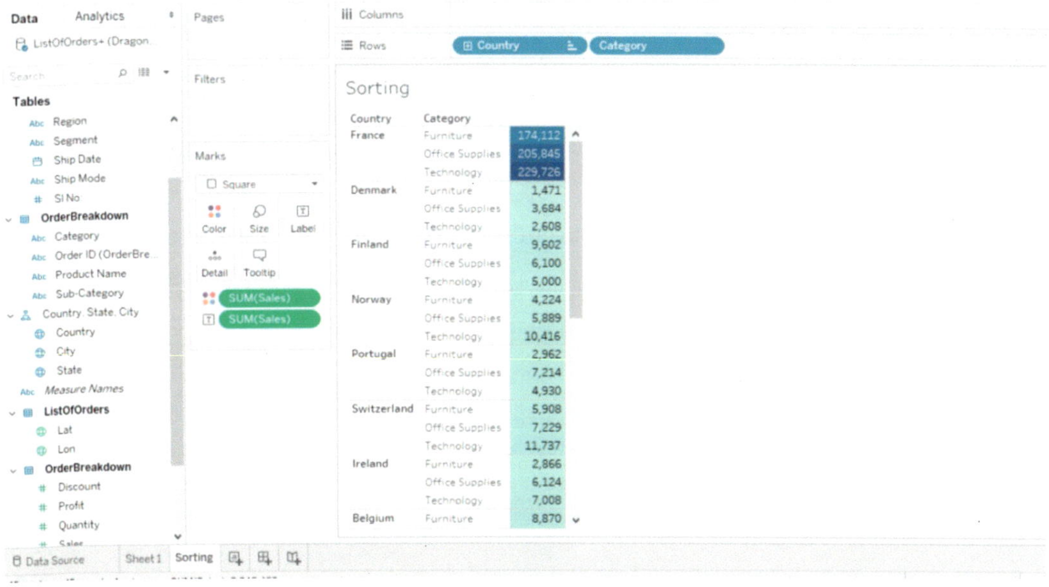

- Hover mouse over Country and right click and select Sort. Select Nested under Sort By-Click on Descending in Sort by order. The below view is created.

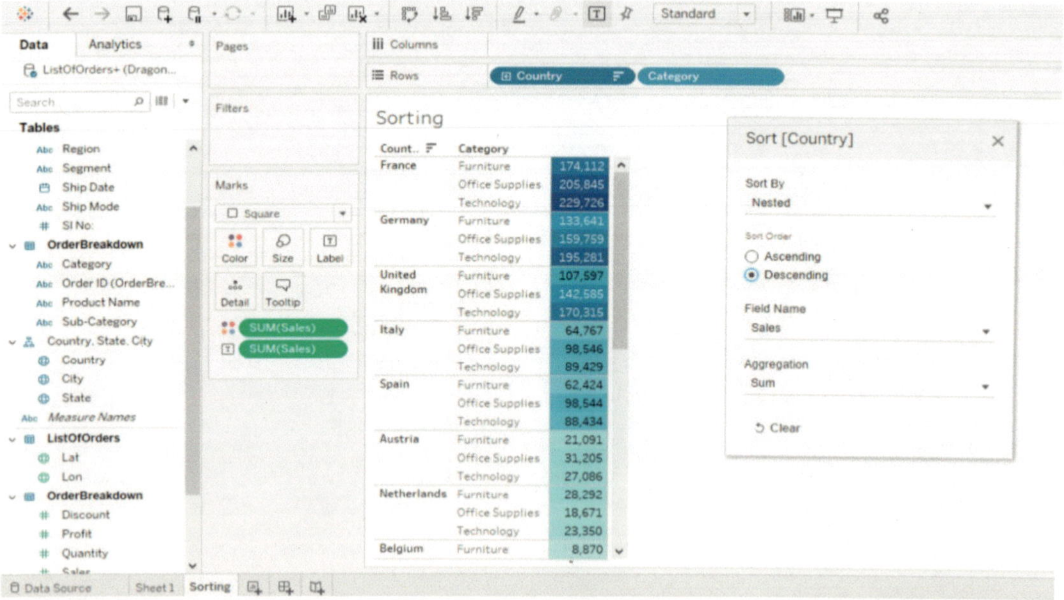

Observation: Both the dimensions are sorted in the descending order based on the measure value. We observe the countries as well as each item in the category are sorted from highest to lowest values based on their total sales.

- Now try a nested sort on Category for a comparison with nested sort on Country.

5.2 Advance Filtering

- Basic filtering was discussed in Section 4.1.2.3 Filters Shelfs.
- Advanced filtering is useful in filtering blended data.
- Create a new view with Country dimensions on the column shelf and double click or drag Sales dimension to the Text shelf in the Marks card to create a table as shown below. Select 'highlight tables' from the Show Me pane.

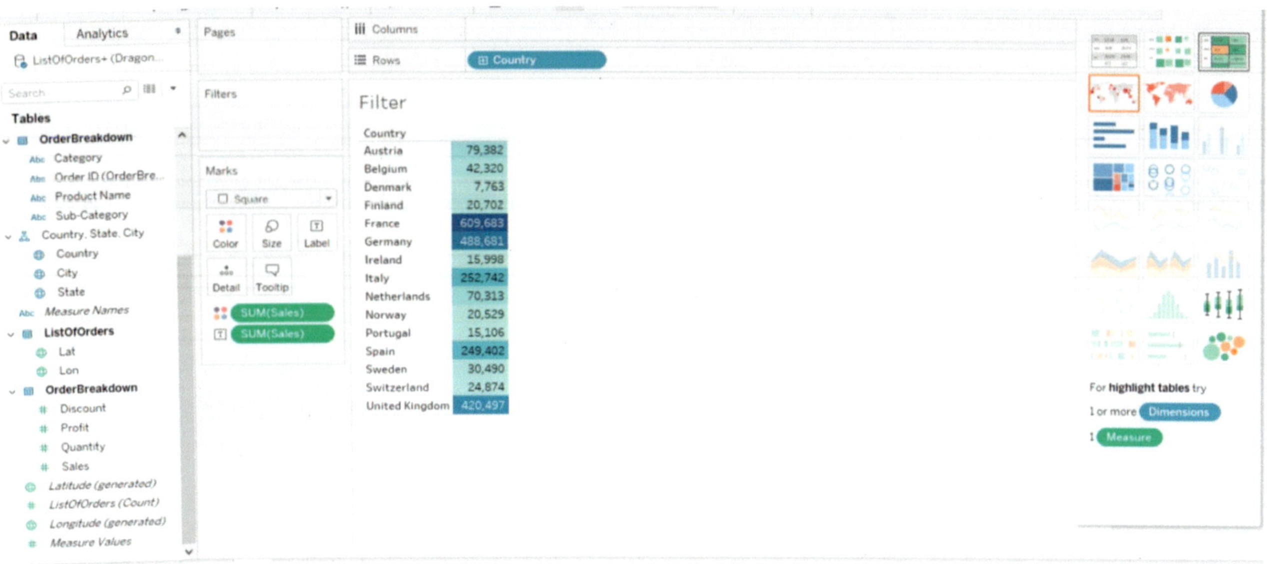

5.2.1 Wildcard Filter

- Wildcard option is used to filter the fields based on a pattern. Users can type the character and filter the field based on the match.
- Hover mouse over the Country dimension in Rows Shelf and right click, a pop-up box appears and select 'Filter'. The Filter dialogue box appears and select the "Wildcard" tab.
- "Wildcard" tab contains the Match value – where the characters to be matched is typed and option to select the type of matches to be used for the filter.

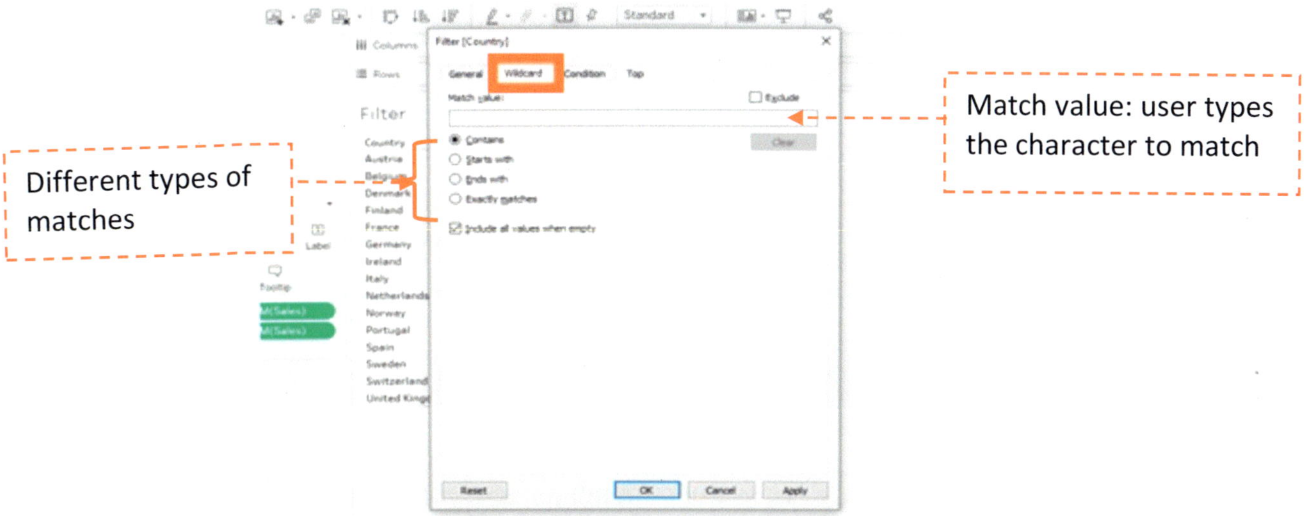

PLEASE NOTE

The match is not case sensitive.

➢ The different types of matches are as follows.

Contains	Select the members if the member name contains typed characters.
Starts with	Select the members if the member name starts with typed characters.
Ends with	Select the members if the member name ends with typed characters.
Exactly matches	Select the members if the member name exactly matches with typed characters.

Source: Tableau Desktop and Web Authoring Help

➢ For example: Right click on Country dimensions – Select Filter – In the filter dialogue box choose 'Wildcard' tab – In Match value : type "Land"- Select Contains and click apply.

Observation: Tableau filters the names of the countries containing the characters "land".

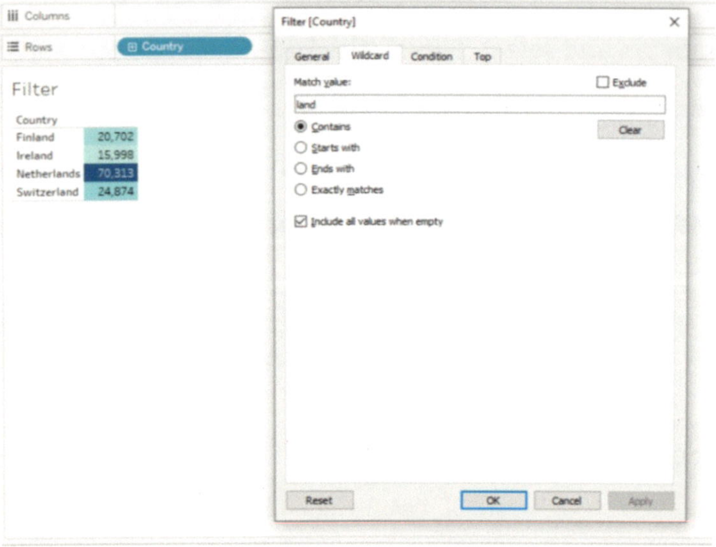

PLEASE NOTE

To remove the filter applied: Click Clear below the Match value and click Ok.

➢ Wildcard filter can also be used to exclude members who contain the typed characters.

➢ Click on the Exclude check box and the types of matches changes to "Does not" as shown below.

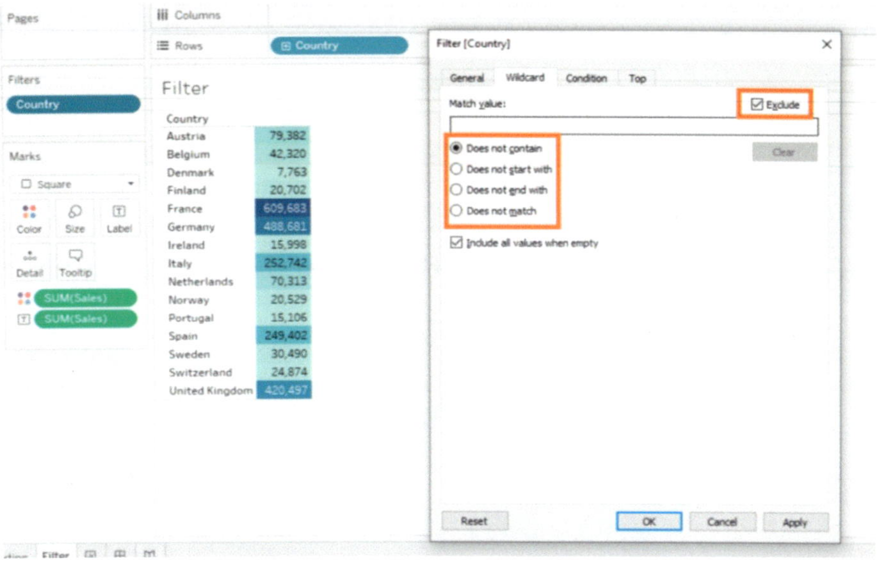

Does not contain	Do not select the members if the member name contains typed characters.
Does not start with	Do not select the members if the member name starts with typed characters.
Does not End with	Do not select the members if the member name ends with typed characters.
Does not exactly matches (Ctrl)	Do not select the members if the member name exactly matches with typed characters.

Source: Tableau Desktop and Web Authoring Help

5.2.2 Condition Filter

➢ Condition Filter is used to filter the dataset by setting conditions.

Types of condition filter:

1. Filter by Field
2. Range of values

3. Filter by formula

5.2.2.1 Filter by Field

- Filter the current view, to display Countries where sum of sales is greater than $300,000.
- Select 'Condition' tab in the Filter Window -Click on radio button 'By field'- Select the name of the field 'Sales' to be filtered from the drop down list -Select the aggregation type 'Sum' from the drop down- Choose the greater than operator from the drop down- Enter the value 300,000 to filter the selected filed 'Sales'- Click OK.

Observation: Only three countries have total sales greater than $300,000

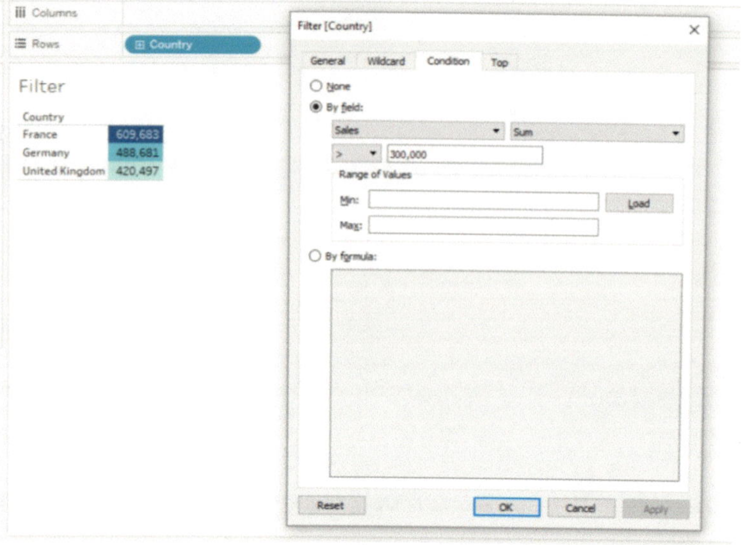

PLEASE NOTE

Note: Filter applied can be cleared by clicking on the radio button 'None'.

5.2.2.2 Range of Values

- Helps analyze data by displaying the minimum and maximum value of the selected field by clicking the "Load" button. It can be used to refer the values.

Observation: In the current view, minimum sale is $7,763 and maximum sale is $609,683

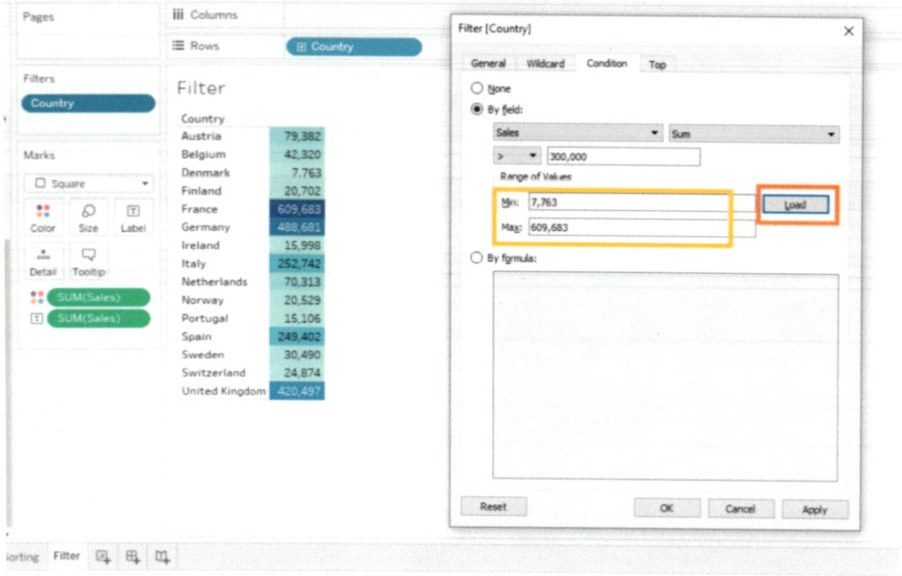

5.2.2.3 Filter by Formula

- Filter dataset by writing formula using this option.
- Click on radio button 'By formula'-Enter formula in the box as shown in the figure - Click Ok.

Observation: Filters and displays the countries whose total sum is greater $300,000

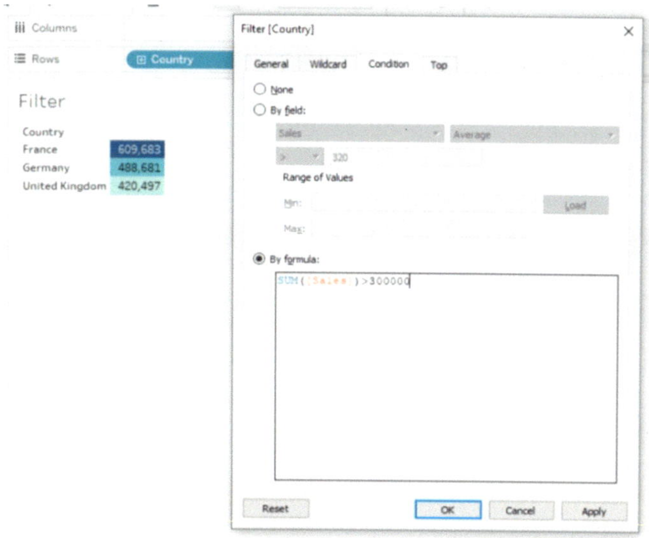

5.2.3 Top Filters

- Filters and displays the top or bottom 'n' number of records.
- Types of Top filters
  1. By Filed
  2. By Formula

5.2.3.1 By Field

- In the example shown, filter restricts the data set to show top 10 records based on the sum of sales.
- Select 'Top' tab in Filter Window- Choose the number of records as 10-Select the field Sales from the drop-down list -Choose the aggregate type as sum- Click Ok.

Observation: Filters and displays the first 10 records in the table.

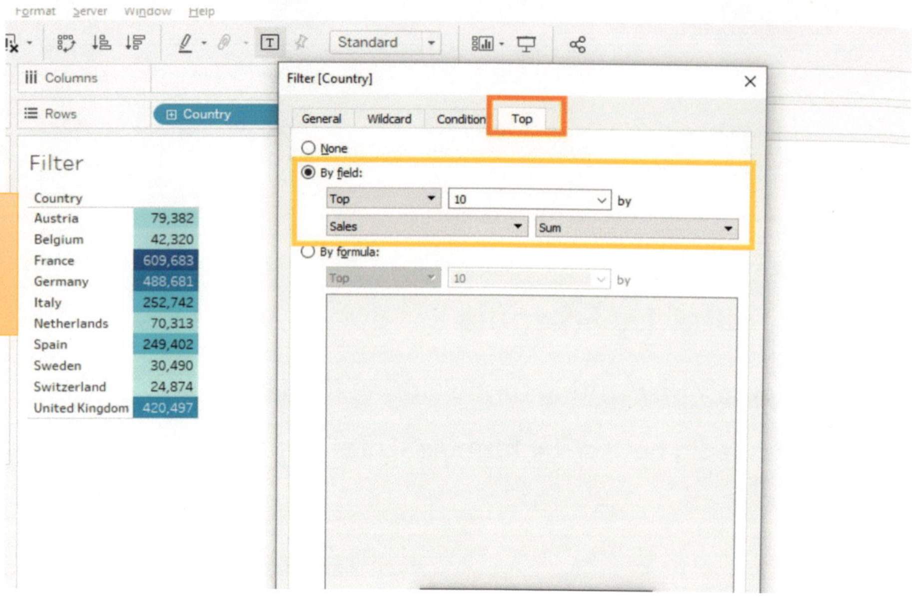

5.2.3.2 By Formula

- The top or bottom condition can also be given through formula
- To display the bottom 5 records of the table: Click on the Top tab of filter window-Click radio button 'By formula'- Select Bottom – Enter number of records as 5- Enter formula: SUM[(Sales)]- Click Ok.

Observation: Bottom 5 records of the table is displayed.

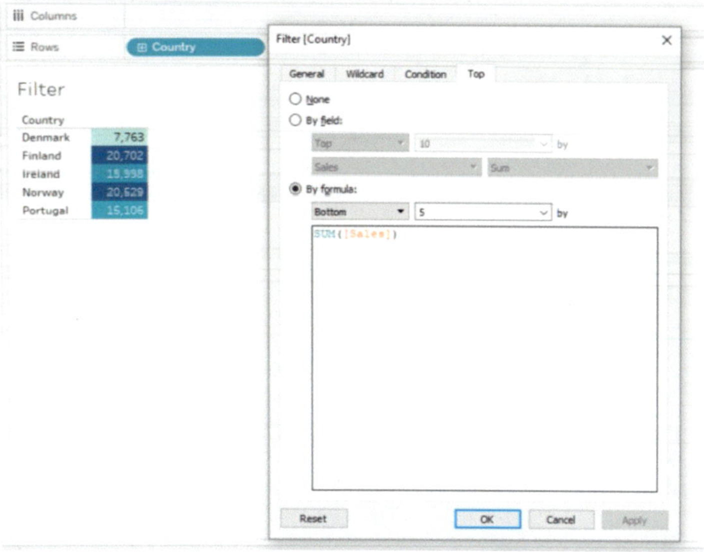

5.2.4 Quick Filter

- Fast and simple filtering is done by quick filters. Filtering by selecting few values can be done using this method.
- To filter based on different countries, Right click on the Country dimensions- Select 'Show Filter'- Filter panel appears on the right-hand side of the page as shown below.

PLEASE NOTE: Sometimes the Show me pane may cover the filter panel. Click on the Show me tab to close the pane.

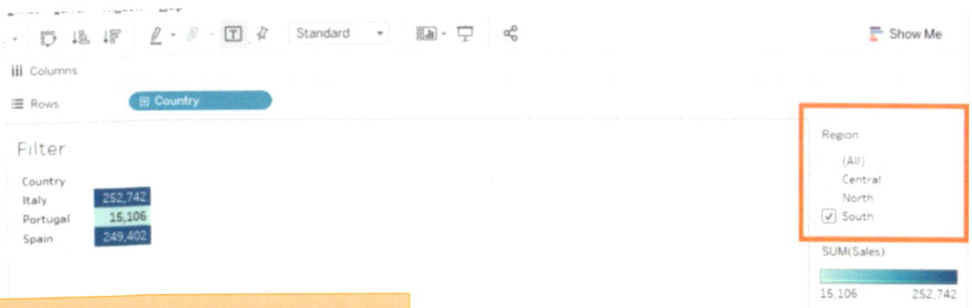

Observation: The table displays the total sales of each country in the south region.

Clicking the check box 'All' either brings all values back if any values are unchecked or if user clicks it again, then all values become unchecked and user can individually select values.

PLEASE NOTE: Options shown in the Quick Filter box may look different as it depends on the type of filter used (e.g., Wildcard, Condition, Top)

Filters can be removed by dragging out the field pill used for filtering from the filter shelf.

6 Organizing Data

6.1 Groups

- Groups are created to combine related members in a field. Grouping helps to simplify large numbers of dimension members by combining them into higher level categories. Grouping helps to organize data according to the requirement.
- Benefits of grouping:
  - Grouping helps you to combine data together in a format that may not exist in the current source data.
  - Groups creates custom combinations and hierarchies to address the inconsistencies that arise when data is pulled from various sources and data is not clean. For example, different business groups may use different names to represent the same data (e.g., spelling variances such as Aus, Aust, and Australia).
  - Groups are added to the data pane and can be applied any of the worksheets.

6.1.1 Create a Group

- Groups can be created in two ways:
  - From fields in the data pane
  - By selecting data in the view and clicking on the group icon.
- Create a view as shown below with Sub-Category dimension in Rows Shelf and Discount measure in Text shelf in Marks card.

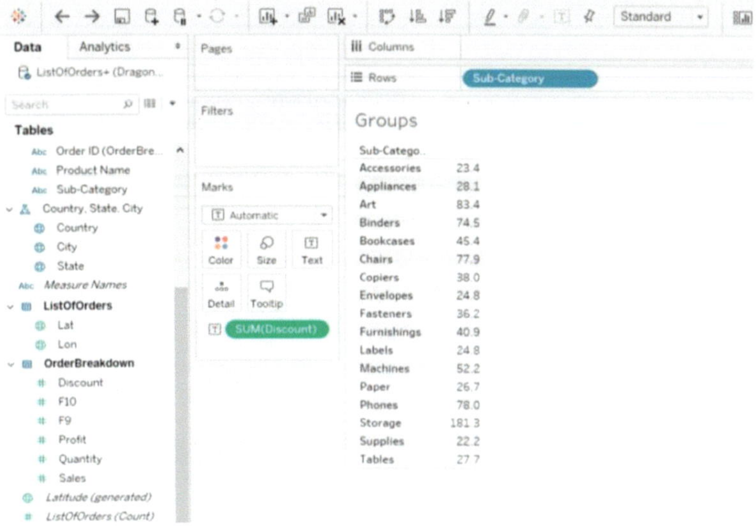

- User wants to group the total discount given to Chairs and Tables under Sub-category dimension:
- To do so, hold Ctrl or Shift key to select Chairs and Tables and click either on the Group icon that appears on the tool tip or select group icon on the toolbar present at the top of the workspace as shown below.

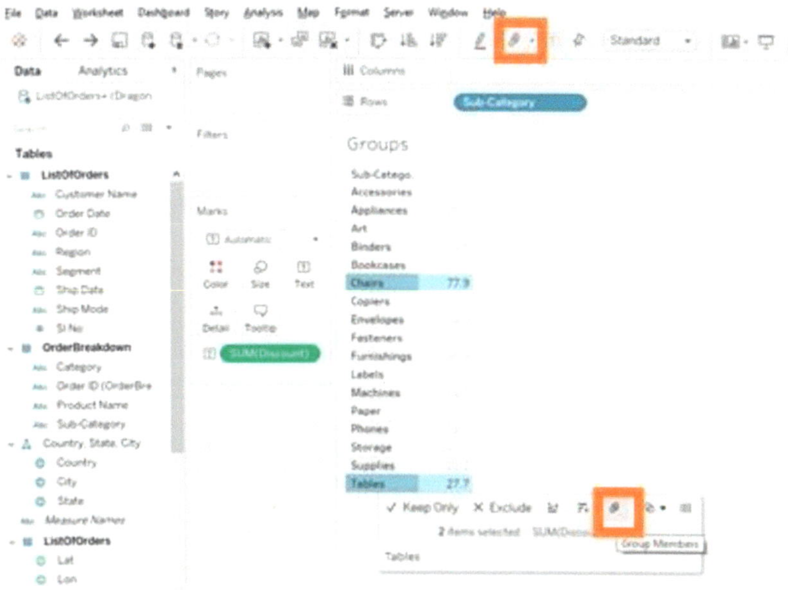

➢ The selected members are combined into a single group. A default name is created using the combined member names as shown below.

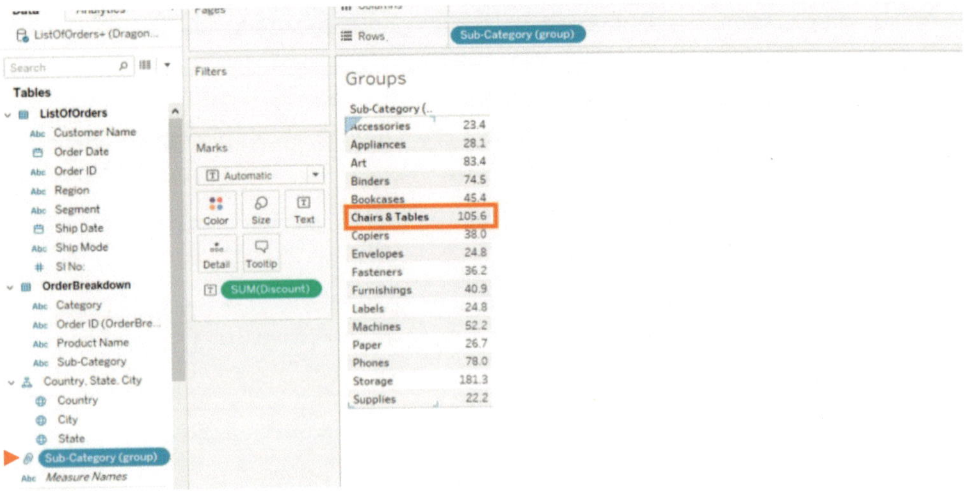

Tableau creates a new dimension adding (group) at the end of the name.

Original dimension remains the same, Tableau creates a new logical dimension based on grouping values.

PLEASE NOTE

To rename the group values, right click on the combined value and select Edit Alias.

To rename the group, right click on the group dimension and select Rename.

➢ Above view can also be created by : Right click on the Sub-Category dimension in the data pane, select Create and click on Group.

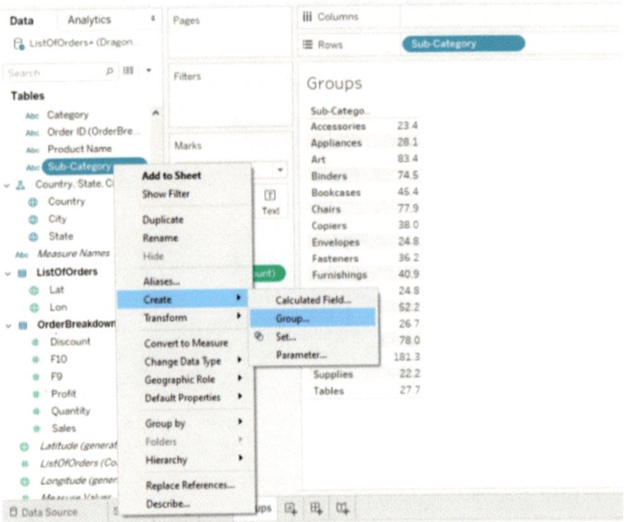

➢ Dialogue box appears. Hold the Ctrl key and select the members to combine - click Group and Click Apply. Sub-category group dimension is created in the Data pane as shown below.

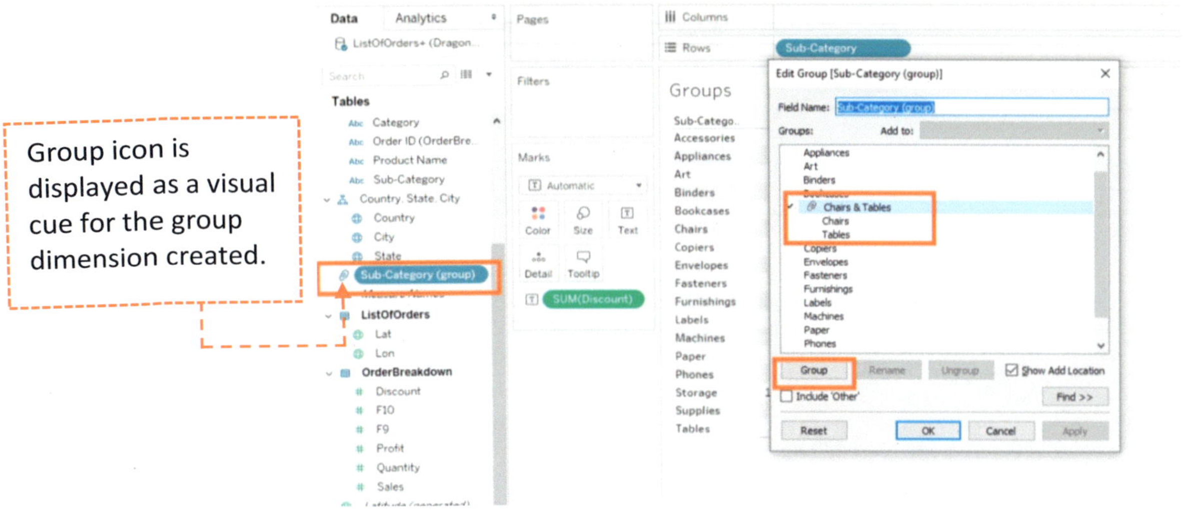

6.1.2 Edit a Group

➢ Grouped fields can be edited through the Edit Group dialog box. New members can be added or removed from the groups, new groups can be created, default group names can be changed, etc.

6.1.2.1 Add members to existing group

➢ Right click on the group field, Sub-Category(group) dimension and click Edit Group as show below.

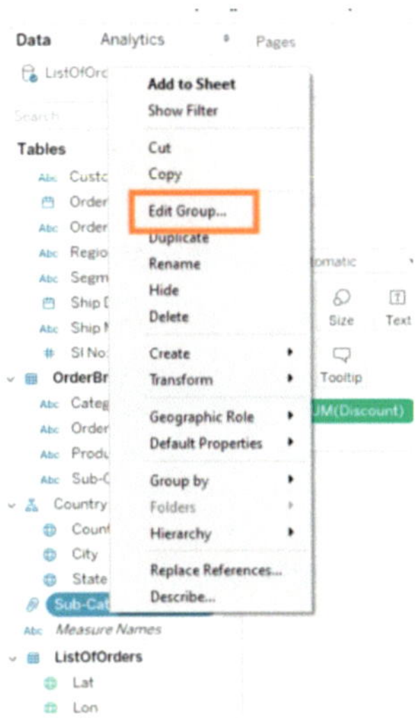

➢ In Edit dialog box, select the members to be added (e.g., Furnishings and Machines) and drag the members into the required group. Click Ok.

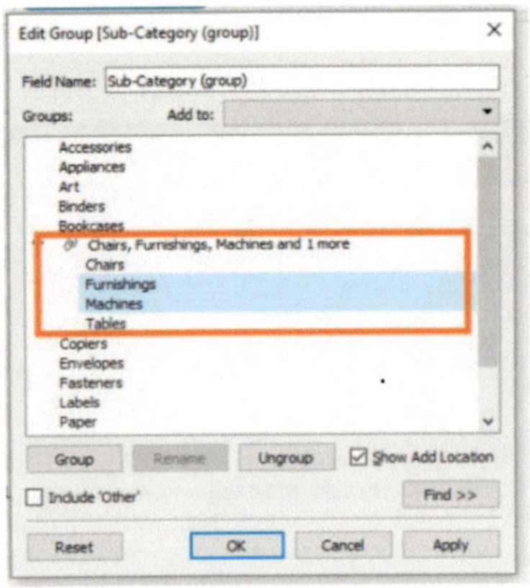

6.1.2.2 Include an 'Other' group

➢ Once a group is created, user has the option to group all remaining or non-group members in 'Other' group. This option is useful for comparing specific groups against remaining members.

➢ To do so, Right click the group field, Sub-Category (group) and select Edit Group. In the Edit dialogue box, select **Include 'Other'.** Click OK

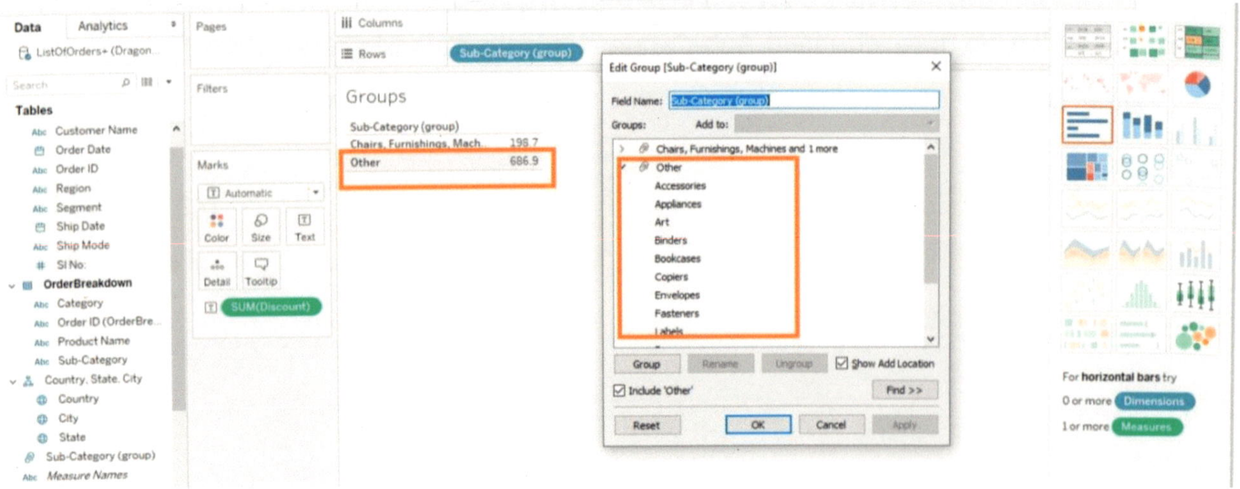

6.1.2.3 Remove members from existing group

- Right click on the group field, Sub- Category (group) and click Edit Group. In Edit dialog box select members Furnishings and Machines and click Ungroup.

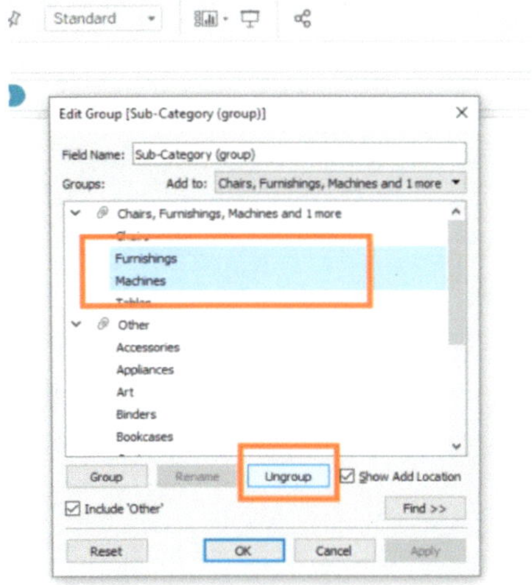

- The members are removed from the current group. Since in this example Other group is created, the members are added to it.

6.1.2.4 Create a new group in a group field

- Right click group field, Sub- Category (group) and click on Edit Group. In Edit dialog box, select members, Binders, Bookcases and Papers, and click on Group. Click Ok.

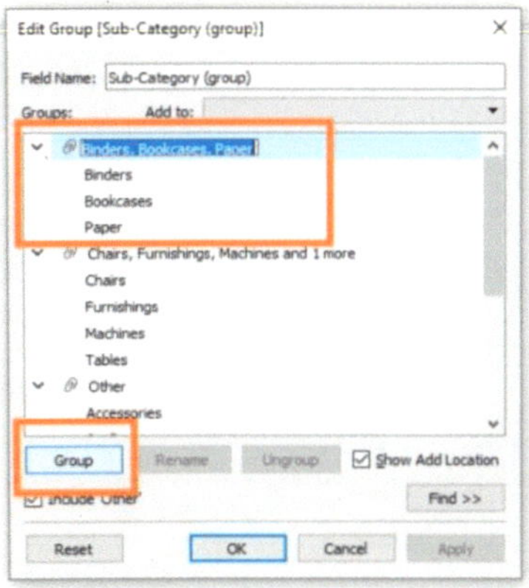

6.1.3 Color View using groups

- In addition to correcting data errors and combining dimensions, you can visually identify groups of related marks by selecting marks directly.
- Create view as shown below, with Sales measure in the Columns Shelf and Profit measures in Rows shelf. Drag Sub-Category on to the Detail Shelf of the Marks card.

- Press and hold the **CTRL** or **Shift** key on the keyboard to select one or more marks in the view as shown below. Click the **Group** button on the toolbar or right-click and select **Group**.

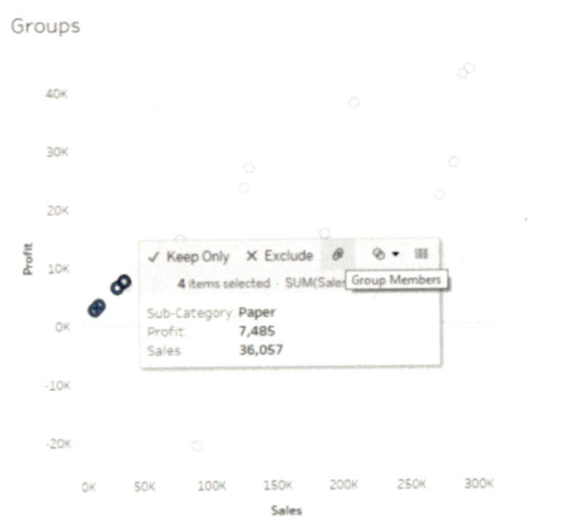

➤ The selected marks are grouped, and all other members are combined into an "Other" category. The new group field is automatically added to Color in the Marks card.

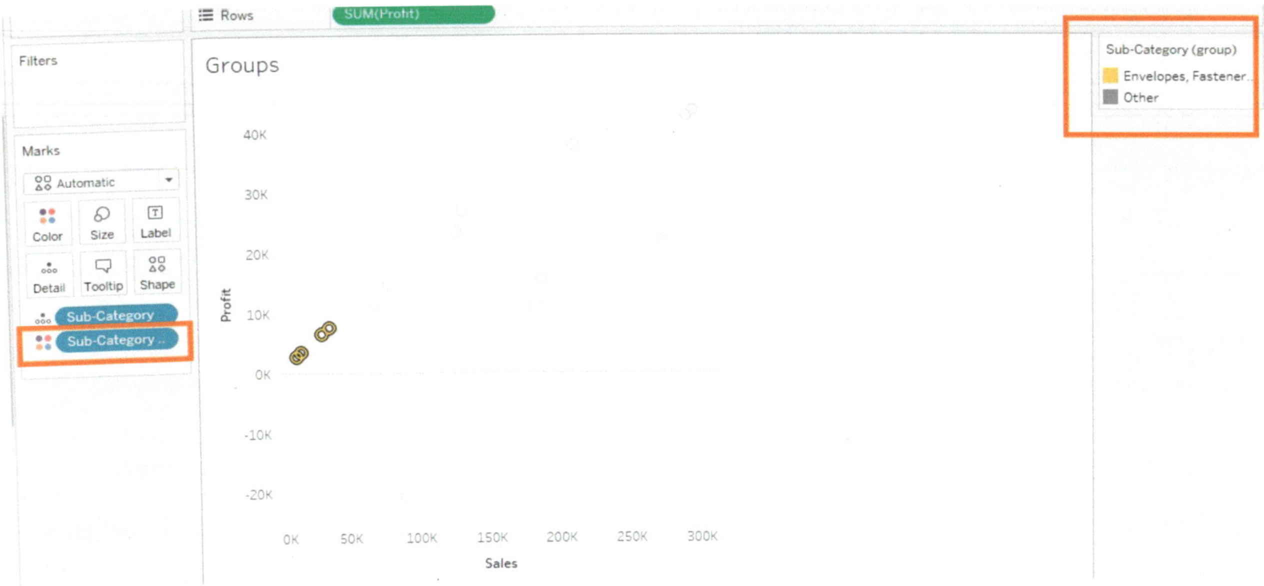

6.1.3.1 Tableau Groups -Custom Maps

➤ Create a new view, by grouping values in a map.

➤ Create the map by double clicking on the Country dimension. Once the map is displayed in the view, Click the mark type to Map so that filled map is shown.

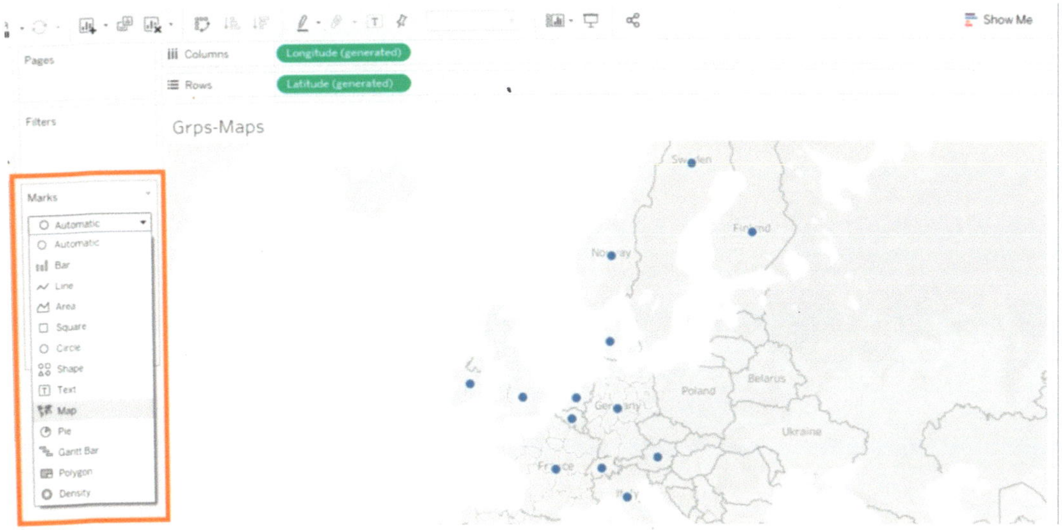

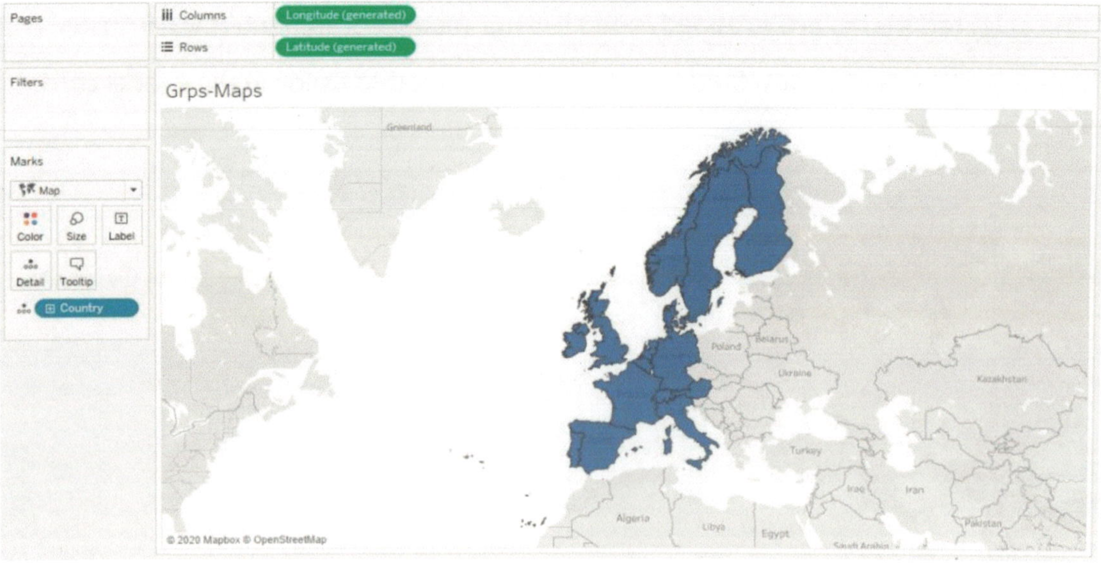

➢ Group the countries into 3 regions North, South and Central (Consider the Region dimension does not exist). To do so, select individual countries by holding Ctrl and click on the paperclip to group all the selected counties together as shown below.

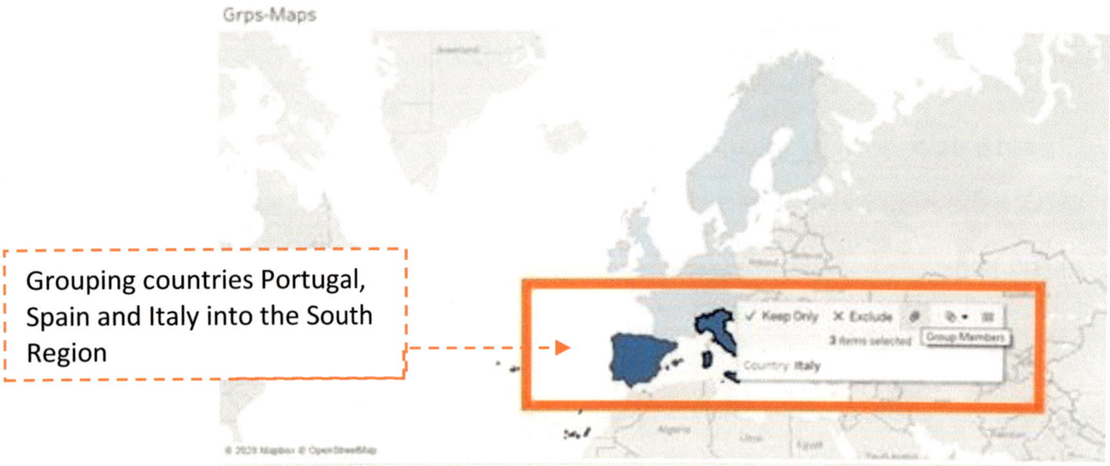

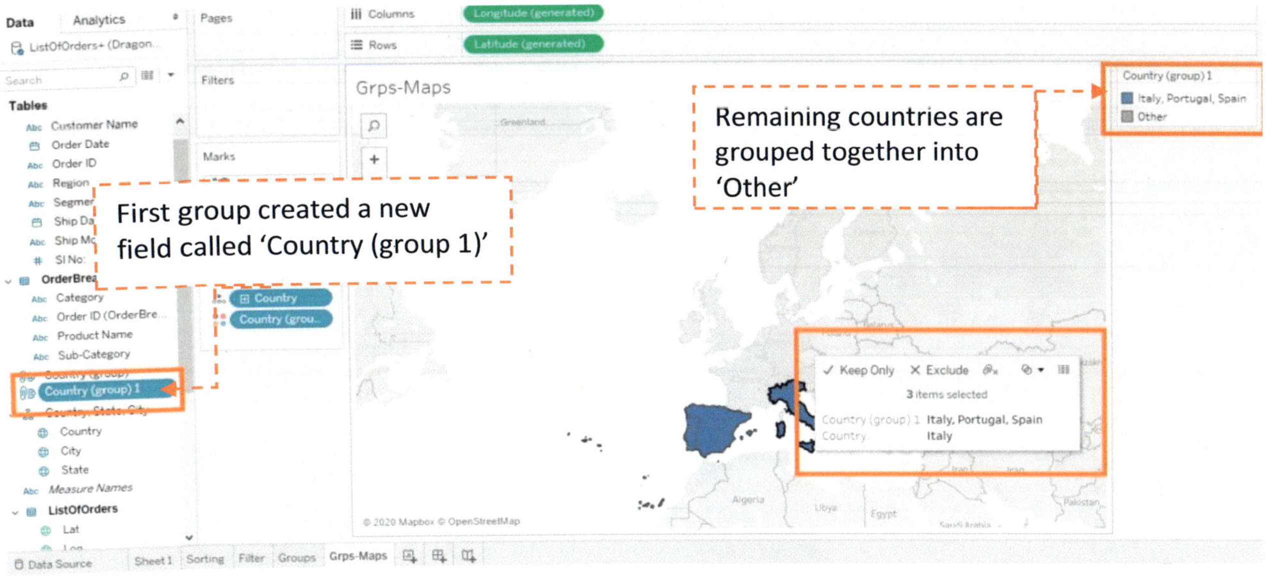

➢ Similarly group together the remaining countries into North and Central regions as shown below.

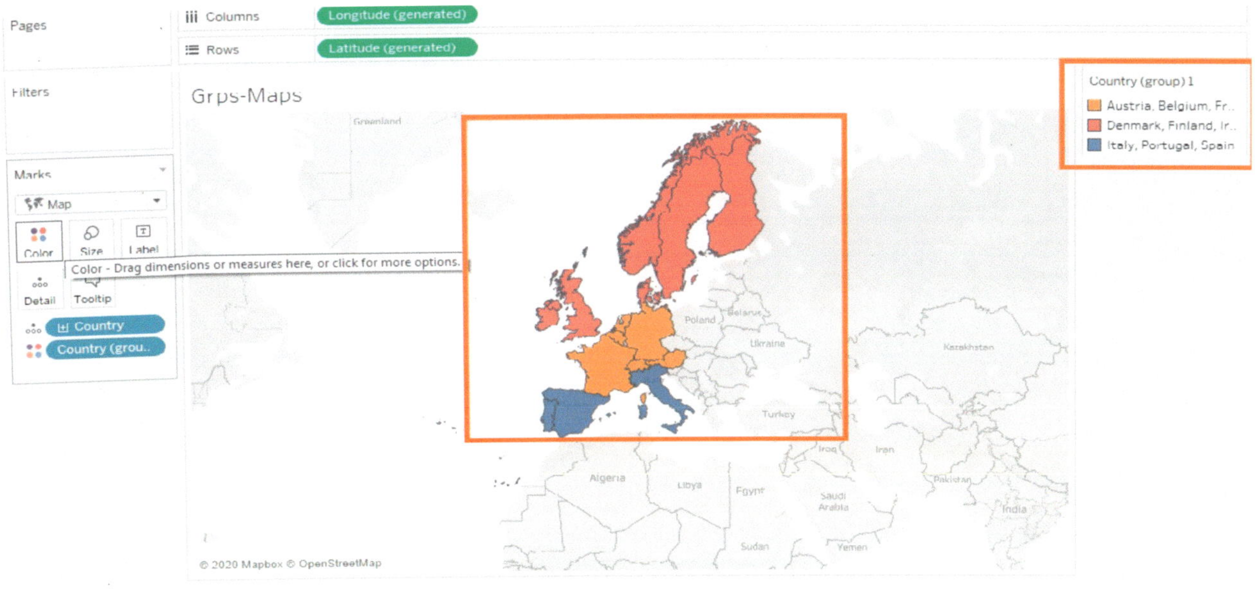

- As seen in the screenshot above, the map consists of three different colors for the three different regions. To rename each group, right click on each value in the color legend and select Edit Alias..., a dialog box appears, type the respective region name and Click Ok as shown below.

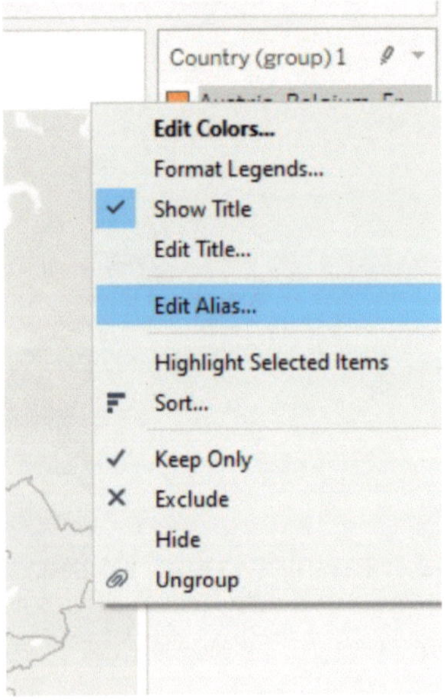

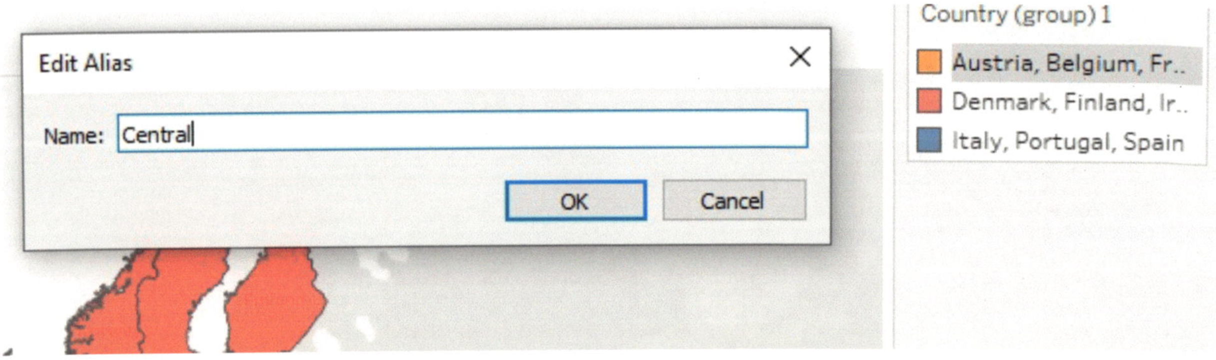

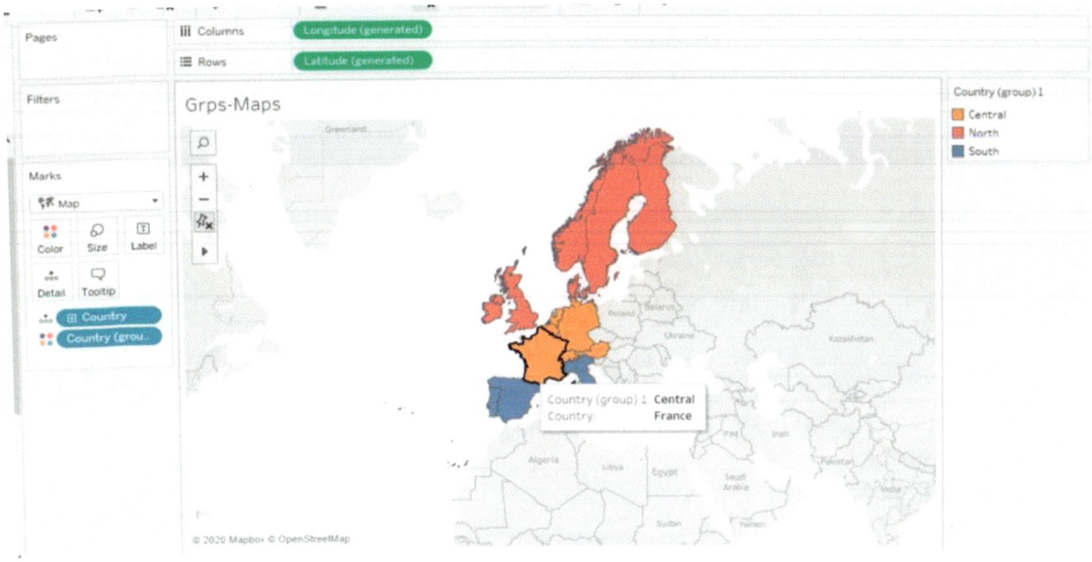

6.2 Hierarchies

- In Tableau, the hierarchy is an arrangement where dimensions are represented at various levels. Hierarchies are created by bringing one or more dimensions as levels under principal dimension.
- When data source is connected, Tableau automatically separates data fields into hierarchies so you can easily break down the viz. You can also create your own custom hierarchies.
- Tableau provides a drill-down action. With the help of + and – symbols, user can navigate from a higher level to a nested level or lower level.
- Having meaningful hierarchies in the analysis is useful as user can expand from and contract to the main dimension as needed.

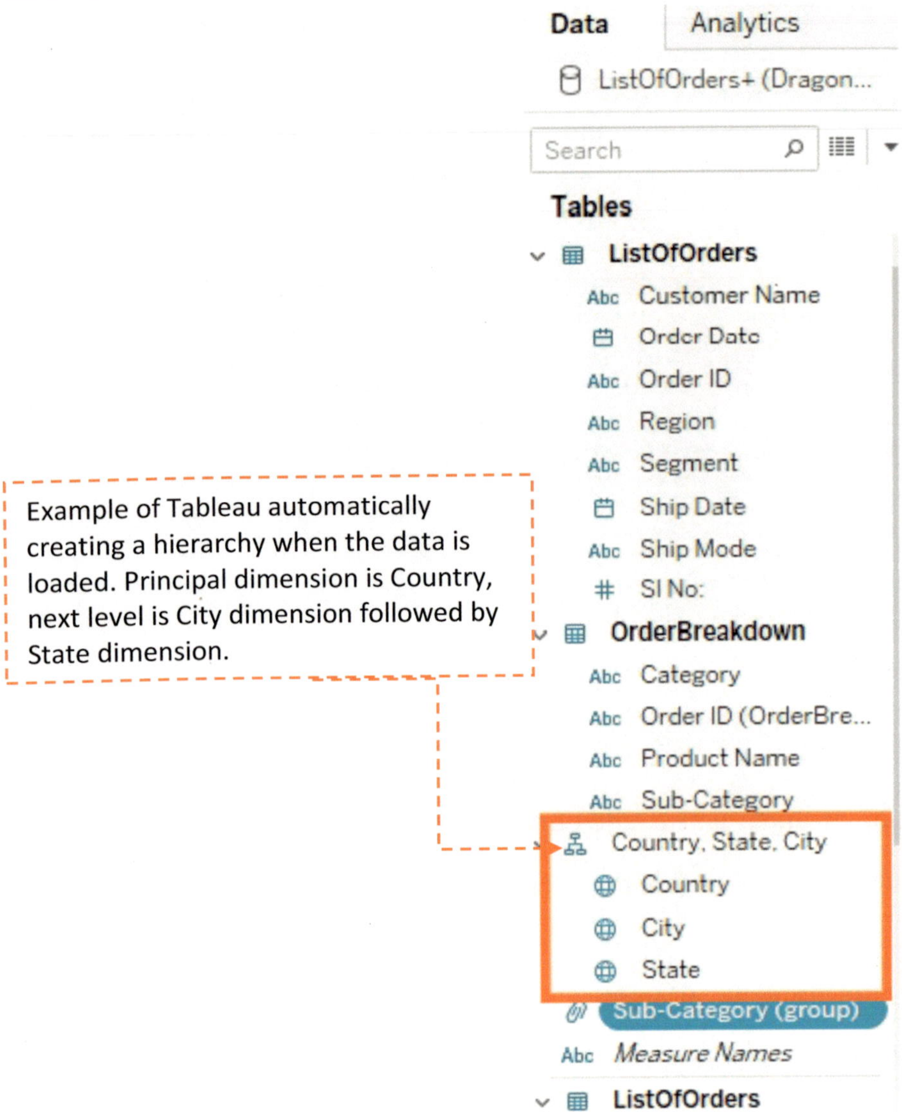

6.2.1 Create Hierarchies

- To create hierarchy (e.g., using Category -> Sub-Category -> Segment), in the Data pane select and right click on the Dimension name Category (principal dimension), on which user wants to create a hierarchy. From the dialog box select Hierarchy and select Create Hierarchy...

PLEASE NOTE

Alternative way to create hierarchy: In **Data** pane, drag a field and drop it directly on top of another field (principal dimension).

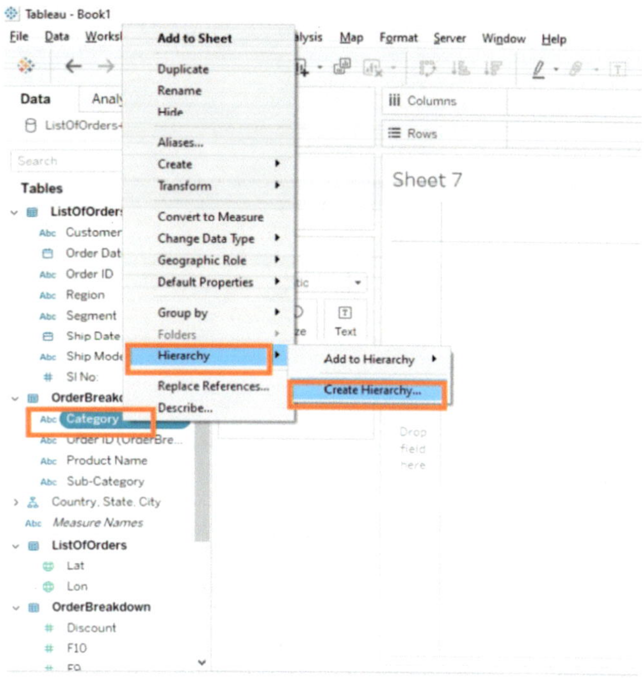

➢ Select **Create Hierarchy..** and a pop window appears to rename the hierarch as shown below. Rename hierarchy as Category_Breakdown.

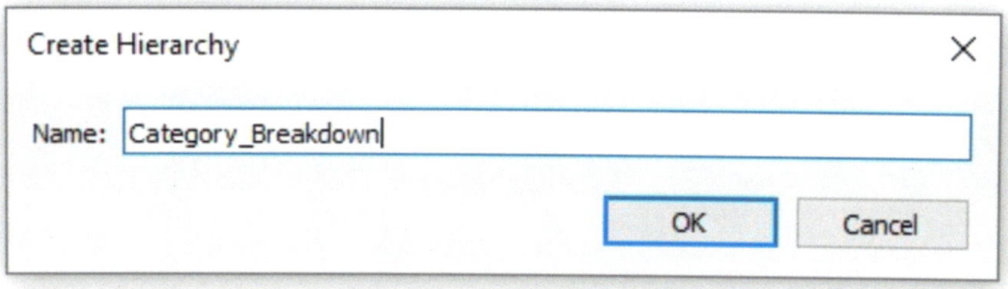

➢ There are two methods to add members to hierarchies:

Method 1: Drag and drop the required dimension to the hierarchy in Tableau. While dropping, Tableau shows a horizontal line representing the member position. In the example, drag Sub-Category dimension onto Category_Breakdown hierarchy.

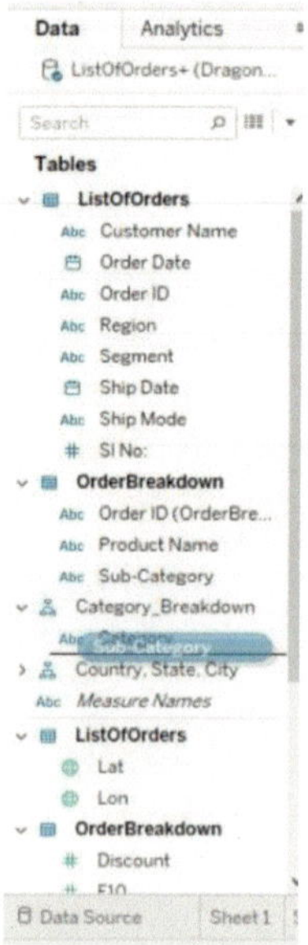

➢ Method 2: Right click on the Dimension name, Sub-Category to add to the existing hierarchy, Category_Breakdown. Select the 'hierarchy' option and select 'Add to hierarchy' and select 'Category_Breakdown'.

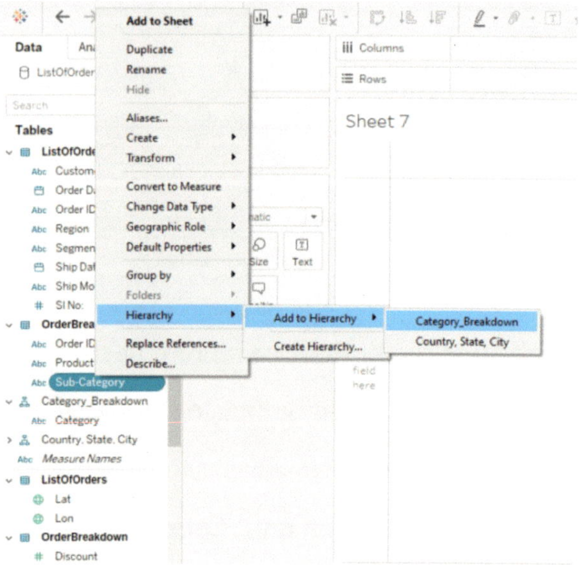

➢ Similarly, add Segment dimension to Category_Breakdown hierarchy using either of the two methods.

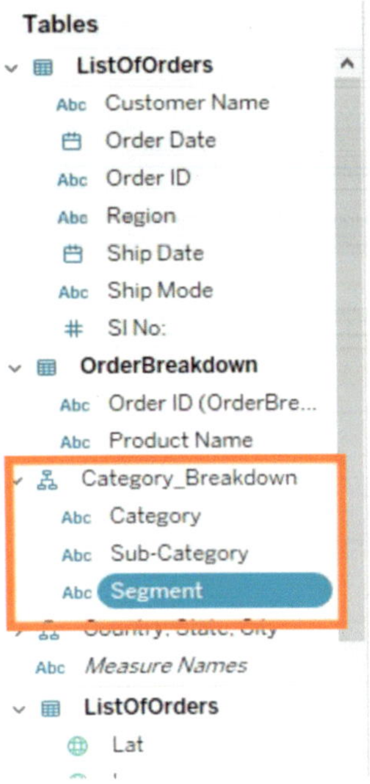

PLEASE NOTE

Positions of the fields in the hierarchy can be rearranged by dragging and dropping in the order required.

6.2.2 Drill-Down or Roll-Up in a hierarchy

- When user adds a field from a hierarchy to the visualization, user can drill-down or roll-up in the hierarchy to add or subtract more levels of detail.
- To drill-down or roll-up in a hierarchy:
    - In the visualization, click the **+** or **-** icon on the hierarchy field.
- In the example, Drag Category dimension from hierarchy/double click Category dimension to Rows Shelf.

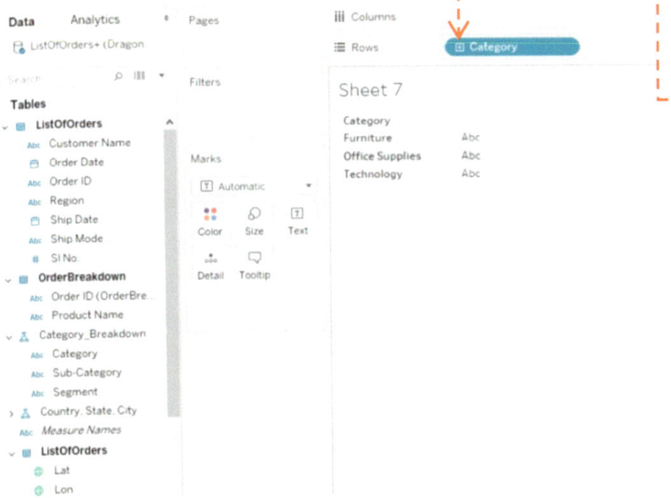

The tiny + symbol next to category helps to perform drill down action.

➢ Create a view with sales across different categories.

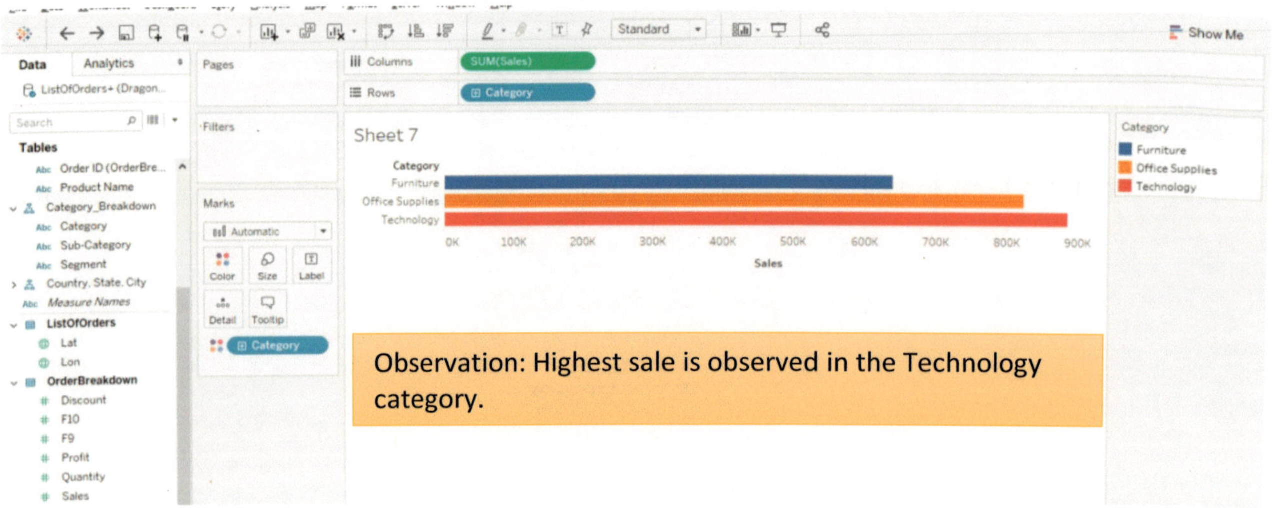

➢ To view visualization of sales across Category and Sub-Category categories, click on the + sign to drill down.

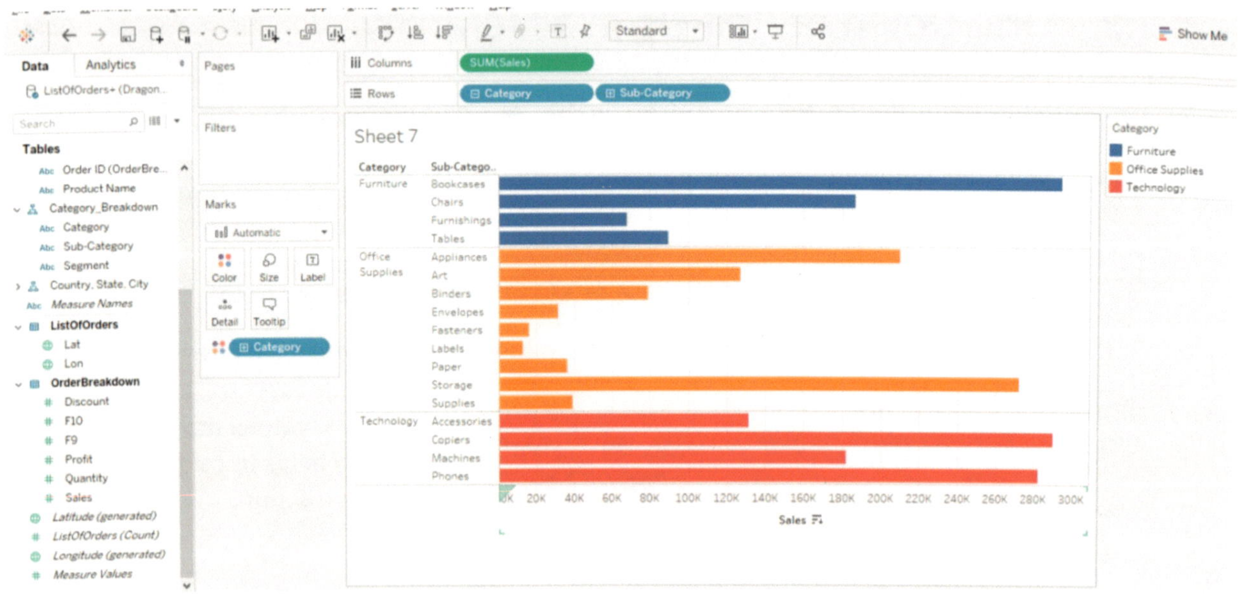

➢ To roll-up click on the – sign next to the Category pill as shown below.

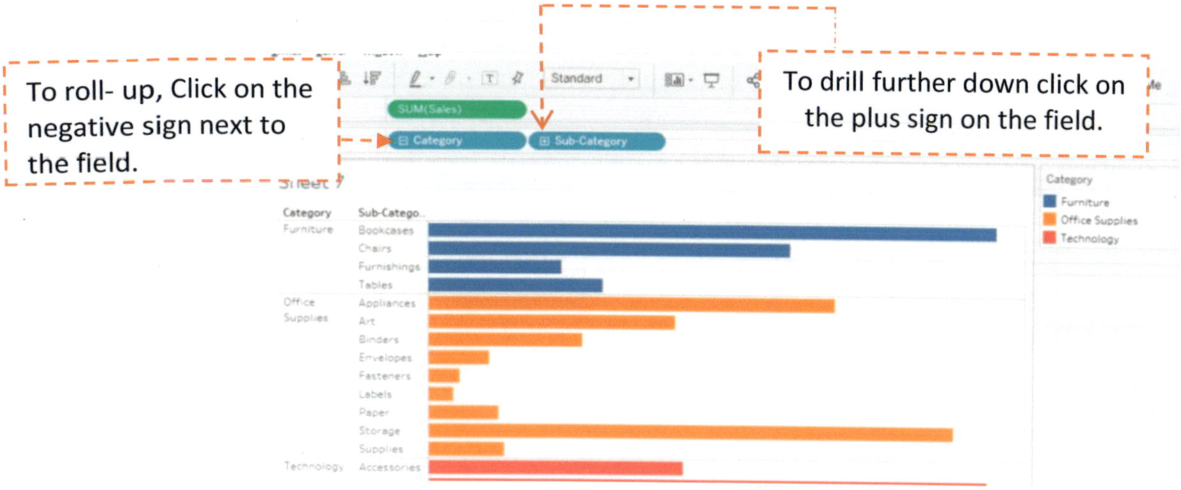

- Once the – sign on the Category field is clicked, the view comes back to the original one with Sales across the Category.

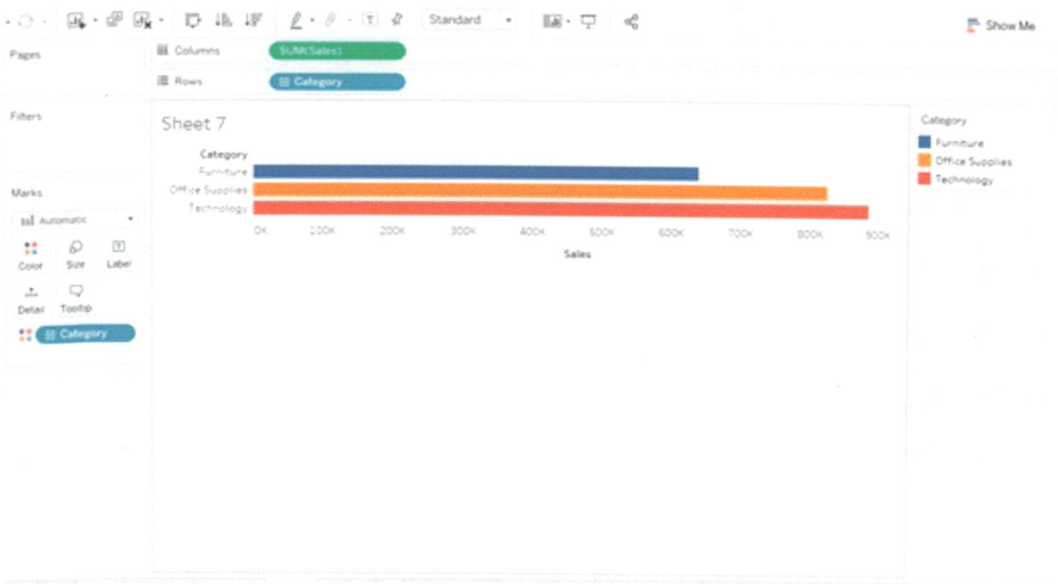

6.2.3 Remove Hierarchy

6.2.3.1 Remove members from Hierarchy

- Select and right click on the Hierarchy member, Segment dimension from the hierarchy. Select Hierarchy and click Remove from Hierarchy as shown below.

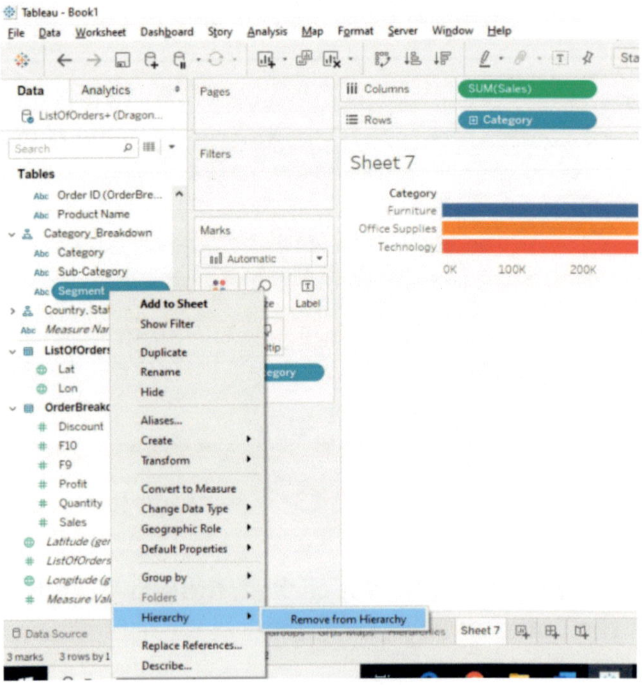

➢ Segment dimension gets removed from the Category_Breakdown division hierarchy as shown below.

PLEASE NOTE

Alternatively, to remove members from Tableau hierarchies, drag members from hierarchy to the dimension pane.

6.2.3.2 Remove Hierarchy

➢ Right click on the hierarchy, Category_Breakdown in the data pane and select option **Remove Hierarchy**.

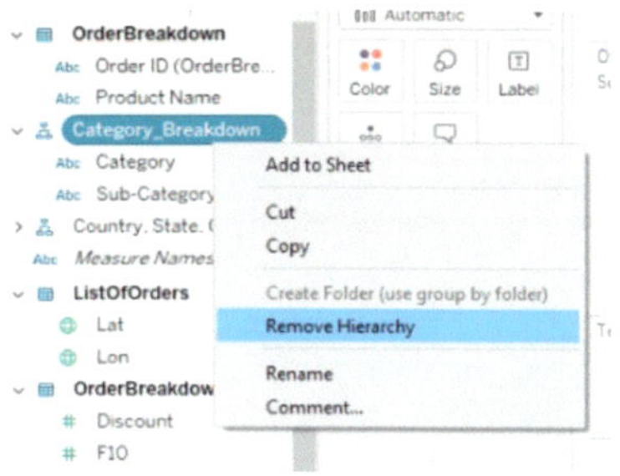

➢ All the fields in the hierarchy are removed and hierarchy name is no longer shown in data pane. The fields are detached from the hierarchy into the data pane as shown below.

6.3 Sets

➢ Sets are custom fields that define a subset of data based on certain conditions.

➢ There are two types of sets:

- Fixed set
- Dynamic set

6.3.1 Create Fixed Set

- Members of fixed sets do not change, even if the underlying data changes. A fixed set can be based on single or multiple dimensions.
- For example, create initial view of profit across different countries as shown below. Drag country to the Rows Shelf and Profit to Columns Shelf, Click on Packed bubbles chart on the Show me tab.

To create a fixed set: In the visualization select the Top three countries with the highest profit. Right click on the selected members and select **Create Set.**

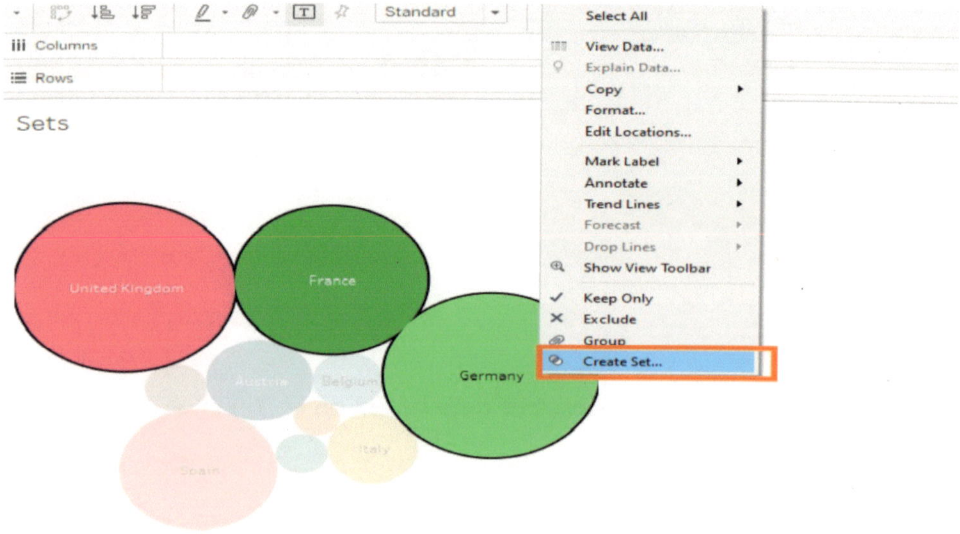

Alternative: Select the members and a dialog box appears. Select the set icon  to create the set.

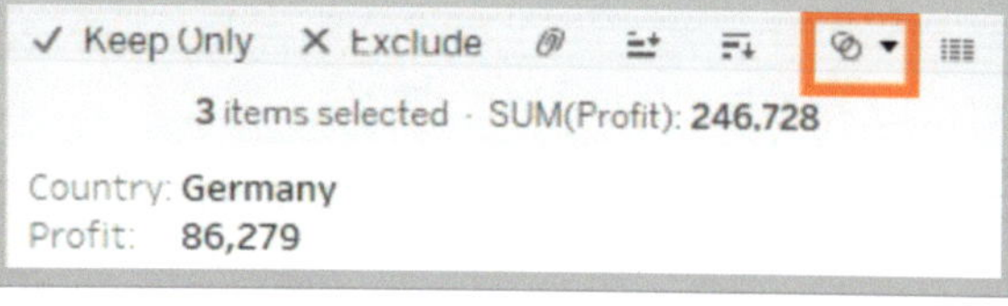

➢ In the Create Set dialog box,

- Name: Enter the Name of the set as Top 3
- By default, members listed in the dialog box is included in the set. The **Exclude** option combines all the members user did not add to the set.
- Remove any Dimensions/selected members by clicking the red "X" icon that appears when mouse hovers over a Column/Row
- **Add to Filters shelf**, automatically moves the set to the Filter shelf once created.

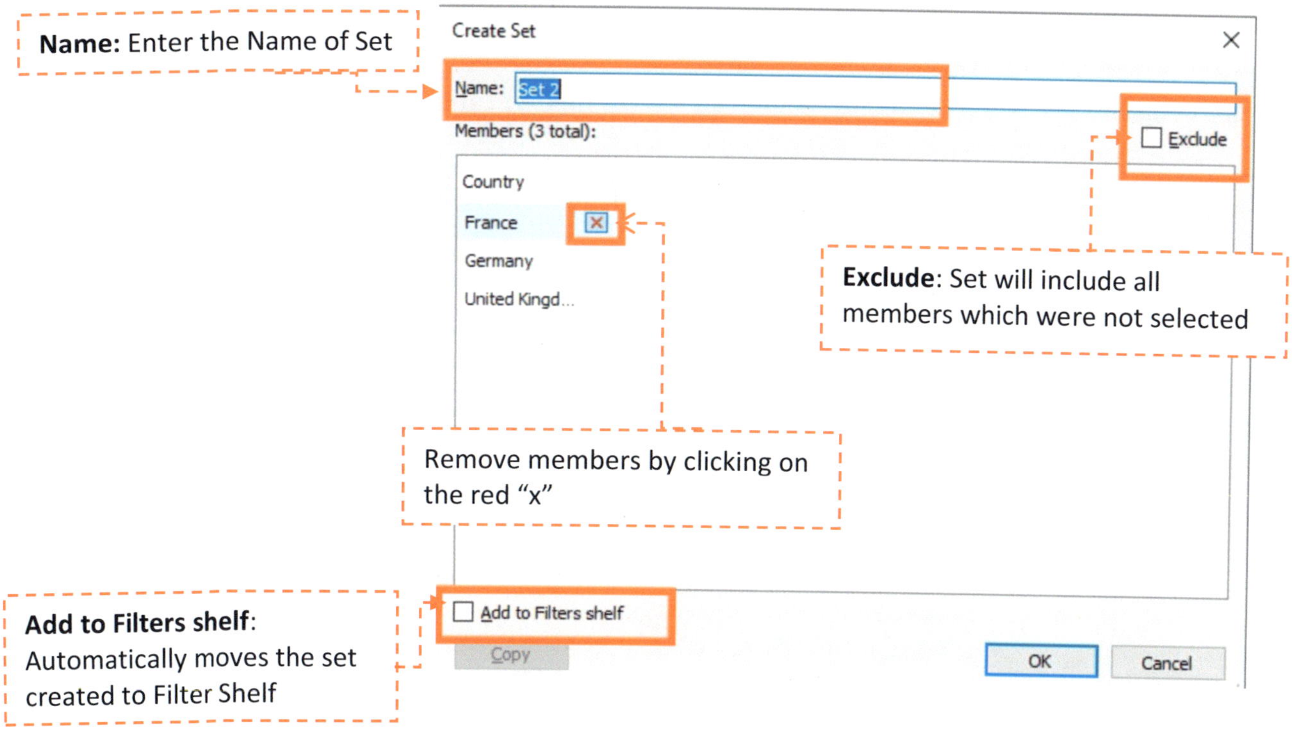

➢ Once done with the options in the Create Set dialog box click **Ok**. The new set, Top 3 is added to the bottom of the pane, under Sets section. A set icon indicates the field is a set.

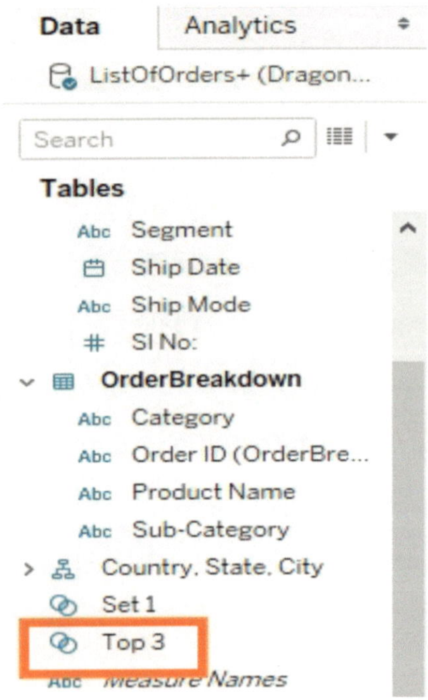

➢ Drag the set **Top 3** to the Rows shelf as shown below. Tableau displays the In/Out mode. This mode separates the set into two categories:

- In: The members in the set
- Out: The members not in the set

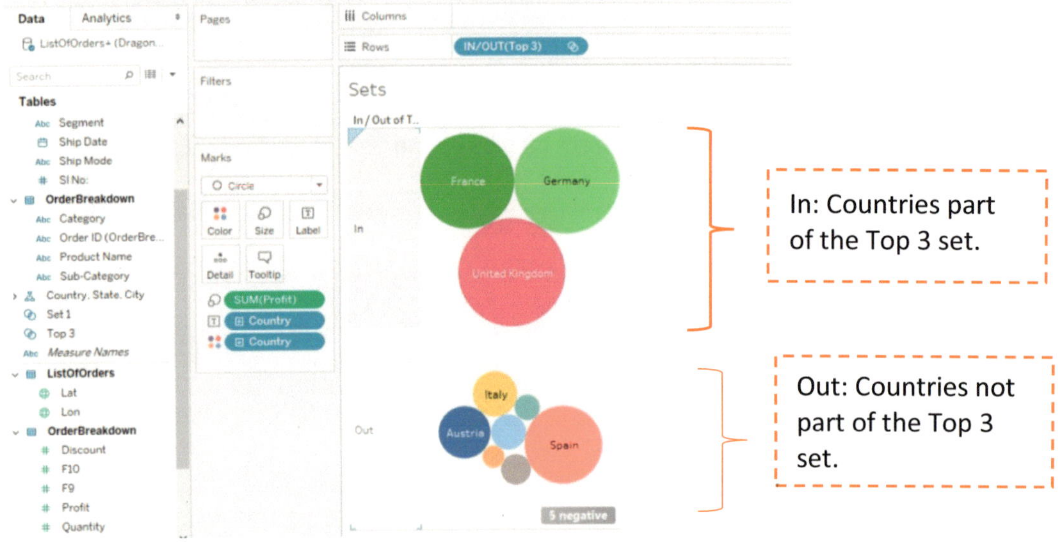

6.3.1.1 Using In/Out Visualization

- Change the existing View to table format by clicking on the Highlight Tables in the Show Me tab. Drag/Remove Country dimension off the Rows Shelf.

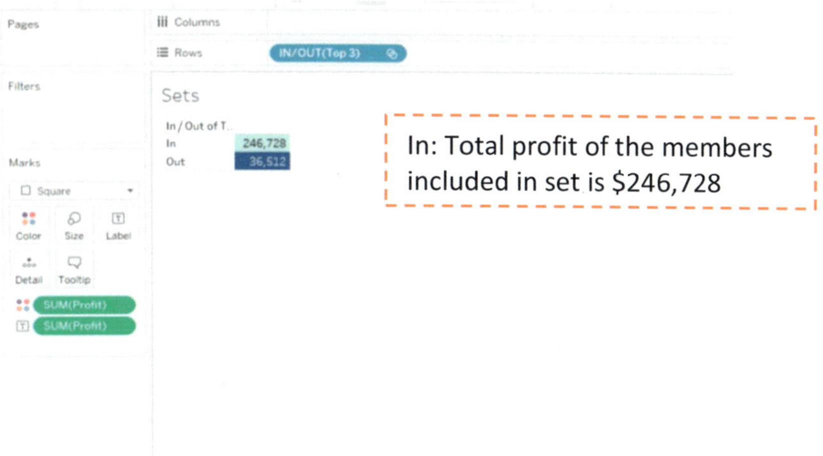

- To show the members selected, click on the Dropdown arrow in the upper right corner of the IN/OUT (Top 3) member present in the Rows Shelf. Next, select the **Show Members in Set** option from the Dropdown menu.

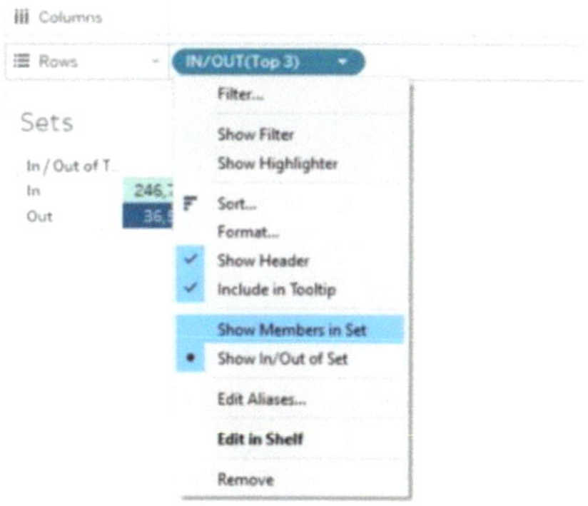

- From the below screenshot, the members present in the set, Top 3 is displayed.

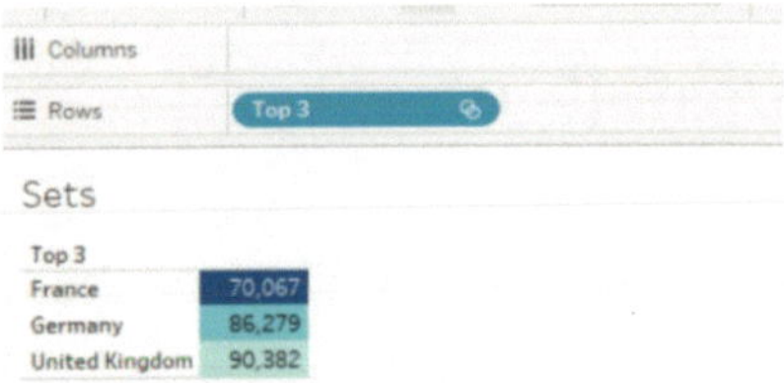

➤ To display the member countries in the In and Out format. Click on the arrow at the bottom corner of the Top 3 pill and select **Show In/ Out of Set**

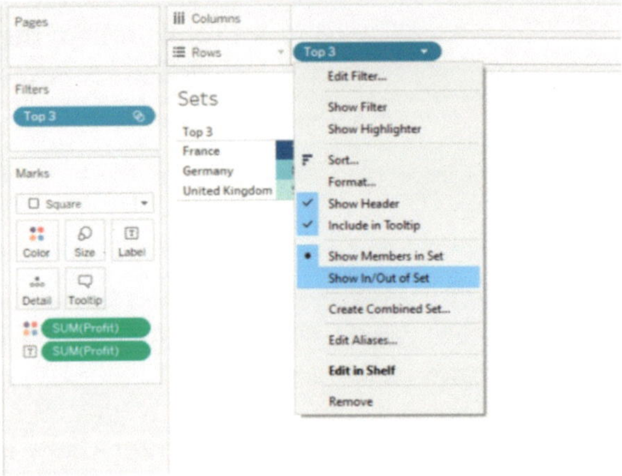

➤ Drag the Country dimension to Rows shelf to display countries in the In and Out Mode.

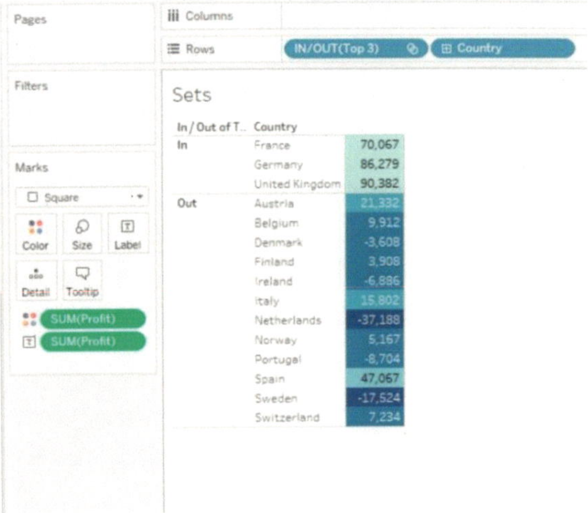

6.3.2 Create Dynamic Set

- Members of dynamic sets change when the underlying data changes. Dynamic sets can be based only on a single dimension.
- To create a dynamic set: In the Data pane, right- click on the dimension, Sub-Category and select **Create** and click **Set**.

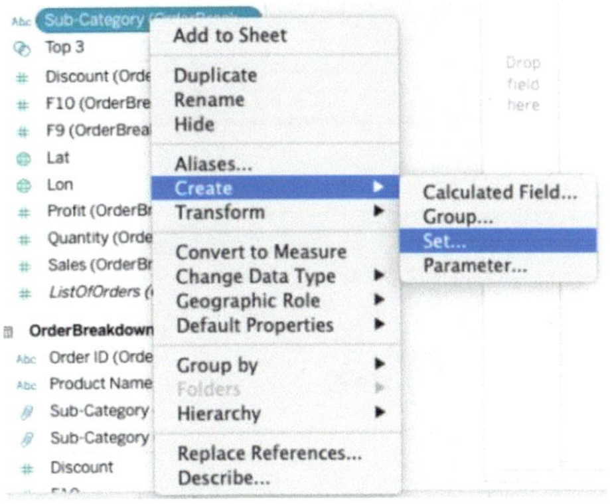

- In the Create Set dialog box,
  - **Name**: Enter the name of the Tableau set
  - **General Tab**: Used to select the required members from the available list.
  - **Condition Tab**: Used to define rules that determine which members to include in the set
  - **Top Tab**: Used to define limit on what members to include in the set.

6.3.2.1 Set using General Tab

- The General tab of a tableau sets consist of three options:
- **Select from List:** This option allows you to choose the required members from the available list.
- **Custom Value List:** This option allows you to add Custom members by typing text.
- **Use all:** This option allows you to select All the available members from the list.

➢ Create a set called Set_General by selecting the first three members or three random members from the list in the Sub-Category dimension as shown below and click Ok. Set_General set is created in the Data pane.

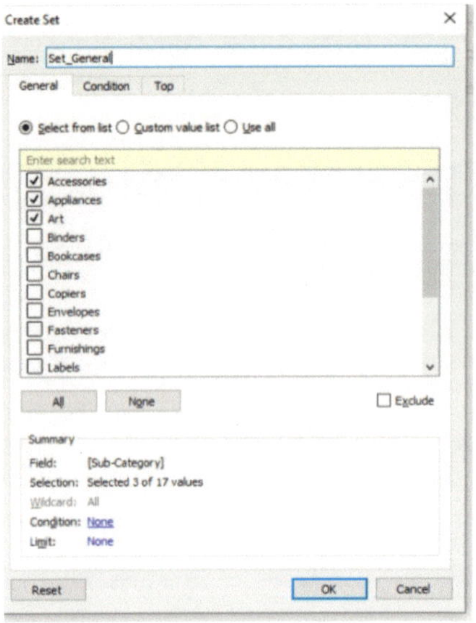

➢ Drag the Set_General set to the Rows shelf and drag Quantity to the Text Shelf of the marks card. Click on the down arrow on the IN/OUT(Set_General) pill and select **Show Members in Set** as shown below.

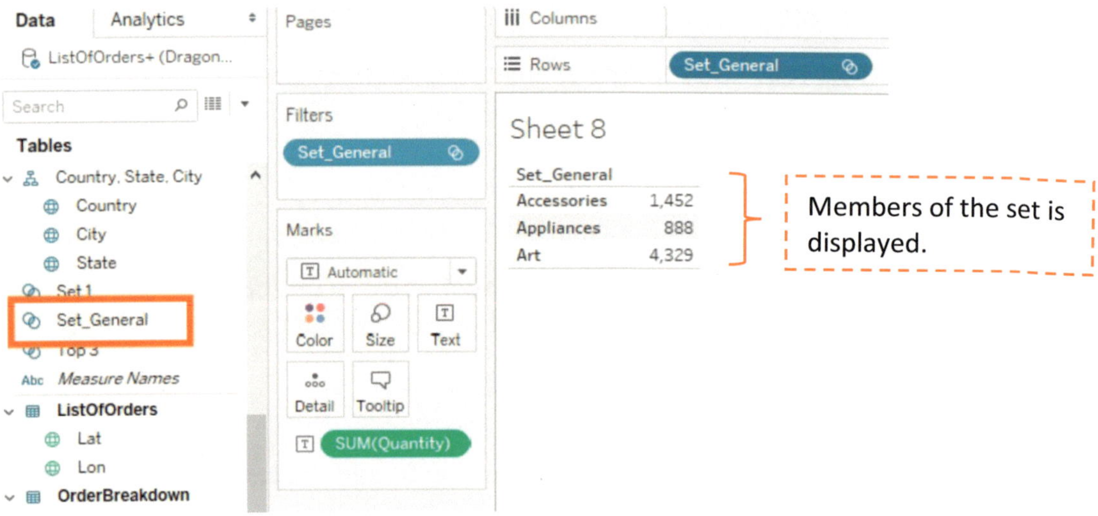

6.3.2.2 Set using Condition Tab

- Members are selected based on certain rules.
- For example, Create a set with members of Sub-Category with quantity > 2500.
- In Data pane, right click on Sub-Category dimension, Select create and click set. Choose the Condition tab. In the condition tab click on the radio button **By field.** In the operator drop down menu select the greater than sign and enter 2500 as shown below.

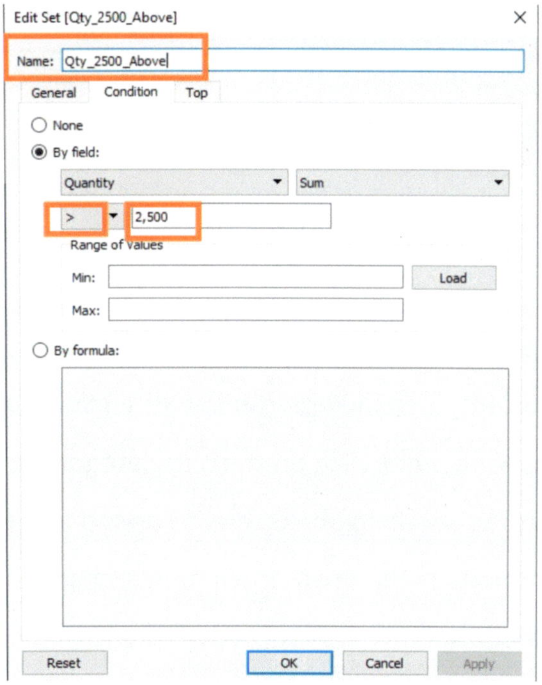

- Click **OK**. The newly created set is found in the Data pane. Drag the Set onto the Rows shelf and click the arrow on the bottom right corner of the set pill and select **Show Members in Set**. The members in the set whose quantity value greater than 2500 is displayed as shown below.

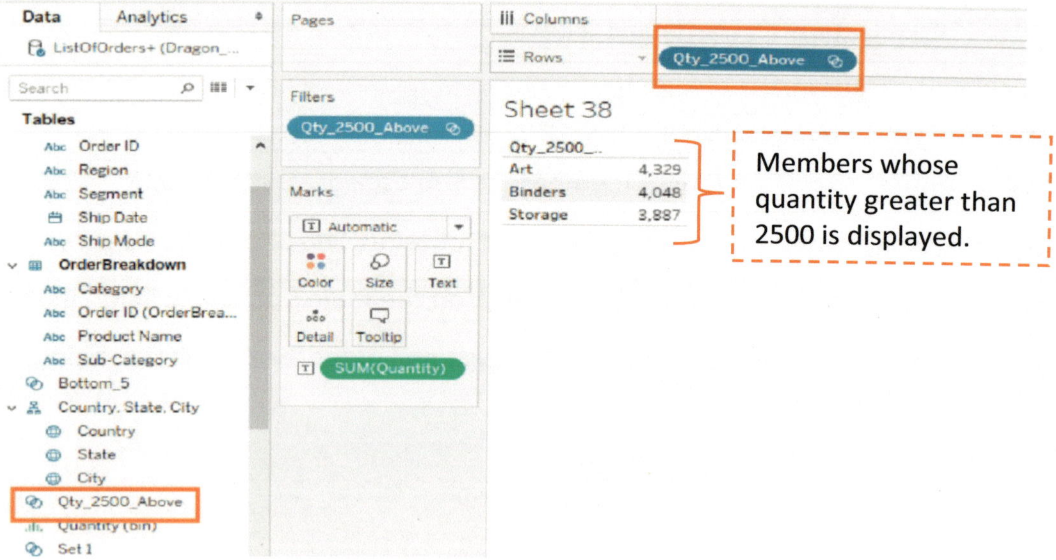

6.3.2.3 Set using Top Tab

- Top tab is used to select the Top and Bottom few records.
- Create a set called 'Bottom_5' to include the bottom 5 Sub-Category products based on their quantity. In Data pane, right click on the Sub-category dimension and select Create and click Set. In the Create set dialog box, select **Top** tab and click on the radio button "By Field". Select Bottom from the drop-down menu, change the number to 5, Select the dimension Sub-Category from the drop-down menu and click **OK** as shown below.

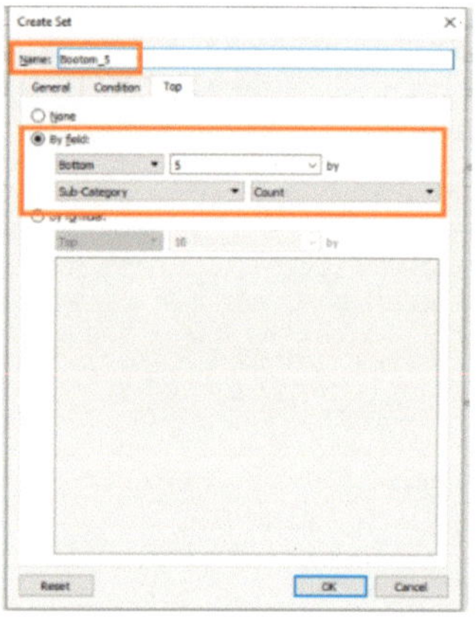

➢ The newly created set, Bottom_5 is found in the Data pane. Drag the Set onto the Rows shelf and click the arrow on the bottom right corner of the set pill and select **Show Members in Set**. The bottom 5 Sub-Categories based on quantity is displayed as shown below.

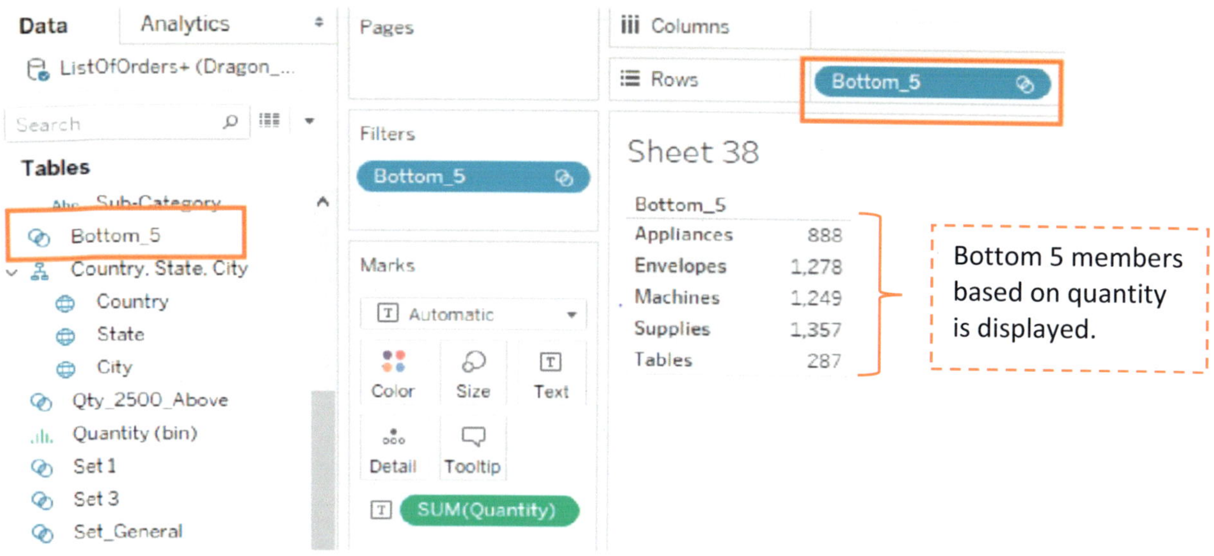

6.3.3 Edit a Set

➢ To edit the existing sets in Tableau, click on the Dropdown arrow in the upper right corner of the Set name and select the **Edit Set...** option from the context menu as shown below.

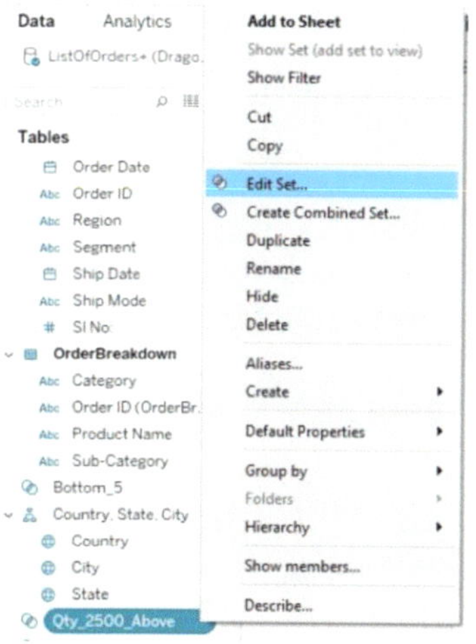

➢ Edit the 'Quantity_2500_Above' to change from 2500 to 4000 and click **OK**. Drag the newly created set to Rows shelf and click on drop down arrow in the upper right corner of the set name and select Show Member set as shown below.

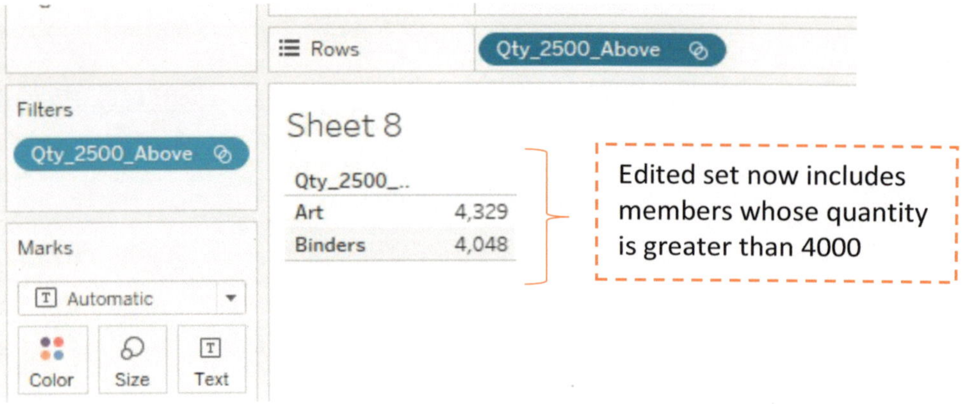

6.3.4 Delete a Set

➢ To delete the existing set in Tableau, click on the Dropdown arrow in the upper right corner of the Set name and select the **Delete** option from the context menu as shown below.

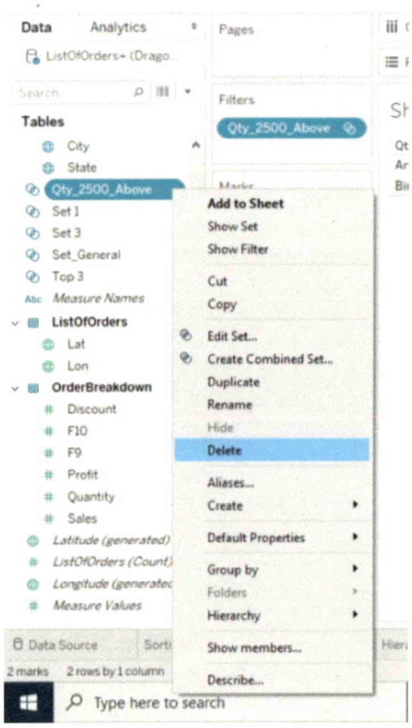

7 Dual and Combined Axis Chart

7.1 Dual Axis Chart

- Dual axis or Combination chart are two independent axes that are layered on top of each other. Dual axis chart is useful when two measures have different scales (example monetary value and percentage) or if measures need to be displayed differently (example one as bar and other as line)
- Positive: Tableau creates two separate mark cards for each of the measures. This enables selection of different mark for each of the measure, thereby creating different charts.
- Negative: Dual axis can be done only with two measures.

- To create Dual axis chart, create the below view. From Data pane, drag Order Date to Columns shelf. On the column shelf right click Order Date and select Month. From the Data drag Sales to Rows shelf and drag Profit to Rows shelf (place it right of SUM(Sales))

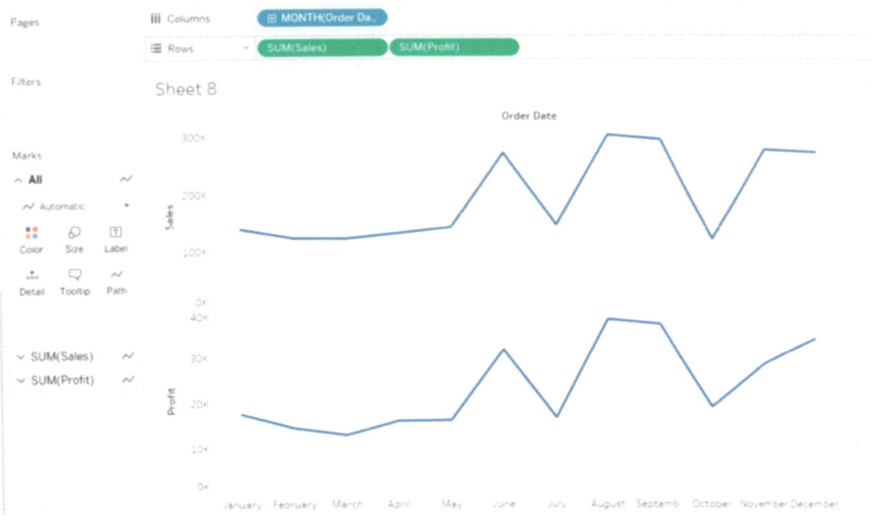

- On the Rows shelf, right-click **SUM(Profit)** and select **Dual-Axis**.

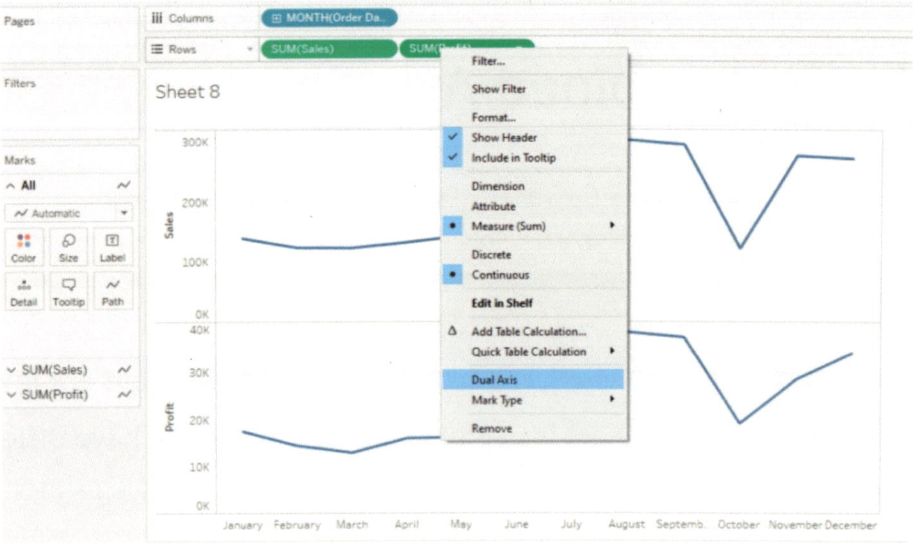

➢ The view updates. Measure Names is added to Color on the Marks card to differentiate the lines as show below.

➢ In the visualization, right-click the **Profit** axis and select **Synchronize Axis**.

➢ Both Axes get synchronized as shown below.

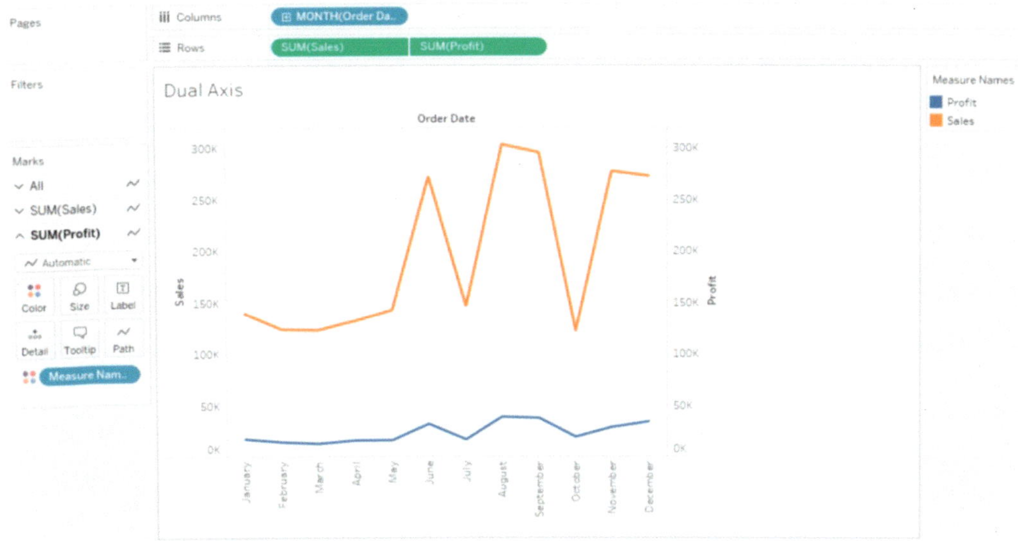

➢ On the SUM(Profit) Marks card, click the Mark Type drop-down and select **Bar**. The updated view as shown below.

7.2 Combined Axis

- A combined axis merges two or more measures into a single axis.
- Positive: Option of adding an additional dual axis to the chart later if user needs another mark type to reflect another measure.
- Negative: limited freedom with the formatting and can only have a single mark type.
- To create combined axis, create the initial view as show below with sales broken down by category and segment.

➢ From **Measures**, drag **Profit** to the vertical **Sales** axis. Drop the field when the mouse icon changes into a double ruler.

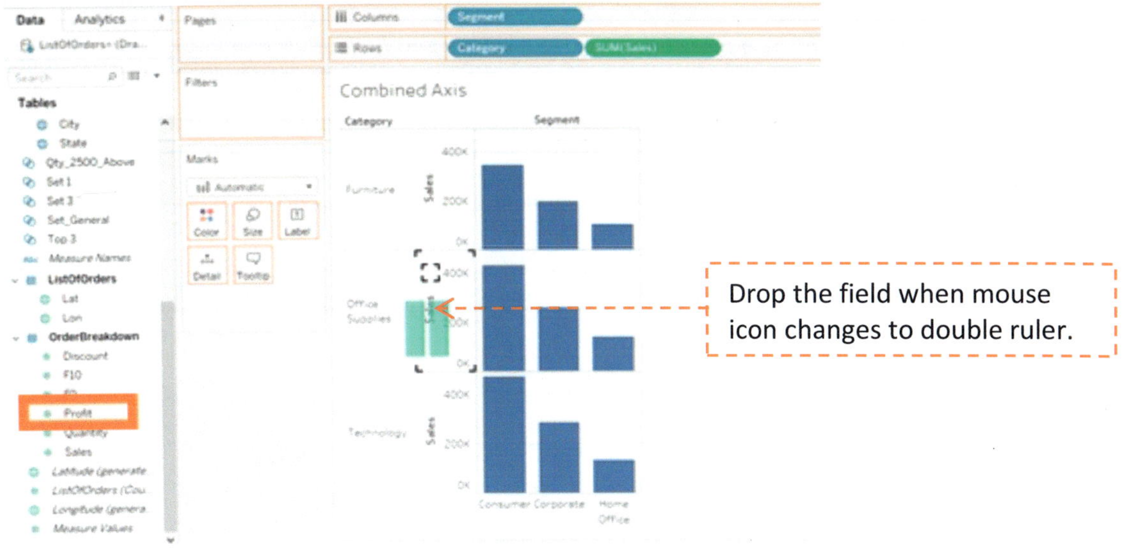

➢ From **Dimensions**, drag **Measure Names** to **Color** on **Marks** card.

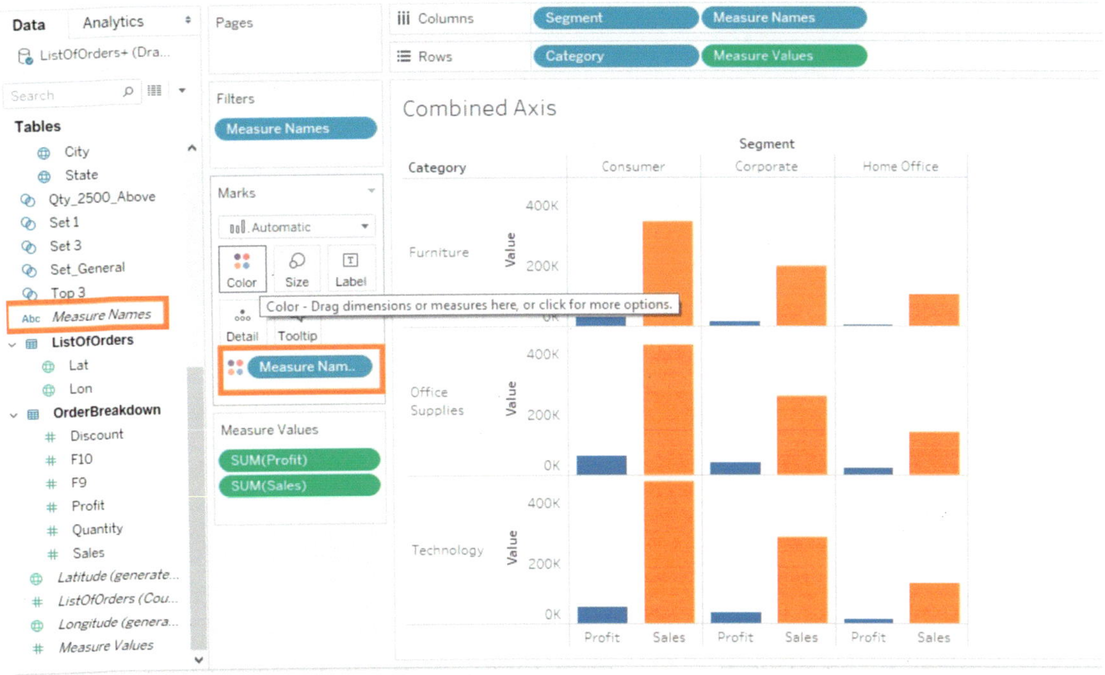

➢ On the axis marked **Value**, right click, select **Edit Axis**, in the **Title** box, type "Dollars" and then click **OK.**

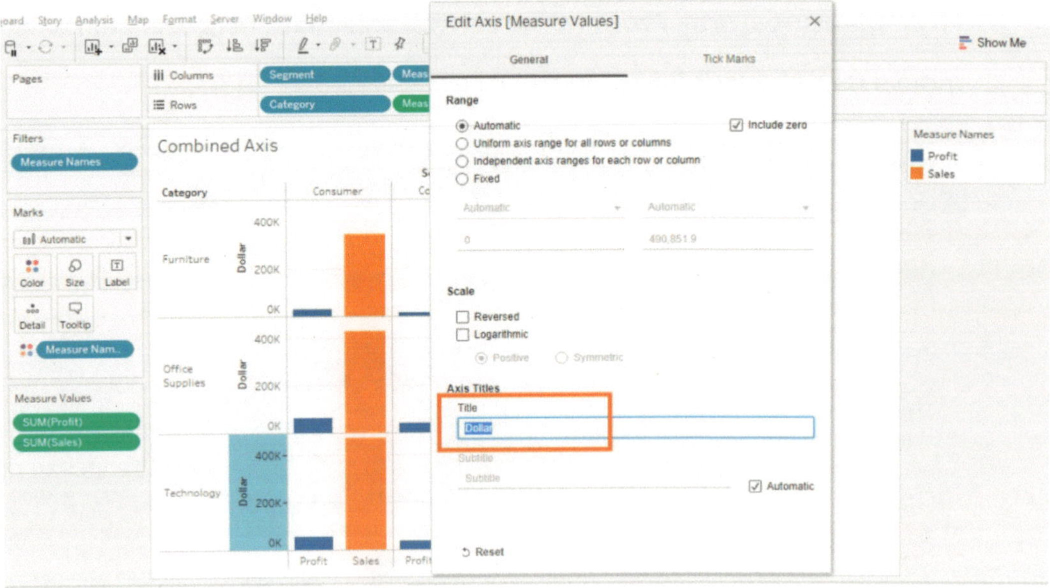

➢ The updated view as shown below.

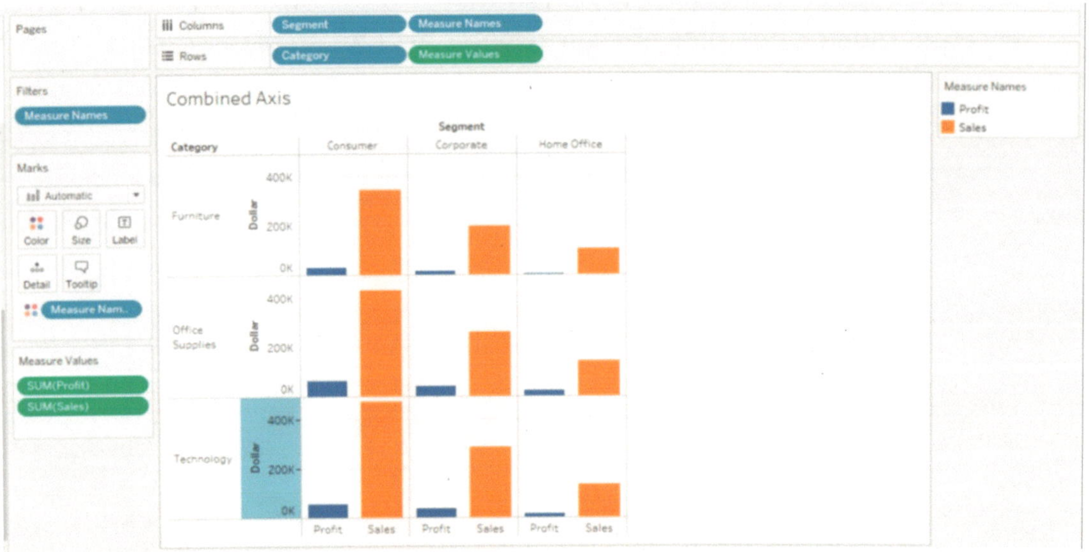

8 Common Chart types

8.1 Area Chart

- An area chart is a line chart where the area between the line and the axis are shaded with a color.
- Area charts are primarily used when the magnitude of the trend is to be communicated (rather than individual data values). To show how one or more groups' numeric values change over the progression of a second variable, the area between the line segments and the axes are highlighted by filling it with color.
- Area charts are commonly used to showcase data that depicts a time-series relationship.
- The basic building blocks for area chart are as follows:

Mark type:	Area
Columns shelf:	Dimension
Rows shelf:	Measure
Color:	Dimension

Source: Tableau Desktop and Web Authoring Help

- To create an area chart, from **Data pane**, drag **Order Date** to the **Columns** shelf. Right click on **YEAR(Order Date)** pill on the column shelf and select **Month** as shown below.

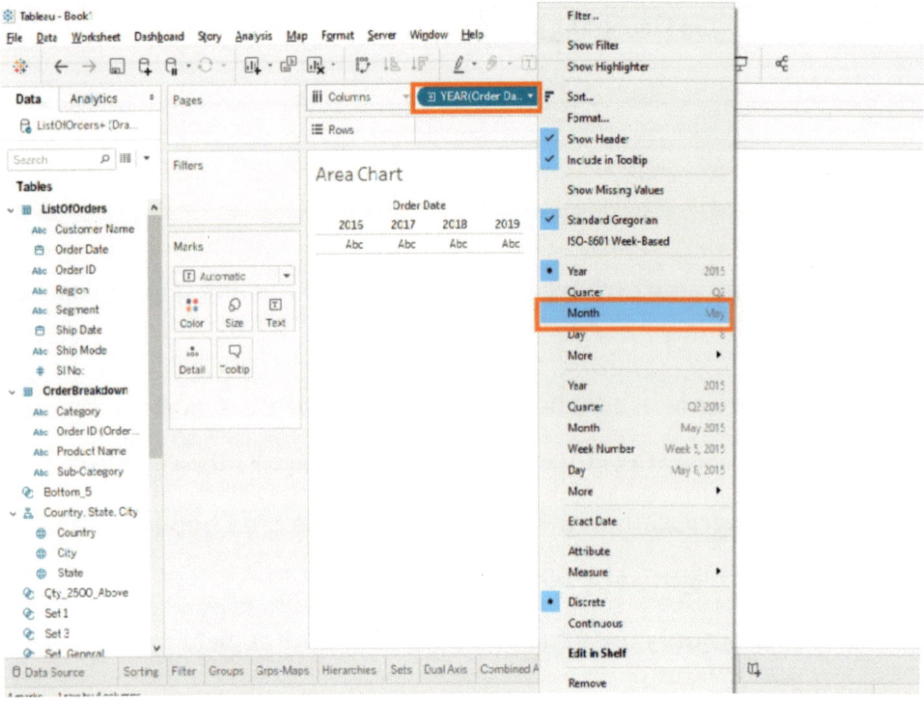

➢ From the **Data** pane, drag **Quantity** to the **Rows** shelf. From the **Data** pane, drag **Ship Mode** to **Color** on the Marks card. On the Marks card, click the Mark Type drop-down and select **Area**.

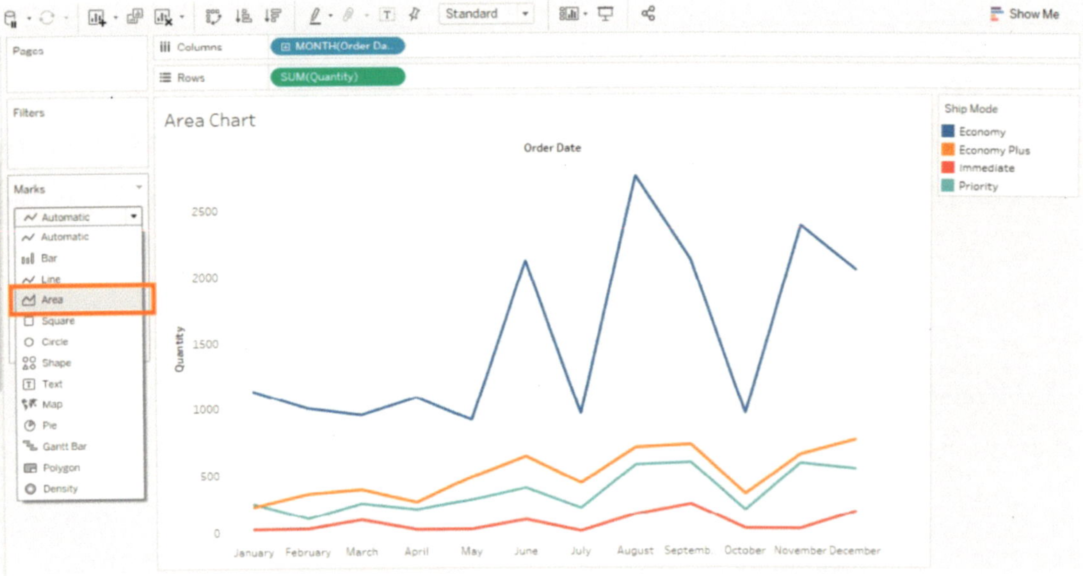

➢ The visualization updates as shown below.

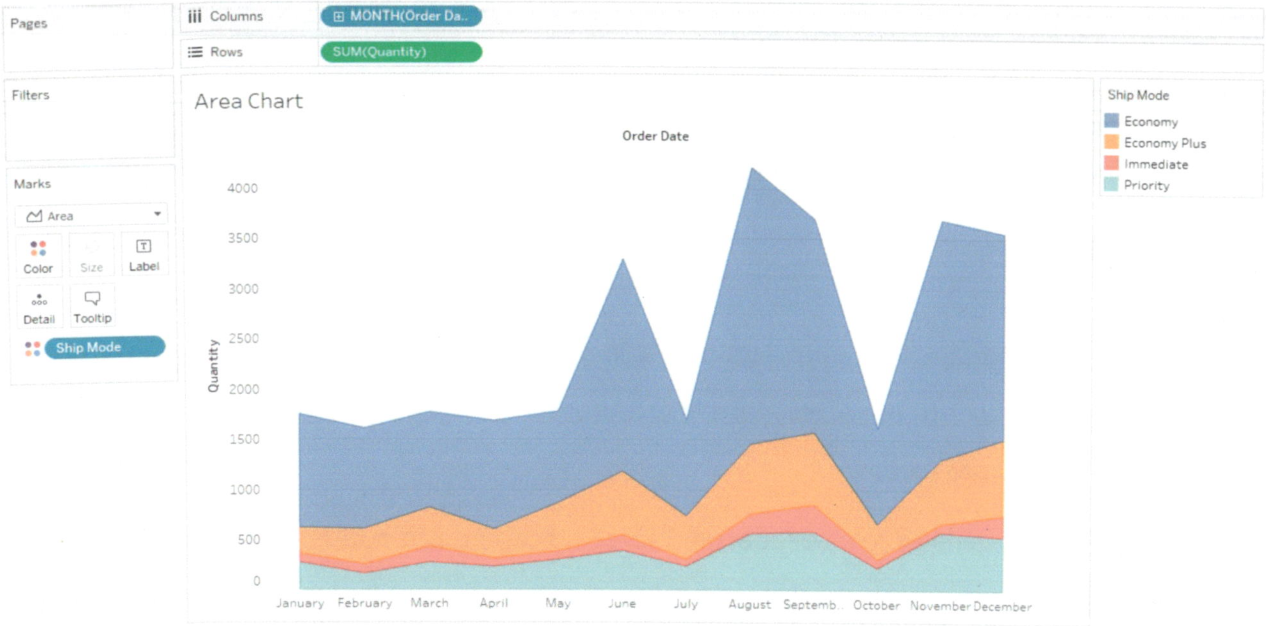

Alternative method to choose bar graph: After dragging Ship Mode dimension from Data pane onto Color Shelf -> From the **Show Me** tab select the bar graph.

8.2 Bar Chart

➢ Bar charts are used to compare data across categories. You create a bar chart by placing a dimension on the **Rows** shelf and a measure on the **Columns** shelf, or vice versa.

Creates Vertical Bars

Creates Horizontal Bars

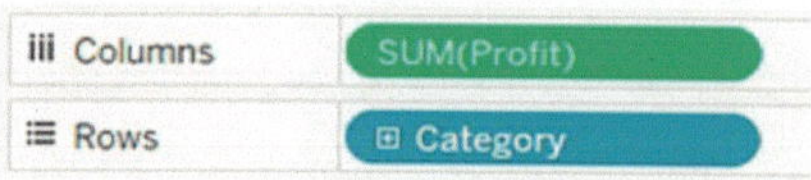

- To create bar chart, see example in Section 4.1.2.1.

8.3 Line Chart

- Line charts connect individual data points in a view. They provide a simple way to visualize a sequence of values and are useful when you want to see trends over time, or to forecast future values.
- A line graph is similar to a bar chart in Tableau, both graphs consist of one or more measures with the option to 'slice and dice' by one or more dimensions. The distinction between the bar chart and line graph is that the line graph must include an element of time.
- To create line chart, see example in section 7.1

8.4 Box Plot

- A box plot or box and whisker plot uses boxes and lines to depict the distributions of one or more groups of numeric data.
- Box limits indicate the range of the central 50% of the data, with a central line marking the median value. Lines extend from each box to capture the range of the remaining data, with dots placed past the line edges to indicate outliers.
- It is used:
    - For a quick understanding of the distribution of a dataset
    - To know whether a distribution is skewed or not
    - To find out unusual observations/errors in the data set

- The basic building blocks for a box and whisk plot are as follows:

Mark type:	Circle
Columns shelf:	Dimension
Rows shelf:	Measure
Detail:	Dimension
Reference Line:	Box Plot

Source: Tableau Desktop and Web Authoring Help

- To create box plot that shows discounts by region and customer segment, drag the Segment dimension to Columns shelf. Drag the Discount measure to Rows shelf.

PLEASE NOTE

Tableau creates a vertical axis and displays a bar chart, which is the default chart type when there is a dimension on the **Columns** shelf and a measure on the **Rows** shelf.

- Drag the Region dimension to Columns and drop it to the right of Segment. Click Show Me in the toolbar, then select the box-and-whisker plot chart type.

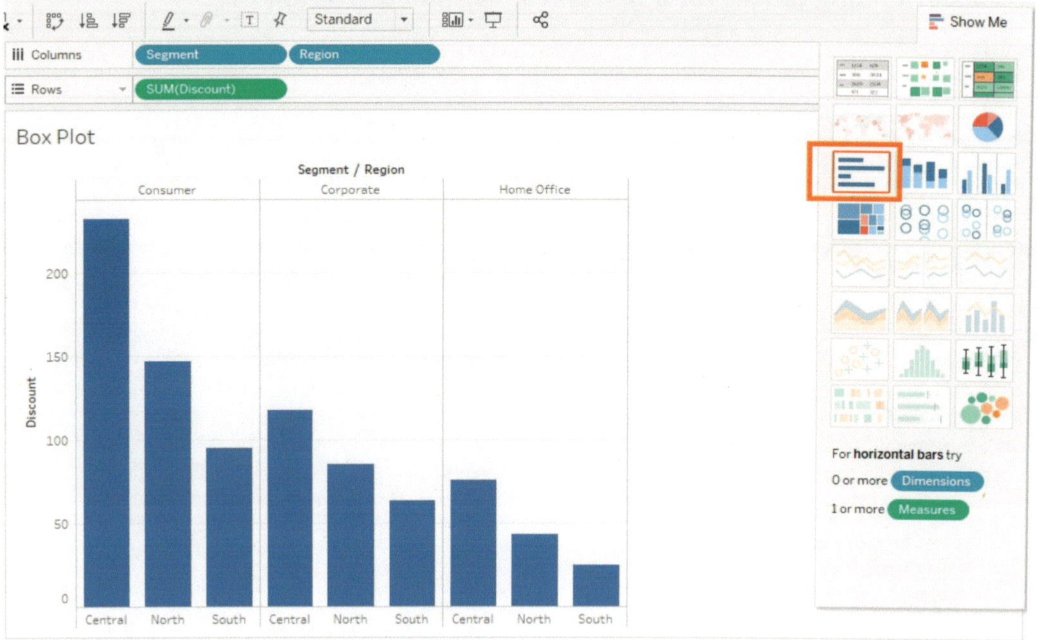

➢ The box plot is created as shown below.

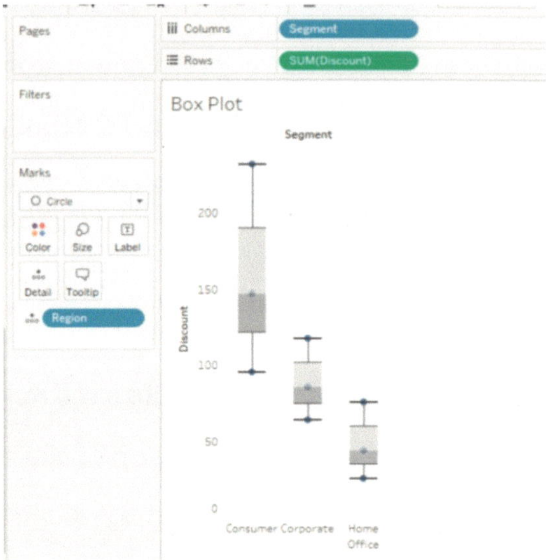

➢ Change the aggregate function of Discount measure from Sum to average. To do so, right click on the SUM(Discount) and select Measure > Average (as shown below).

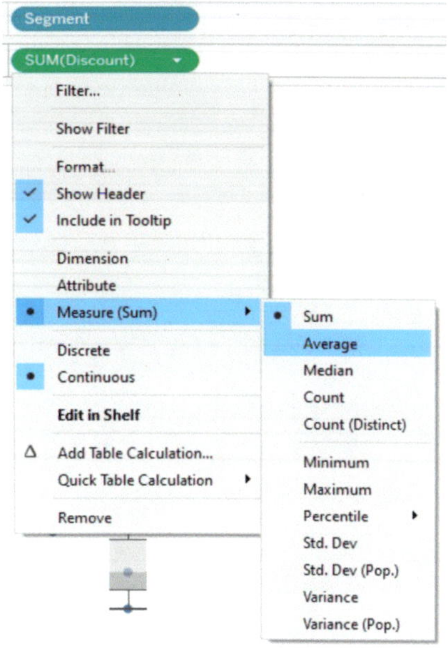

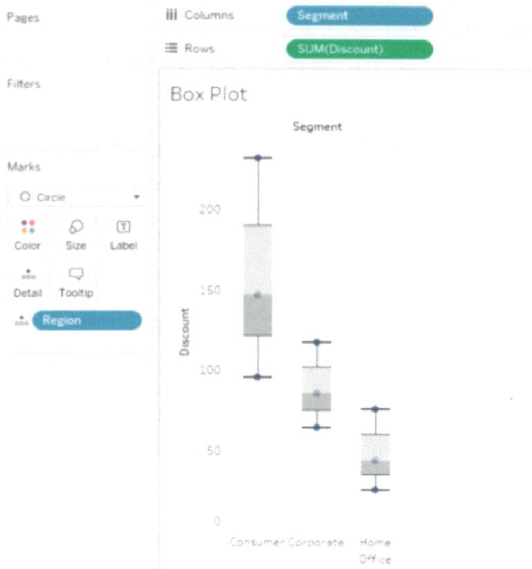

Observation: There are only a few marks in each box plot. Also, Tableau by default reassigned **Region** from the **Columns** shelf to the **Marks** card when chart type was changed to Box plot.

- Drag **Region** from the **Marks** card back to **Columns**, to the right of **Segment**.
- Change aggregate function for Discount as SUM

Observation: Box plots are used to show distribution of data, the flattened box plots in the current view is because the data is aggregated.

➢ To disaggregate data, from the main menu, select **Analysis** > **Aggregate Measures**.

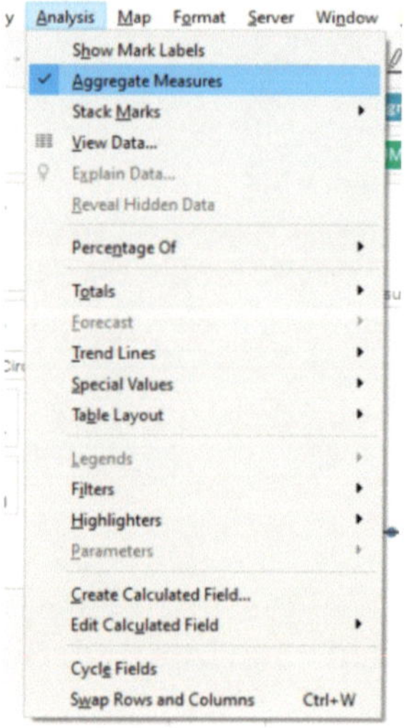

Observation: In the above view, instead of a single mark for each column, range of marks are observed, one for each row in the data source.

- To make the view easier to read. Click on the Swap button on the axes. The view turns into horizontal box plots.

8.5 Heat Maps or Density Marks

- Heat maps are visualizations where marks on a chart are represented as colors. As the marks "heat up" due their higher values or density of records, a more intense color is displayed.
- In Tableau, you can create a chart using the density mark by placing at least one continuous measure on the Columns shelf, and at least one dimension or measure on the Rows shelf (or vice versa), and then adding a field to the Marks card.
- The basic building blocks for a density chart are as follows:

Mark type:	Density
Rows and Columns:	At least one continuous measure, and at least one measure or dimension
Marks card:	At least one continuous measure

Source: Tableau Desktop and Web Authoring Help

- To create Heat Maps of Sub-Category Sales by month of Order Date, from the Data pane drag Order Date dimension onto Columns shelf and right click on YEAR(Order Date) and select month. From the Data pane drag Sales measure onto Rows shelf and drag Sub-Category to Colour shelf in Marks Card as shown below.

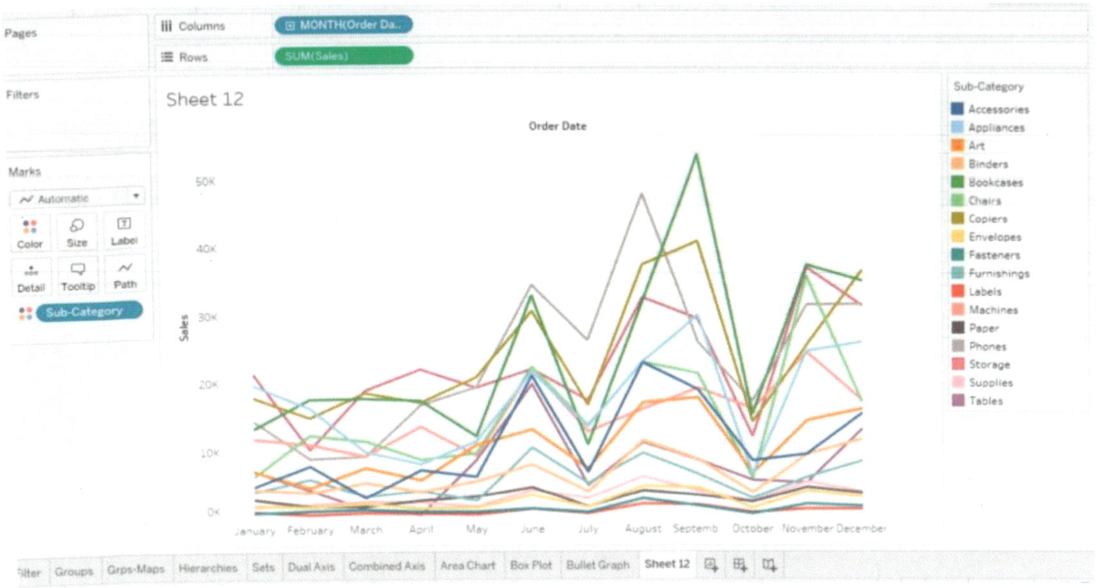

Graph contains 17 lines overlapping and several of the Sub-categories at the bottom are on much smaller in scale than the rest, making it challenging to gain insights. In this case, heat map maybe better.

- From the Show Me tab click on the Heat Map as shown below.

- The view is updated as shown below.

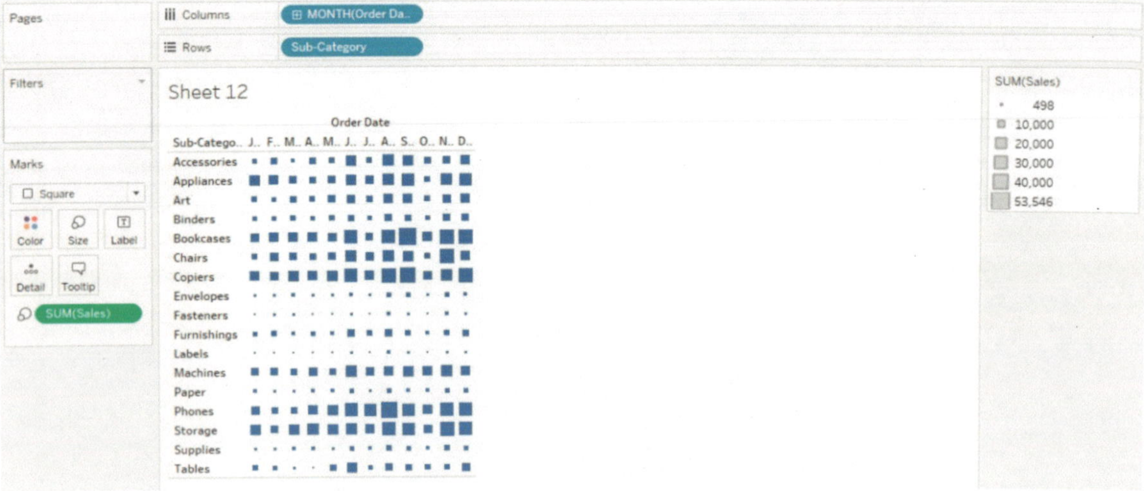

➢ By default, mark type is set to Square. As shown below change mark type to circle.

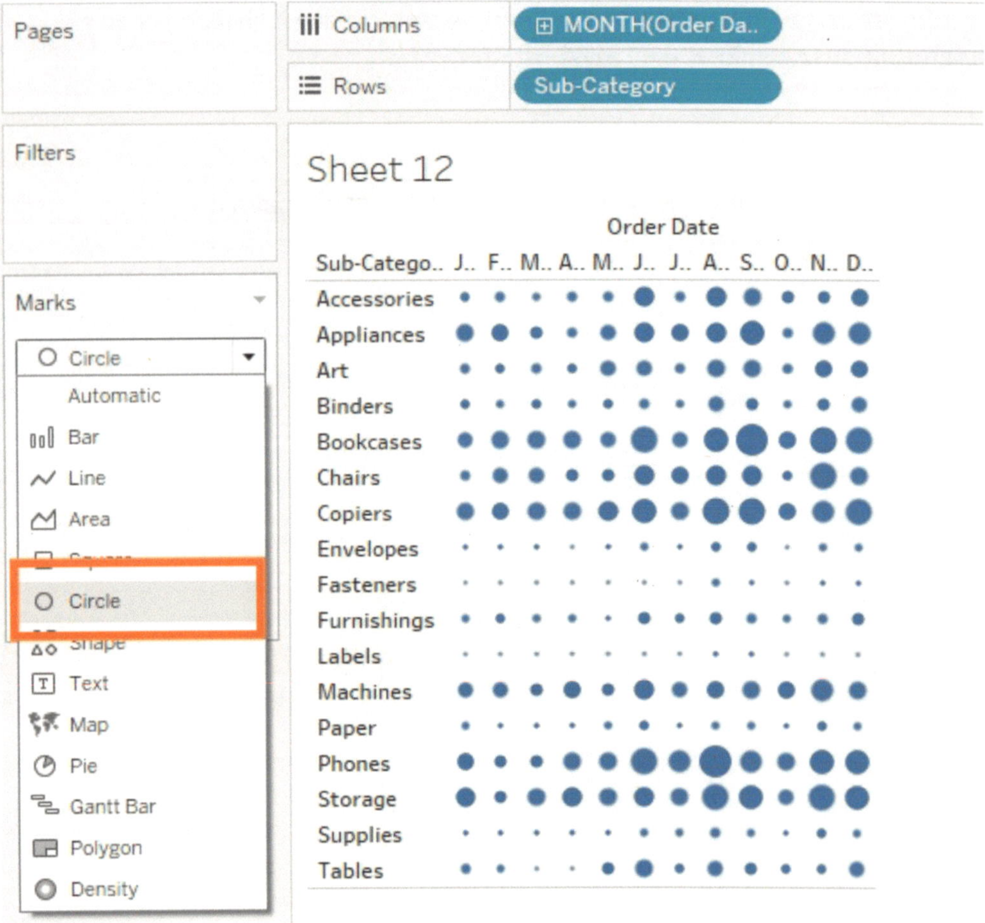

Each intersection of Sub-Category and Month of order Date is shown by a mark (circle).

➢ For better visualization, increase the size of the marks as shown below.

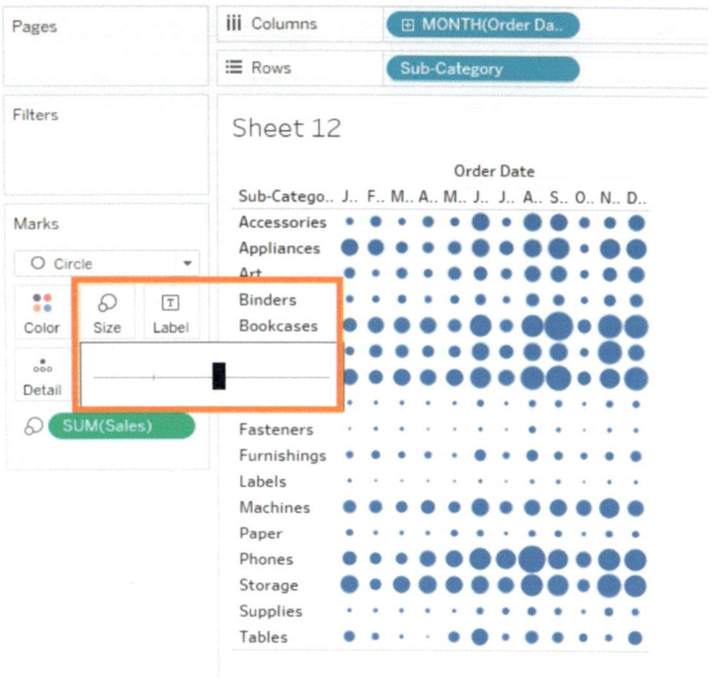

➢ Observations can be made easier by the color intensity of the marks as show below. Drag Sales measure to color Marks card to get the updated chart.

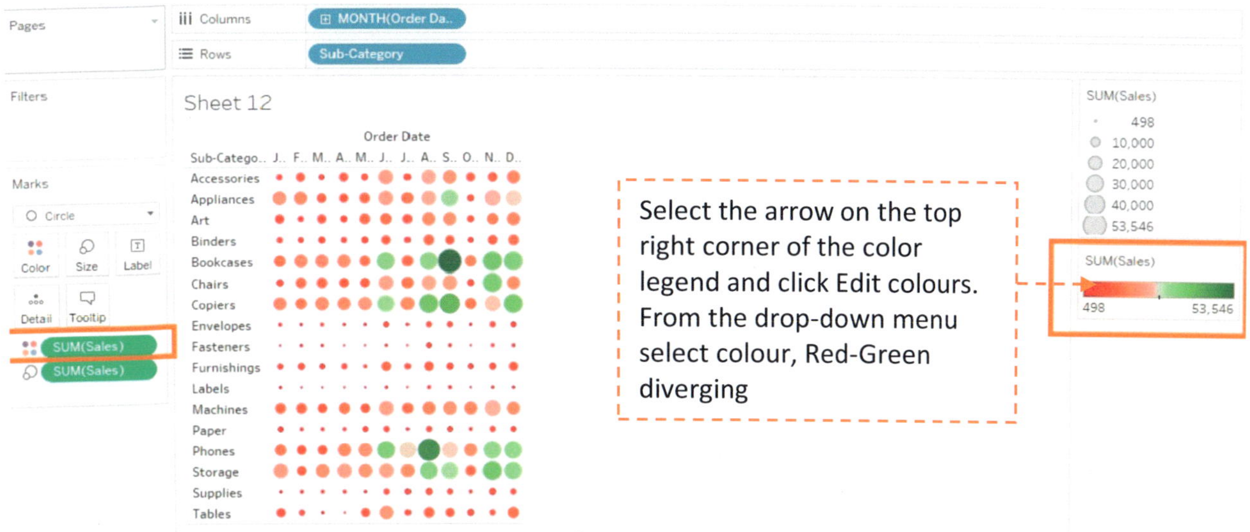

Observation: This visualization uses the exact same fields as the line graph above, but it is now much easier to compare sub-categories within a specific month (reading the chart vertically) or compare the seasonality across each sub-category (reading the chart horizontally).

➢ One more option, use one measure for the size, and a different measure for the color. For example, if we size the circles by the Quantity measure instead of sales, the heat map updates as shown below.

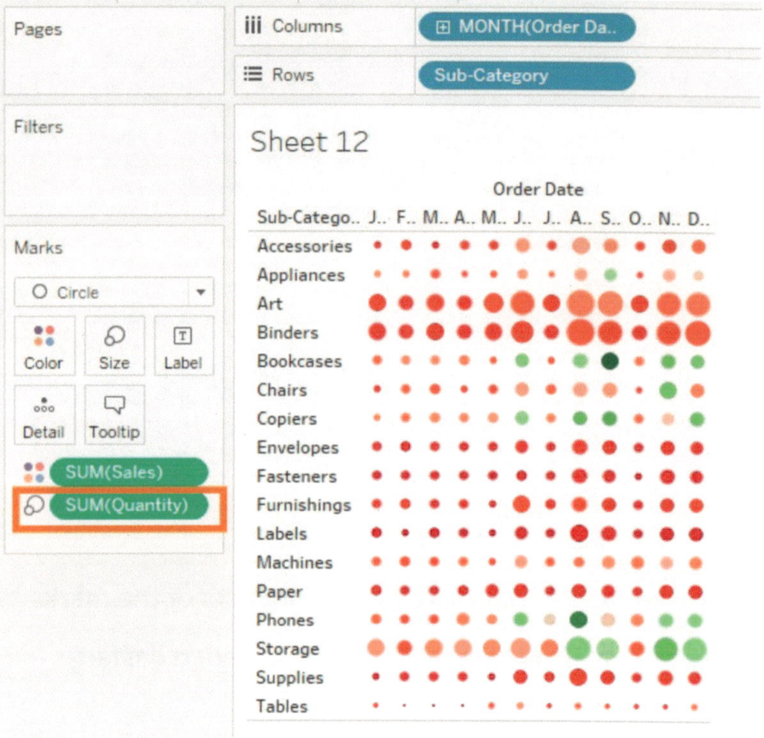

With this analysis, large and light circles would mean that a sub-category sold a relatively large quantity but made a relatively low amount of revenue: low sales per item. Conversely, small and dark circles would mean the sub-category sold a relatively small quantity, but generated a relatively high revenue: high sales per item.

8.6 Highlight Tables

➢ Highlight tables are used to compare categorical data using color.

➢ Highlight tables consist of one or more dimensions and exactly one measure (the color).

➢ Highlight tables are used for:

- Quickly identifying highs and lows or other points of interest in your data.
- A means of enhancing a crosstab.

➢ To create highlight map to observe how profit varies across regions, product sub-categories, and customer segments, drag Segment dimension to Columns Shelf. Drag the **Region** and **Sub-Category** dimensions to **Rows**, dropping **Sub-Category** to the right of **Region**. Drag Profit measure to Label shelf in Marks card. Click on the Highlight Tables in Show Me tab.

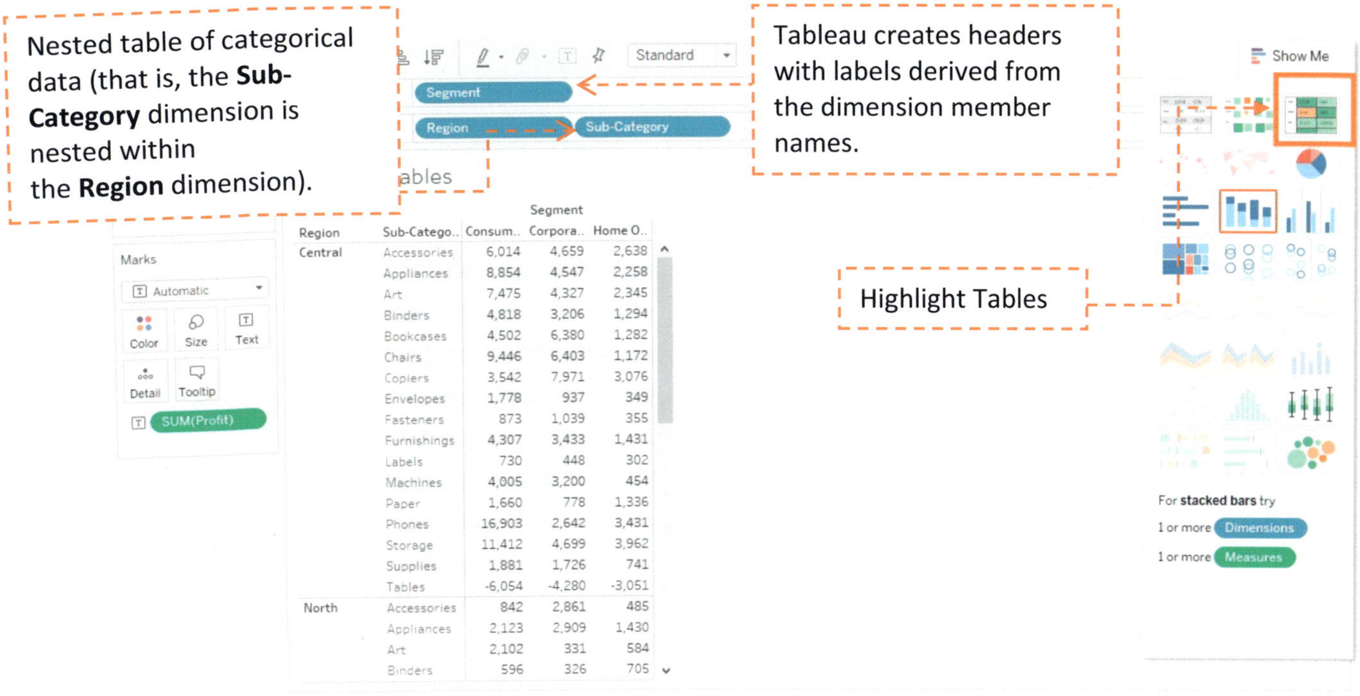

➢ The view converts to highlight table as shown below.

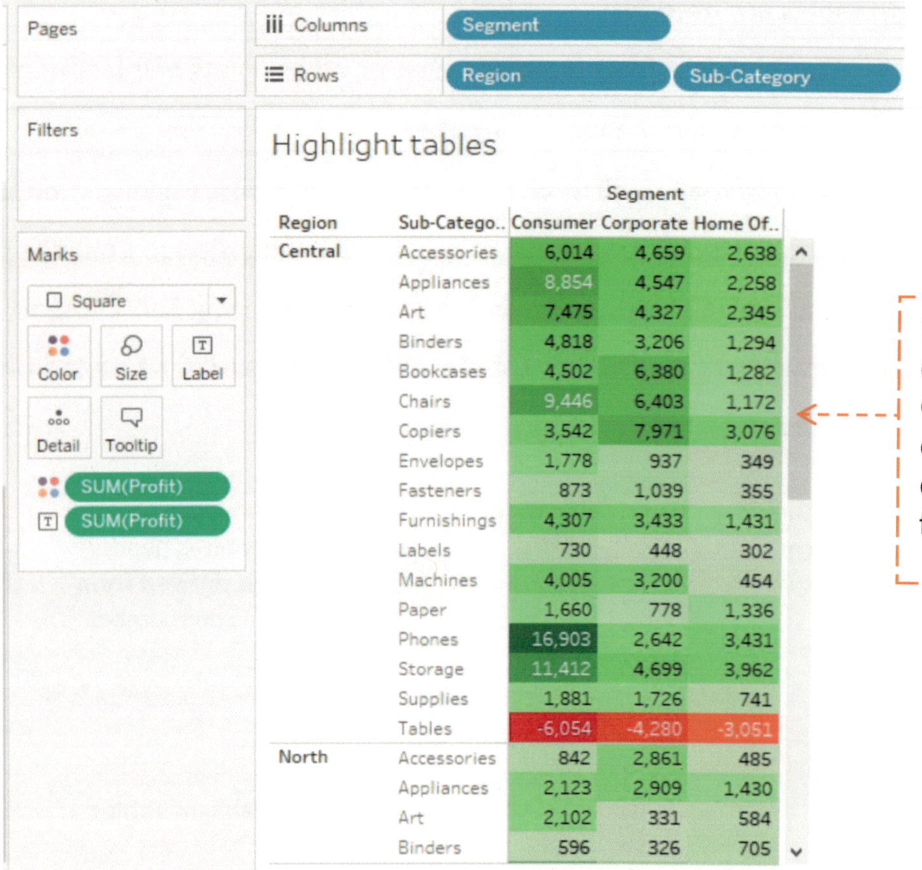

		Segment		
Region	Sub-Catego..	Consumer	Corporate	Home Of..
Central	Accessories	6,014	4,659	2,638
	Appliances	8,854	4,547	2,258
	Art	7,475	4,327	2,345
	Binders	4,818	3,206	1,294
	Bookcases	4,502	6,380	1,282
	Chairs	9,446	6,403	1,172
	Copiers	3,542	7,971	3,076
	Envelopes	1,778	937	349
	Fasteners	873	1,039	355
	Furnishings	4,307	3,433	1,431
	Labels	730	448	302
	Machines	4,005	3,200	454
	Paper	1,660	778	1,336
	Phones	16,903	2,642	3,431
	Storage	11,412	4,699	3,962
	Supplies	1,881	1,726	741
	Tables	-6,054	-4,280	-3,051
North	Accessories	842	2,861	485
	Appliances	2,123	2,909	1,430
	Art	2,102	331	584
	Binders	596	326	705

In this view, the data for only the Central region is observed. Scroll down to see data for other regions.

Observation: In Central region, Phones with darker shades of green are observed to be the most profitable Sub-Category, and Tables with shades of red the least profitable.

8.6.1 Difference between Highlight tables and Heat Maps

- Highlight tables consist of one or more dimensions and exactly one measure.
- Heat maps consist of one or more dimensions and one or two measures.

8.7 Gantt Chart

➢ Gantt charts are used to show the duration of events or activities. In a Gantt chart, each separate mark (usually a bar) shows a duration.

➢ Grant chart are created with one date, one or more dimensions, and zero to two measures.

Mark type:	Automatic or Gantt Bar
Columns shelf:	Date or Time field (continuous measure)
Rows shelf:	Dimension(s)
Size:	Continuous measure

Source: Tableau Desktop and Web Authoring Help

➢ To create a Gantt chart that shows how many days elapse on average between order date and ship date, drag the **Order Date** dimension to **Columns**. On the **Columns** shelf, click the **Year (Order Date)** drop-down arrow, and then select **Week Number**.

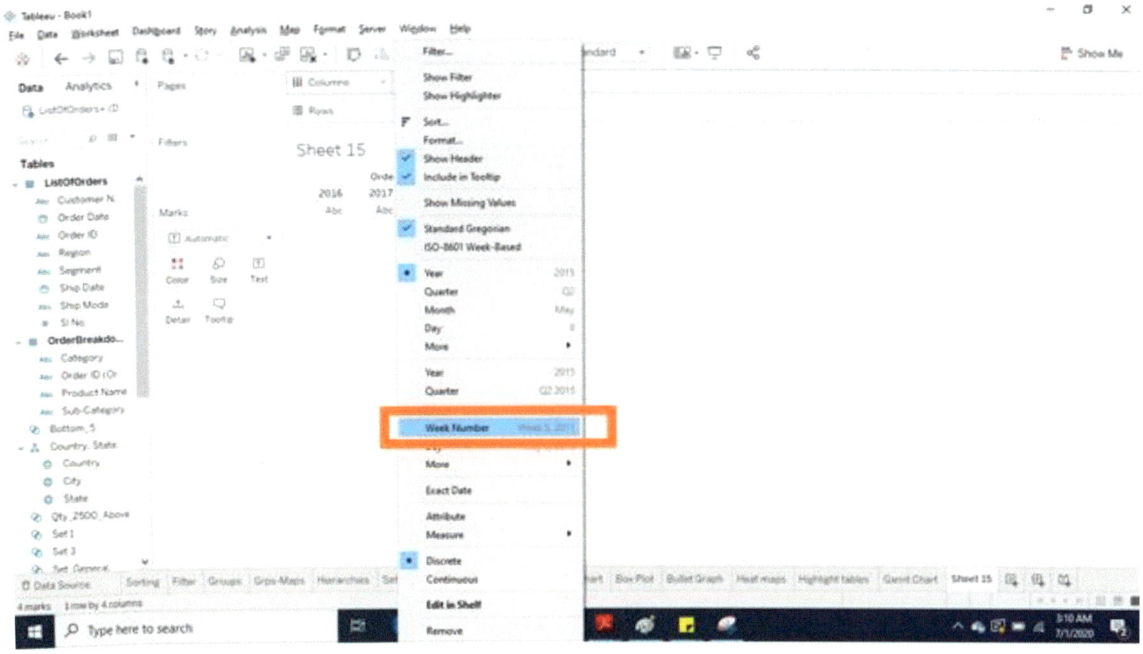

➢ Drag the **Sub-Category** and **Ship Mode** dimensions to the **Rows** shelf. Drop **Ship Mode** to the right of **Sub-Category**.

To observe the length of the interval between the order date and ship date, a calculated field is created to capture the interval. In the toolbar menu, click **Analysis > Create Calculated Field**. Alternatively, right-click on any field in the **Data** pane and select **Create** > **Calculated Field**.

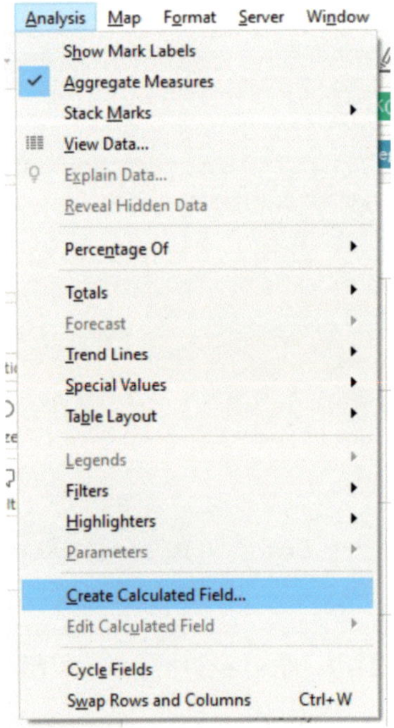

➢ In the calculation dialog box, name your calculated field **OrderUntilShip**. Clear any content that's in the **Formula** box by default. In the **Formula** box, enter the following formula and then click **OK**:

```
DATEDIFF('day',[Order Date],[Ship Date])
```

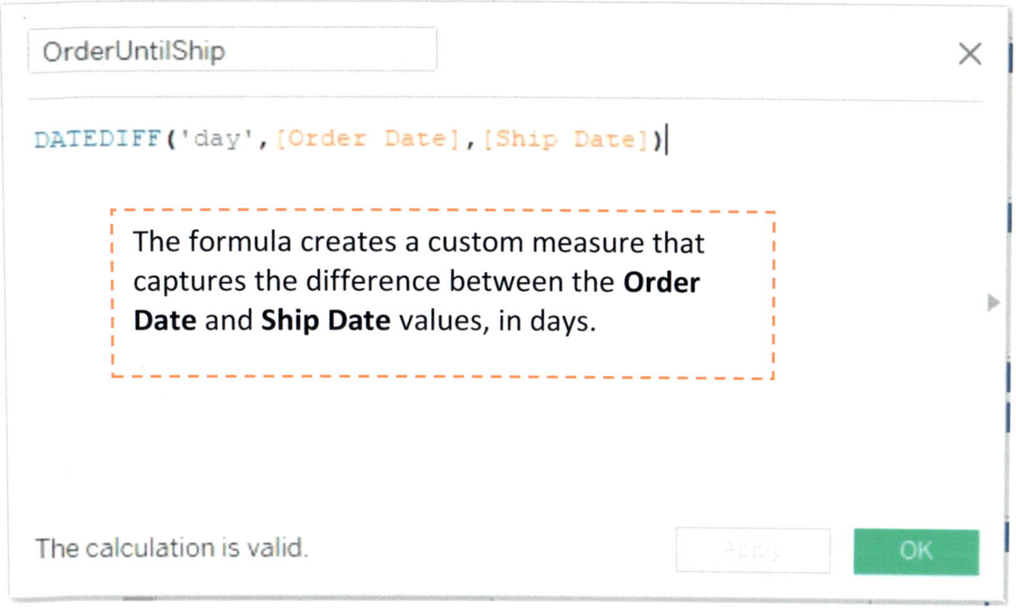

➢ From the Data pane, drag the **OrderUntilShip** measure to **Size** on the **Marks** card. The default aggregation for **OrderUntilShip** is **Sum**, but in this case, it makes more sense to average the values. Right-click the **SUM(OrderUntilShip)** field on the **Marks** card, and then select **Measure (Sum)** > **Average**.

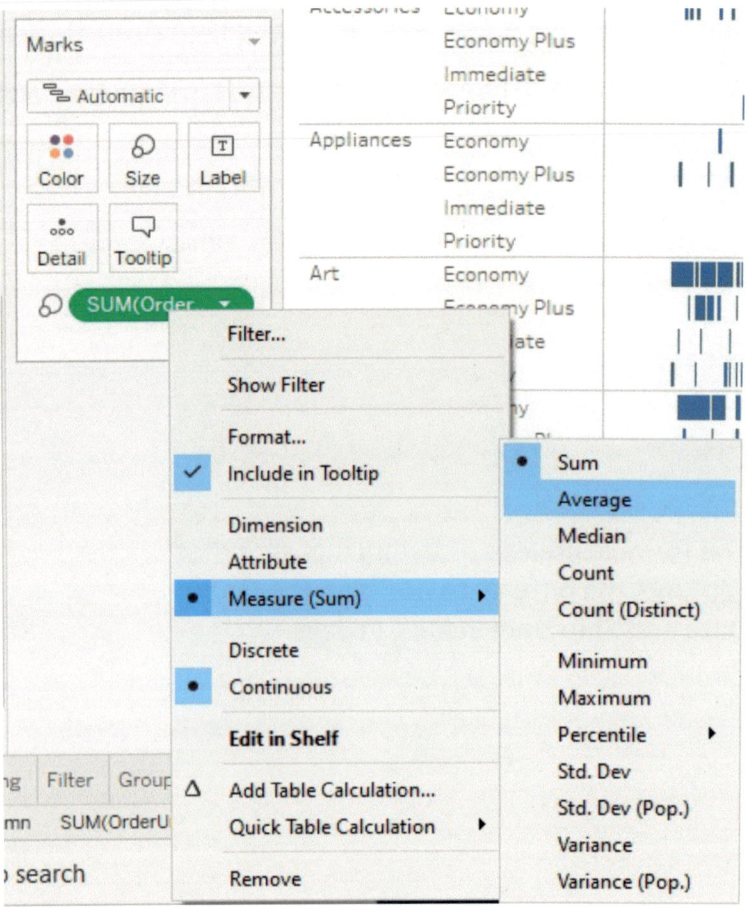

➢ The view consists of too many views making it difficult to read. Data can be made more readable by filtering in a smaller time window. Hold down the Ctrl key (Command key on Mac) and drag the **Week(Order Date)** field from the **Columns** shelf to the **Filter** shelf. A dialog box appears, select **Range of Dates > Next.**

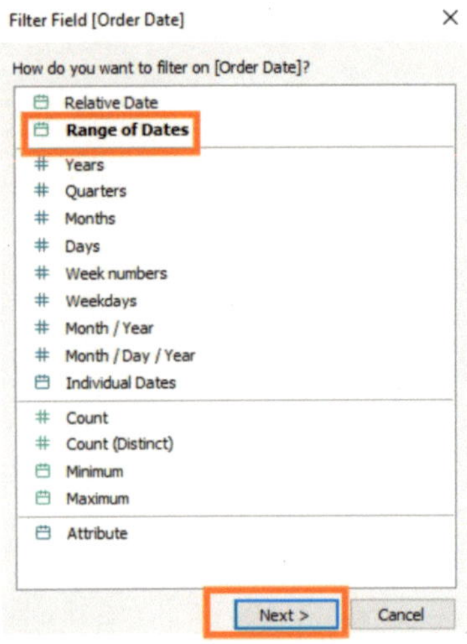

- Select the range to a twelve-month time interval, such as 1/1/2016 to 1/1/2017, and click **OK**.

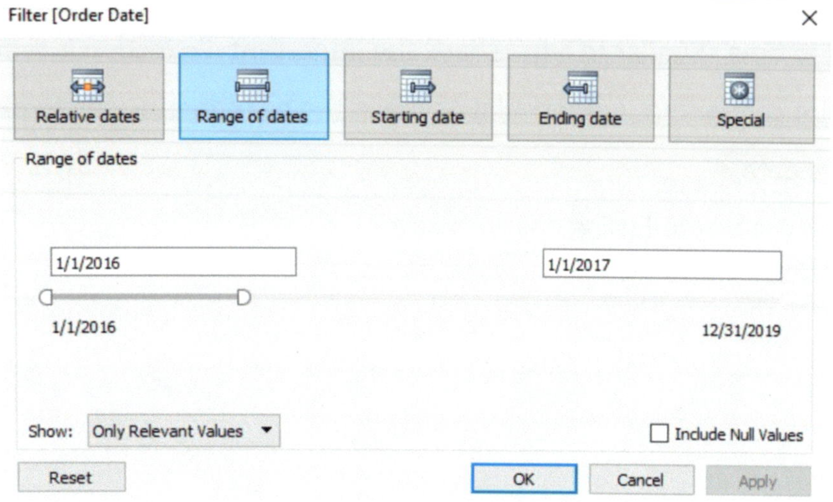

- Drag the **Ship Mode** dimension to **Color** on the **Marks** card.

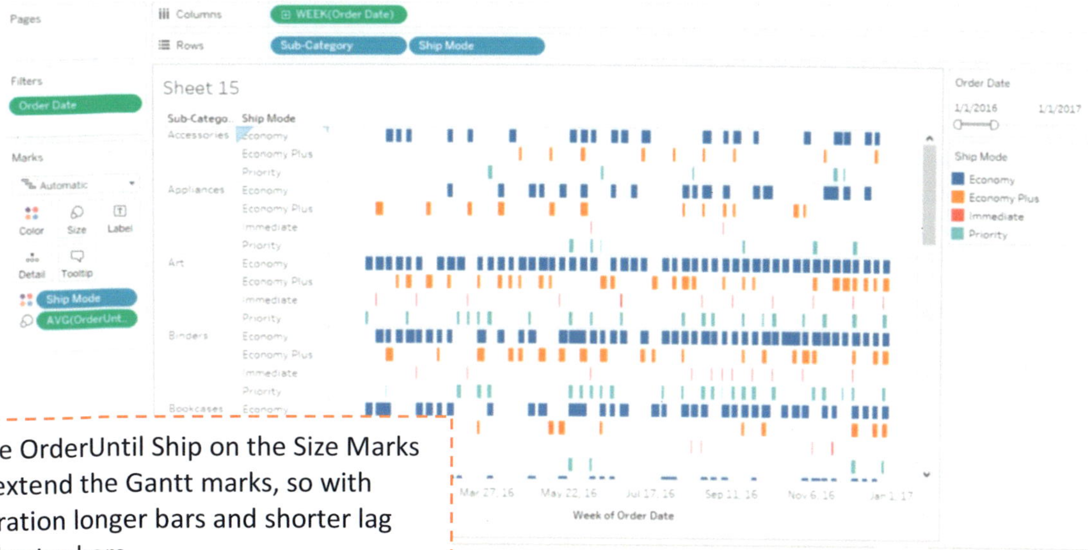

Placing the OrderUntil Ship on the Size Marks Card will extend the Gantt marks, so with longer duration longer bars and shorter lag leads to shorter bars.

Observe: From the view, we can observe which ship modes are more prone to longer lag times, whether lag times vary by category, and whether lag times are consistent over time.

8.8 Histogram

- A histogram is a chart that displays the shape of a distribution of a quantitative data at one point in time. Similar to a bar chart, the important distinction is that histograms are used to plot continuous, numerical data while the bar chart is used to plot discrete, categorical data.
- Histograms are created using one measure.

Mark type:	Automatic
Rows shelf:	Continuous measure (aggregated by Count or Count Distinct)
Columns shelf:	Bin (continuous or discrete).

Source: Tableau Desktop and Web Authoring Help

- To create a histogram, pre-select the measure that you want to visualize the distribution for by clicking on it in the Measures Shelf in the Data pane. Then navigate to the Show Me options and choose "histogram".

Tableau automatically creates the dimension "Quantity (bin)" to provide the equally-sized ranges which are required to create a histogram.

The **Quantity** measure captures the number of items in a particular order. The histogram shows that about 3,900 orders contained two items (the second bar), about 2,000 orders contained 4 items (the third bar), and so on.

PLEASE NOTE

You do not have to drag the measure to the Columns or Rows Shelf. Instead, imply pre-select the measure (quantity) and chose Histogram from the Show Me options.

- Depending on how the distribution looks, size of the bins can be changed. From the Data pane, right click on the newly created Quantity (bin) dimension and select “Edit”. Edit Bins [Quantity] dialog box appears that shows the current bin size and if required user can change the equal ranges:

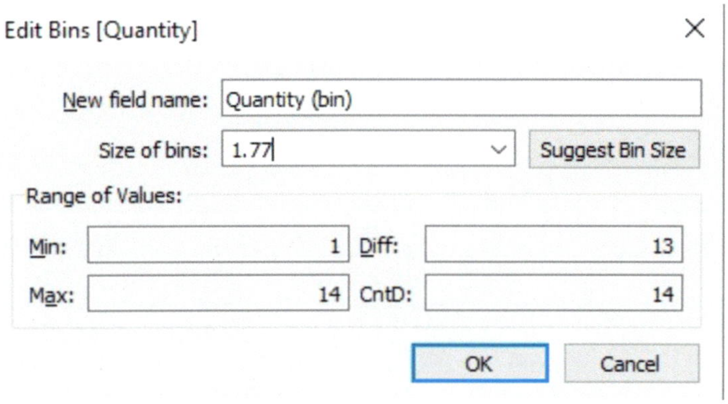

8.9 Scatter Plot

- Scatter plots are used to visualize relationships between numerical variables.
- Scatter plots are created with zero or more dimensions, and two or four measures.
- In Tableau, a scatter plot is created by placing at least one measure on the **Columns** shelf and at least one measure on the **Rows** shelf.
- Scatter plot can use several mark types, the two additional measures and/or dimensions can leverage the Color and/or Size Marks Cards.

➢ To create scatter plot that compares Sales to Profit across different Categories and Regions, from the data pane drag Sales and Profit measures to the Rows and Columns shelf respectively as shown below.

Observation: When two measures are used Tableau by default creates scatter plot as seen in this example.

➢ Drag the **Category** dimension to **Color** on the Marks card.

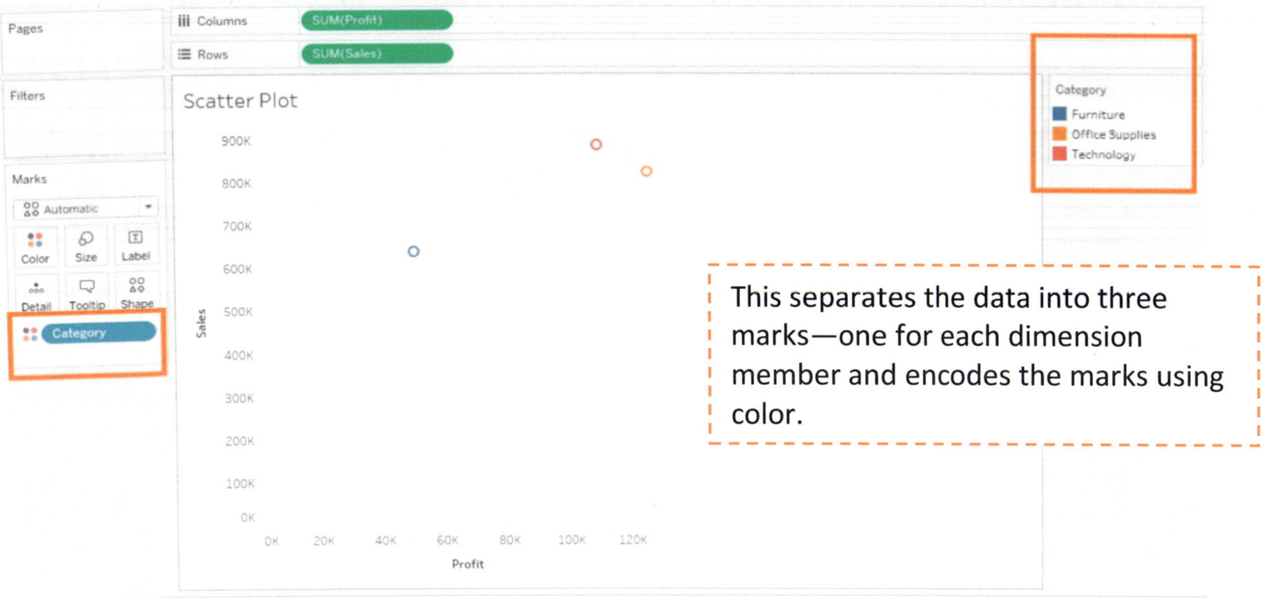

➢ Drag the **Region** dimension to **Shapes** on the **Marks** card. The view is updated as shown below.

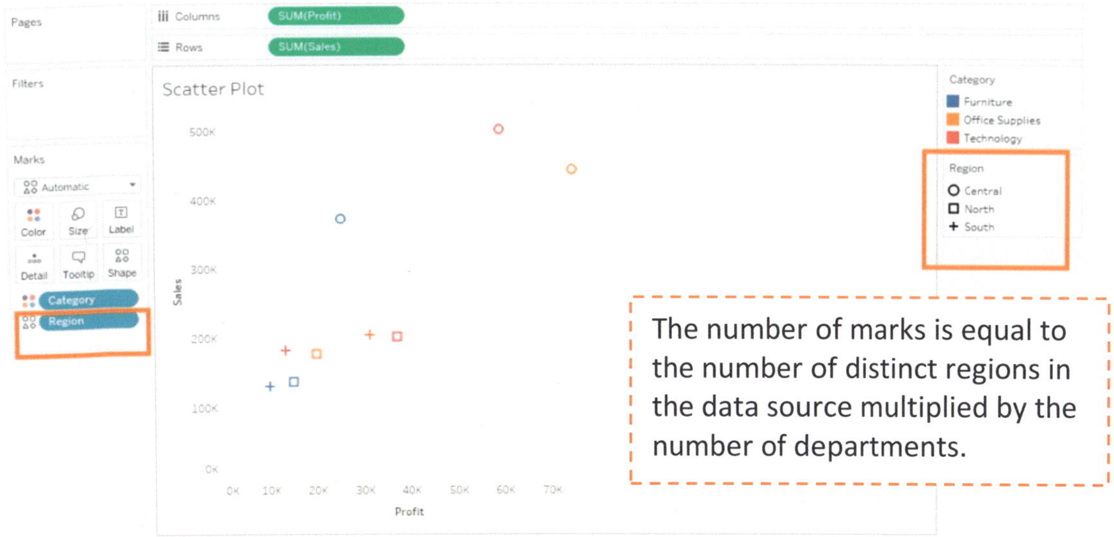

Observation: From the graph we can infer, among the three categories, Furniture as the lowest sales in turn lowest profit value in all the regions. The remaining two departments, Office supplies and Technology have high sales in turn high profit in the Central region.

8.10 Treemap

- Treemaps are used to display data in nested rectangles.
- Dimensions are used to define the structure of the treemap, and measures to define the size or color of the individual rectangles.
- Treemaps consist of 1 or more Dimensions and 1 or 2 Measures

Mark type:	Automatic or Square
Color:	Dimension or Measure
Size	Measure
Label or **Detail**:	Dimension(s)

Source: Tableau Desktop and Web Authoring Help

- To create a treemap that shows aggregated sales totals across a range of product categories, Drag the **Sub-Category** dimension to **Columns**. Drag the **Sales** measure to Rows.
- Tableau displays a bar chart—the default chart type when there is a dimension on the Columns shelf and a measure on the Rows shelf. Click Show Me on the toolbar, then select the treemap chart type.

➢ The below Treemap is displayed.

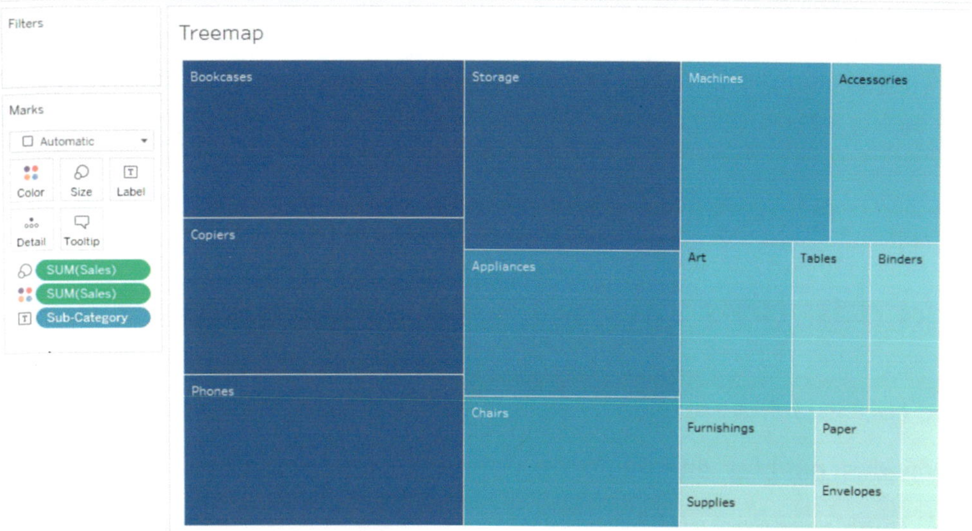

Observation: In the above treemap, both the size of the rectangles and their color are determined by the value of **Sales**—the greater the sum of sales for each category, the darker and larger its box.

➢ Drag the **Ship Mode** dimension to **Color** on the **Marks** card.

Observation: In the resulting view, **Ship Mode** determines the color of the rectangles—and sorts them into four separate areas accordingly. **Sales** determines the size of the rectangles:

PLEASE NOTE

- Measures can be placed only on **Size** and **Color shelf** on the Marks card, placing a measure on any other shelf in marks card as no effect.
- Treemaps can accommodate any number of dimensions, one or even two on **Color**. But beyond that, adding dimensions only breaks the map into greater number of smaller rectangles.

8.11Packed Bubble Chart

➢ Packed bubble charts are used to display data in a cluster of circles. Dimensions define the individual bubbles, and measures define the size and color of the individual circles.

➢ Packed bubbles consist of 1 or more dimension and 1 or 2 measures.

Mark type:	Circle
Detail:	Dimension
Size:	Measure
Color:	Dimension or Measure
Label (optional):	Dimension or Measure

Source: Tableau Desktop and Web Authoring Help

- To create packed bubble chart, see example in section 6.3.1.

8.12 Geographic Mapping

- Maps are used in Tableau to analyze the data geographically. To plot a map, it is essential to have one geo date.
- Geographic mapping consists of one geo date, zero or more dimensions, and 0 to 2 measures.
- Two types of Geographic maps:
    - Point Map
    - Filled/Polygon Maps

8.12.1 Point Map

- To create a basic map, in the Data pane, double-click Country. Tableau by default creates point map.

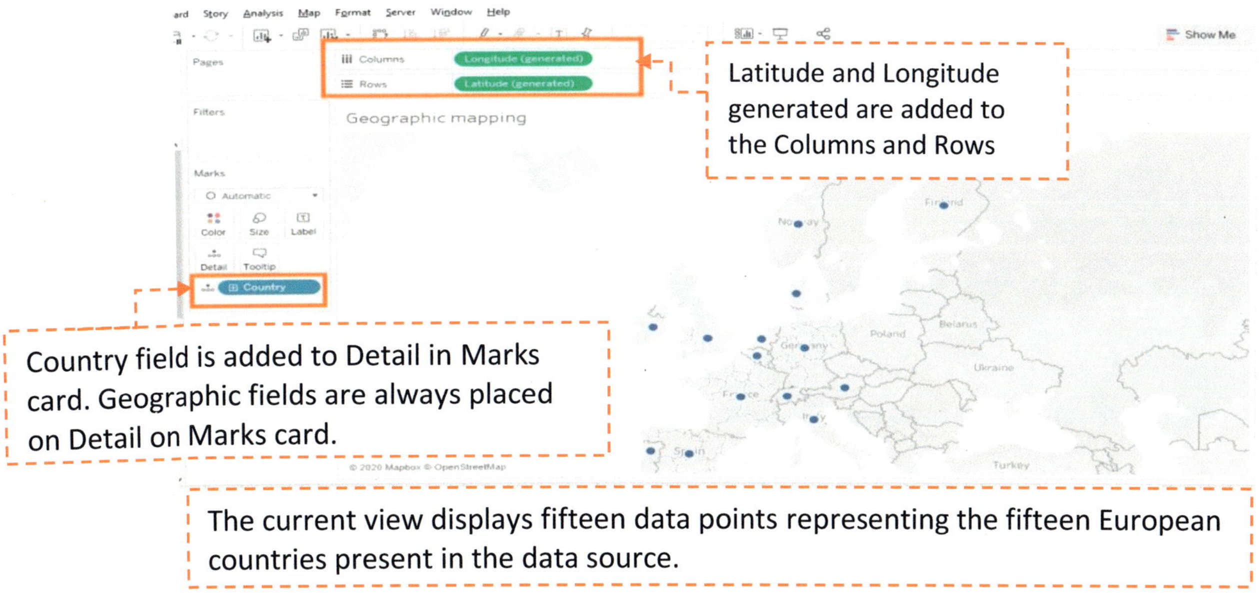

➢ On the Marks card, click the **+** icon on the **Country** field. The State field is added to Detail on the Marks card.

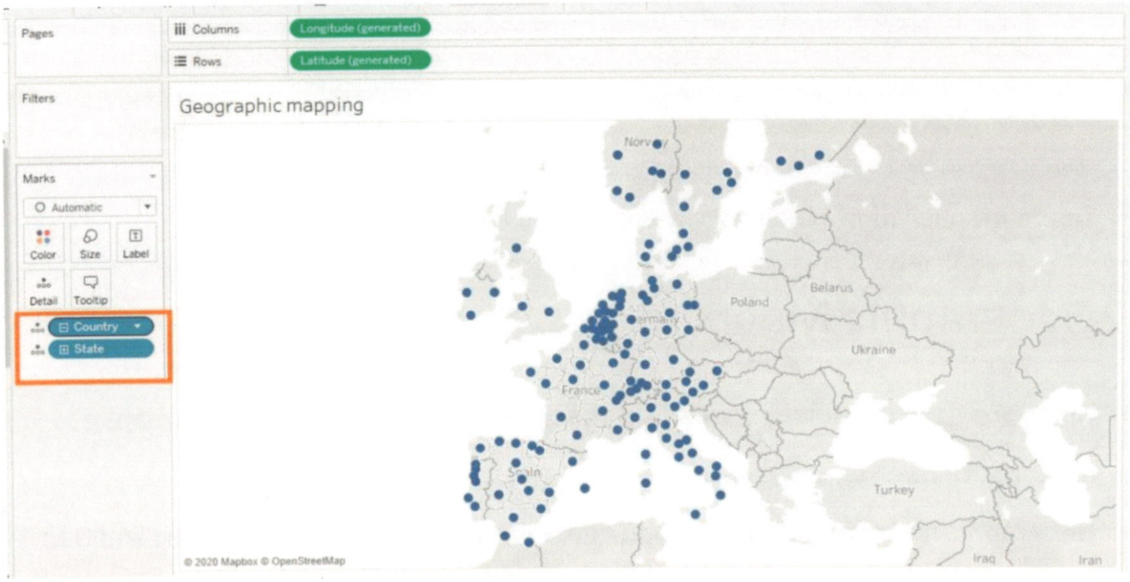

Observation: Map updates to include a data point for every state in the data source.

8.12.2 Filled/Polygon Map

➢ In the above view, on the Marks card, click the Mark Type drop-down and select **Map.** Map updates to filled map.

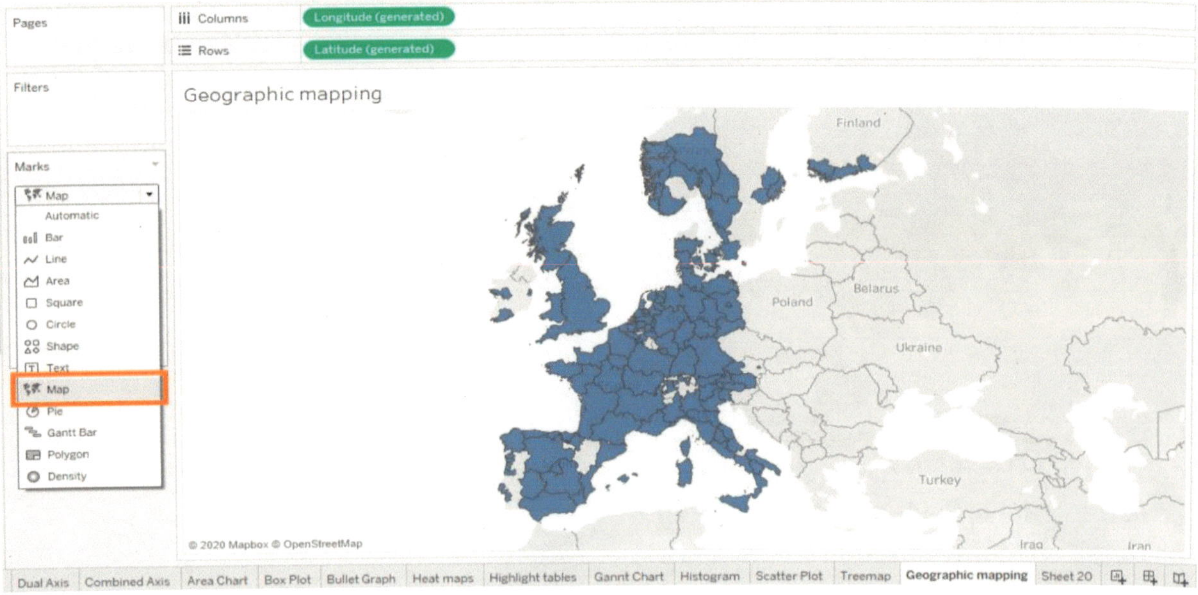

➢ Add measures and dimensions to the Marks card to add visual detail to the view. From Measures, drag **Sales** to **Color** on the Marks card.

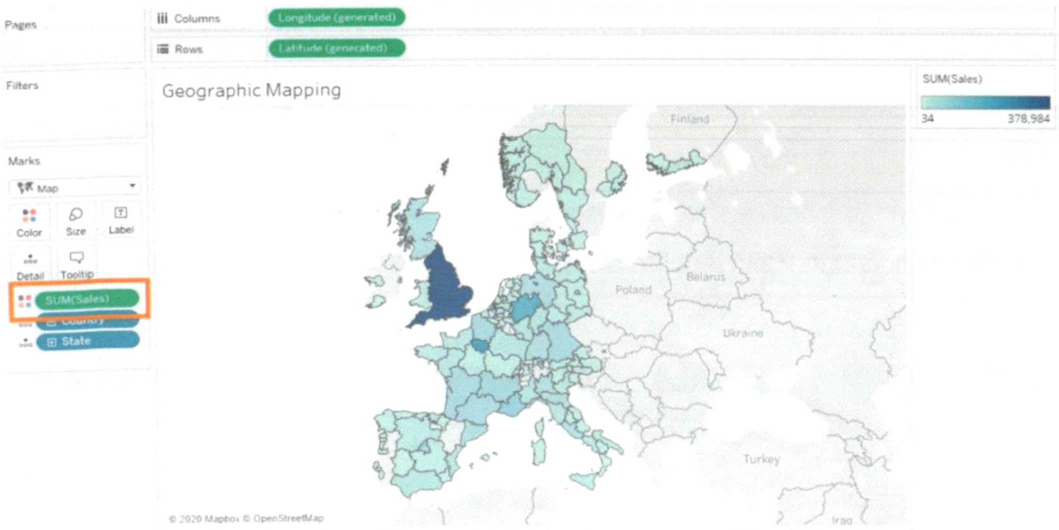

Observation: Each state is colored by sum of sales.

8.12.3 Geographic Groups

➢ Custom territories can be created using maps.
➢ To create custom territories, see section 6.1.3.1 Tableau Groups -Custom Maps

9 Specific Values

9.1 Totals

➢ For the example of Totals, create a Crosstab as show below with Region dimension on the Columns Shelf, Category and Sub-Category dimension on the Rows Shelf and Sales on the Text in Marks Card.

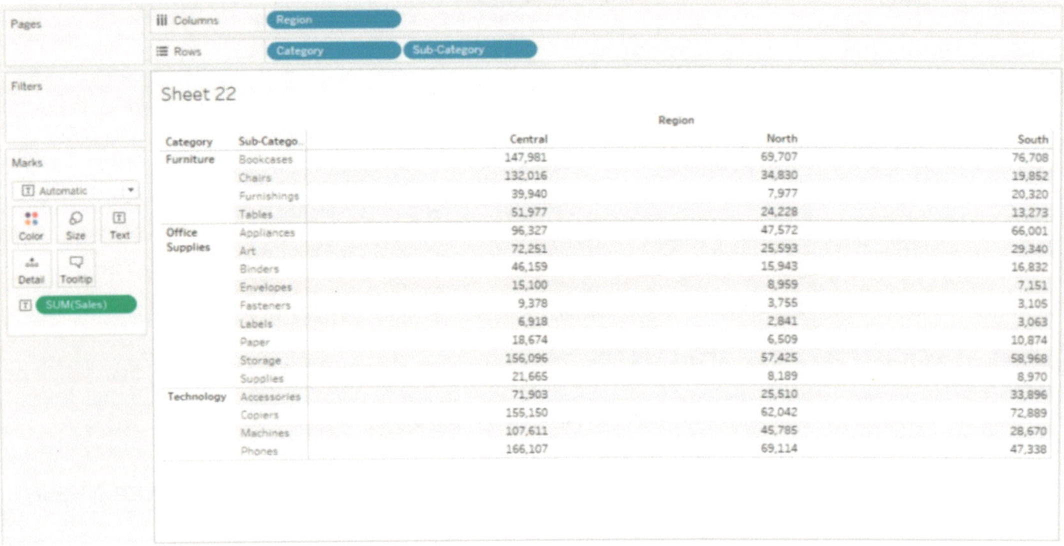

Category	Sub-Catego..	Central	North	South
Furniture	Bookcases	147,981	69,707	76,708
	Chairs	132,016	34,830	19,852
	Furnishings	39,940	7,977	20,320
	Tables	51,977	24,228	13,273
Office Supplies	Appliances	96,327	47,572	66,001
	Art	72,251	25,593	29,340
	Binders	46,159	15,943	16,832
	Envelopes	15,100	8,959	7,151
	Fasteners	9,378	3,755	3,105
	Labels	6,918	2,841	3,063
	Paper	18,674	6,509	10,874
	Storage	156,096	57,425	58,968
	Supplies	21,665	8,189	8,970
Technology	Accessories	71,903	25,510	33,896
	Copiers	155,150	62,042	72,889
	Machines	107,611	45,785	28,670
	Phones	166,107	69,114	47,338

9.1.1 Grand Totals

➢ On the **Analysis** Main menu, Select **Totals** as shown below.

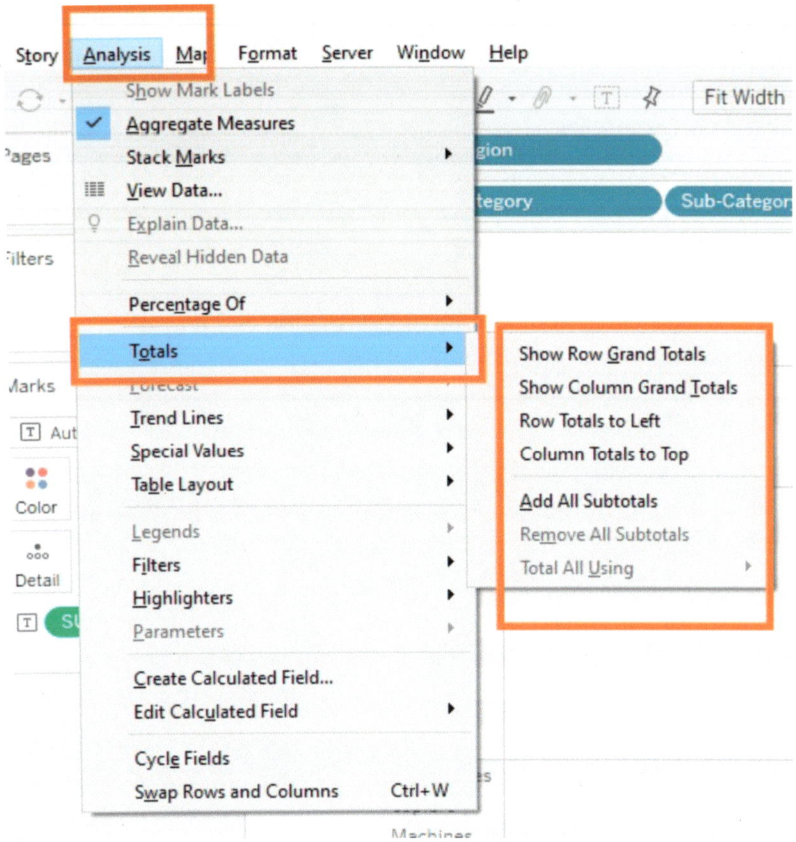

- Under **Totals**, there are multiple options to choose from:
  - **Show Row Grand Totals:** If row headers are displayed, calculates grand totals for rows. Row grand totals appear automatically on the right-side of the visualization.
  - **Show Column Grand Totals:** If row headers are displayed, calculates grand totals for columns. Column grand totals appear automatically at the bottom of the visualization.
  - **Row Totals to Left:** Row grand totals appears on the left-side of the visualization.
  - **Column Totals to Top:** Column grand totals appears at the top of the visualization.
  - **Add All Subtotals:** Calculates the totals of each row category across each column heading.

➢ From Analysis menu, Select Totals, Select **Show Row Grand Totals, Show Column Grand Totals, Add All Subtotals** to create the below view

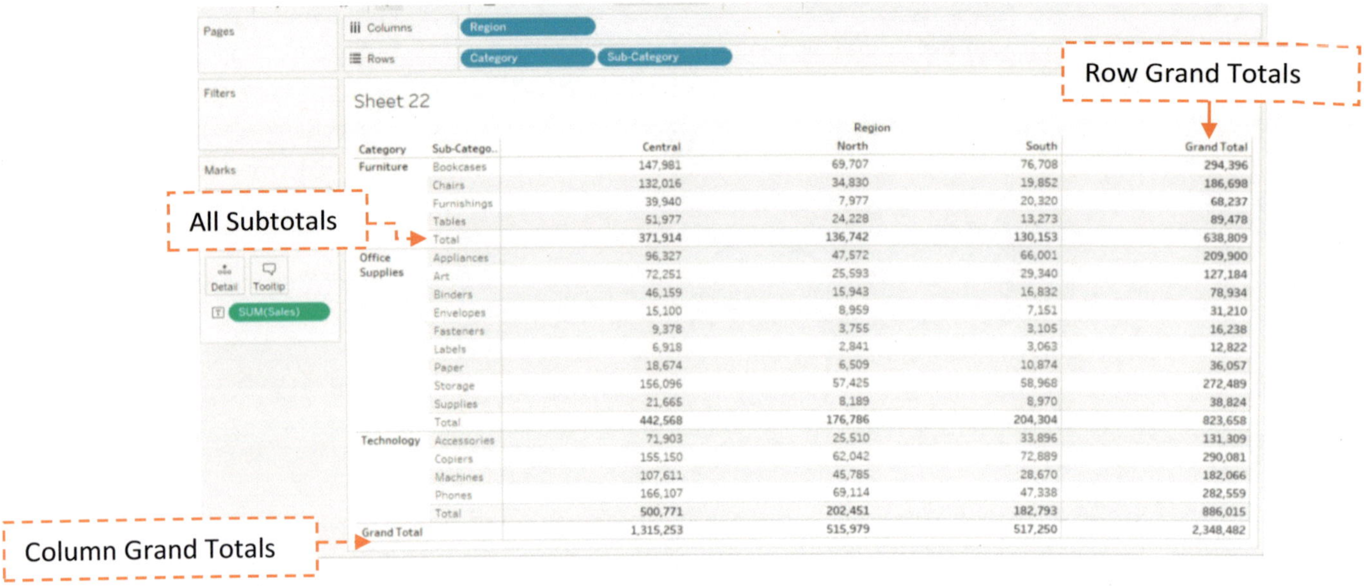

Category	Sub-Catego..	Central	North	South	Grand Total
		Region			
Furniture	Bookcases	147,981	69,707	76,708	294,396
	Chairs	132,016	34,830	19,852	186,698
	Furnishings	39,940	7,977	20,320	68,237
	Tables	51,977	24,228	13,273	89,478
	Total	371,914	136,742	130,153	638,809
Office Supplies	Appliances	96,327	47,572	66,001	209,900
	Art	72,251	25,593	29,340	127,184
	Binders	46,159	15,943	16,832	78,934
	Envelopes	15,100	8,959	7,151	31,210
	Fasteners	9,378	3,755	3,105	16,238
	Labels	6,918	2,841	3,063	12,822
	Paper	18,674	6,509	10,874	36,057
	Storage	156,096	57,425	58,968	272,489
	Supplies	21,665	8,189	8,970	38,824
	Total	442,568	176,786	204,304	823,658
Technology	Accessories	71,903	25,510	33,896	131,309
	Copiers	155,150	62,042	72,889	290,081
	Machines	107,611	45,785	28,670	182,066
	Phones	166,107	69,114	47,338	282,559
	Total	500,771	202,451	182,793	886,015
Grand Total		1,315,253	515,979	517,250	2,348,482

PLEASE NOTE

The totals applied in the view can be removed by: Analysis menu > Select Totals and Uncheck the selected totals.

9.2 Aggregation

➢ In Tableau, measures or dimensions are aggregated, though it is more common to aggregate measures.

➢ When measure is added to view, Tableau automatically aggregates its values. Sum, average, and median are common aggregations. The type of aggregation applied varies depending on the context of the view.

➢ For example, **Sales** becomes **SUM(Sales)**. Every measure has a default aggregation which is set by Tableau when you connect to a data source.

9.2.1 Configure Total Aggregation

➢ When totals are selected in the visualization (either grand totals, subtotals, or both), aggregations are used to specify the totals displayed in the view.

➢ **To configure all totals:** Select **Analysis** > **Totals** > **Total All Using**, and select an aggregation from the list.

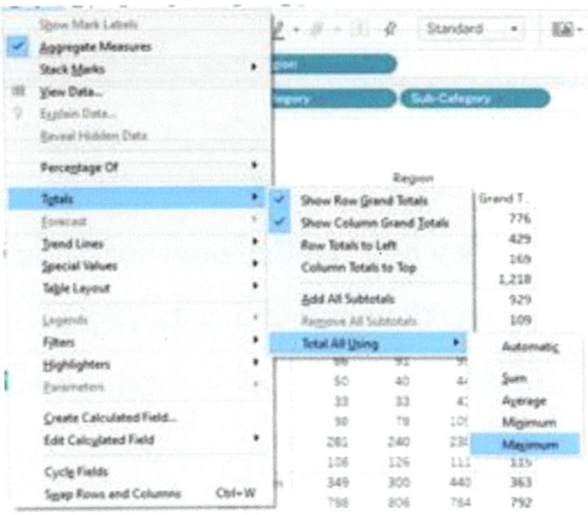

PLEASE NOTE

Total All Using does not get highlighted until either or both Rows Grand Total or Columns Grand Total is selected.

➢ In the existing view, Select **Analysis >Totals** > **Total All Using,** select **Maximum.** The view is updated as shown below.

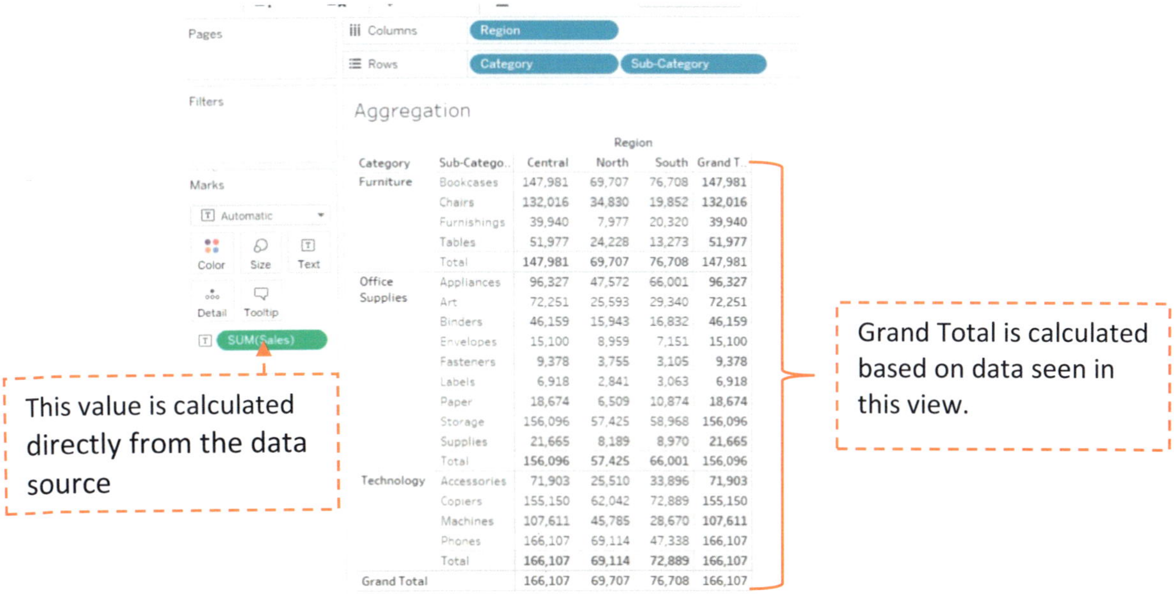

Observe: In the current view, the row totals, column totals and subtotals are showing the maximum or highest sum of sales in the respective rows, columns and subtotals.

PLEASE NOTE

Aggregates calculated based on Grand Total might differ from aggregates calculated directly from data source. This is because the Grand Total is calculated based on data sliced to create the view.

10 Calculations in Tableau

10.1Calculated Field

- Calculated field helps to create a new field/column not present in the existing data source using the available data. The newly calculated field is saved in the Tableau data source without making any changes to the original data source.
- Examples where calculated field is used:
  - To segment data
  - To convert a datatype of a field
  - To calculate ratios
- For an example of calculated field, create a new field **Discount Ratio**. To do so, Select Analysis > Click Calculated Field as seen below.

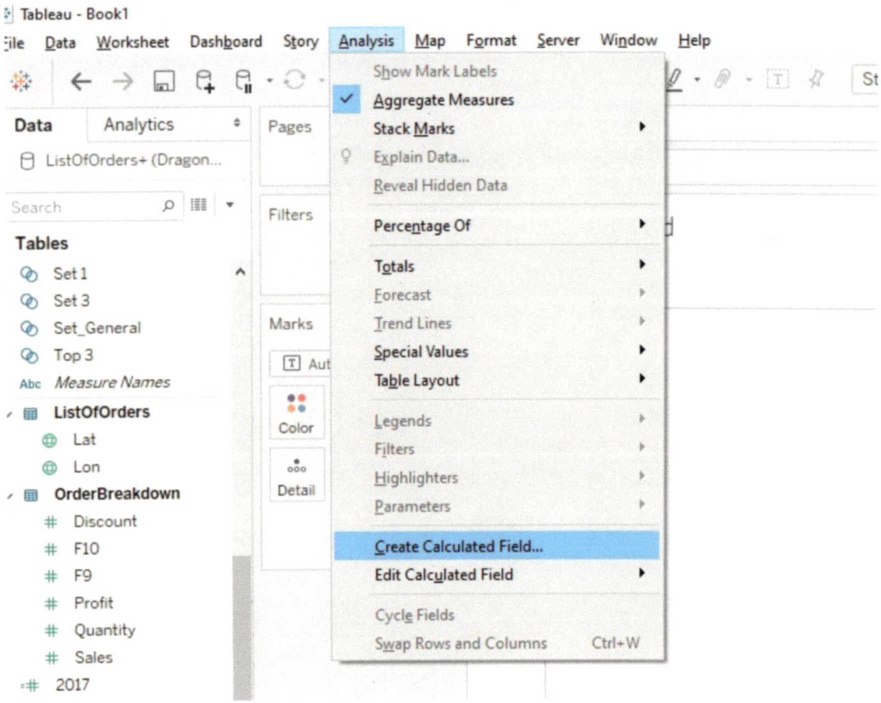

- The Calculation Editor opens up as seen below.

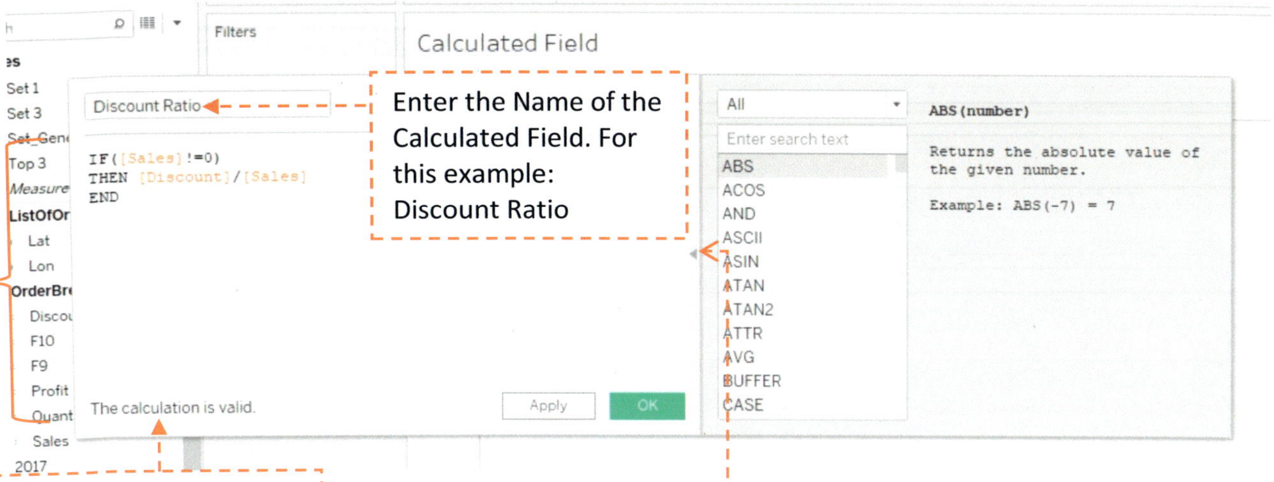

Enter the Name of the Calculated Field. For this example: Discount Ratio

Enter a Formula

Displays message: whether the calculation is valid or not.

Click on the Triangle icon: Includes a list of functions. Each Function include syntax, description and example.

To add the Function to the formula: Double Click on the function in the list

The formula in the example checks If sales is not equal to zero. If true returns Discount ratio else zero.

- Once done Click OK. The newly created calculated field, Discount Ratio is added to the Measures in Data pane (as the field returns numerical value) as show below.

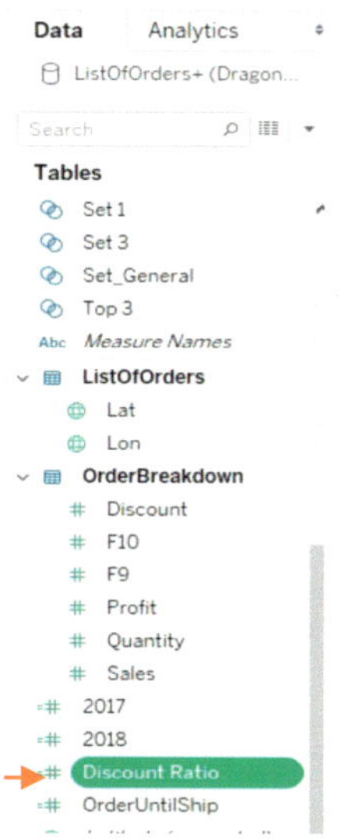

An equal (=) to sign appears next to the newly created field in the Data pane. The equal to sign represents Calculated Field

➢ To use the calculate field in the view, build the below view. From Dimensions drag Region to the Columns Shelf and drag dimensions Category and Sub-category to the Rows shelf. The update view is as shown below.

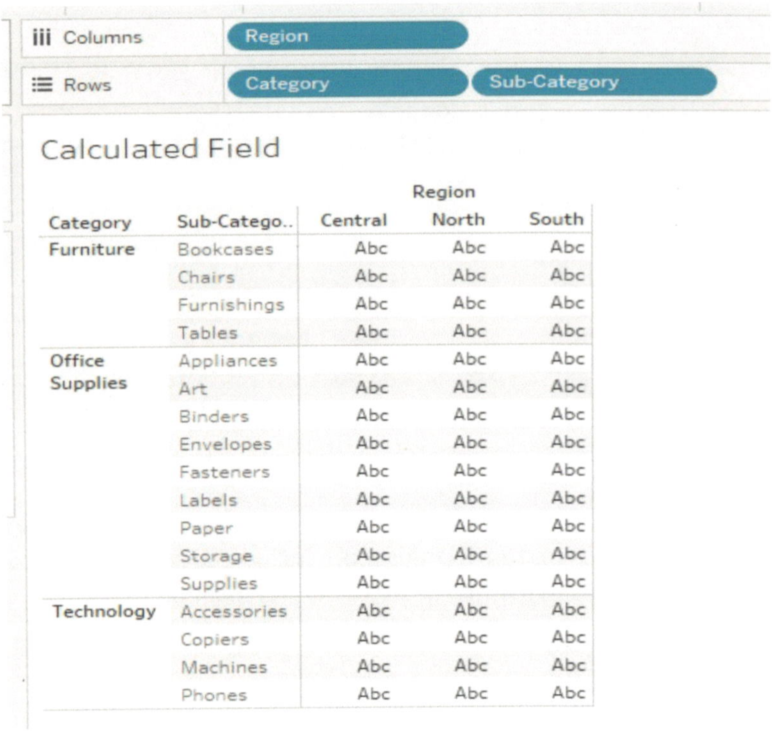

➢ To add the calculated filed to the view, from the Data pane drag Discount Ratio measure to the Color Shelf on the Marks card. The view updates to highlight table as seen below

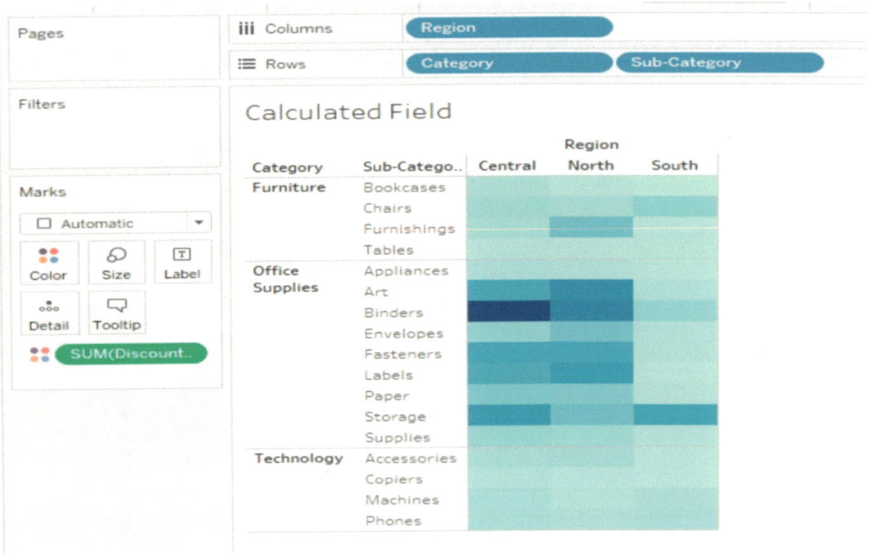

➢ The Discount ratio by default is aggregated as Sum. For the below calculation, aggregate Discount Ratio by average. Click on the down arrow on the SUM (Discount Ratio) pill in the marks card. Select Measure (Sum) > Select Average as seen below.

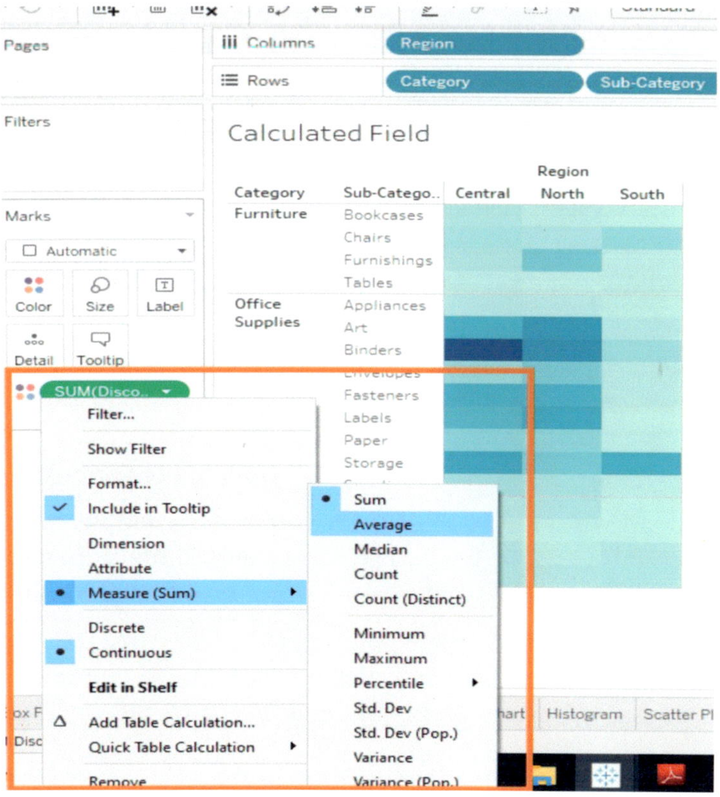

➢ The view updates with average of Discount ratio.

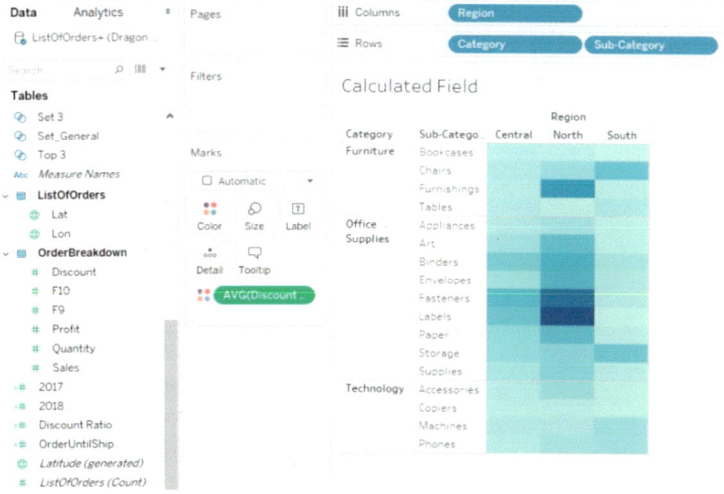

Observation: Overall discount is higher in North region when compared to the other two regions. Labels in the North region is heavily discounted.

10.1.1 Edit Calculated Field

- The calculations in the Calculated field can be edited anytime.
- To edit calculated field: In the Data pane, right click the calculated field, discount ratio and select Edit.
- The Calculation Editor opens up, the following changes can be made

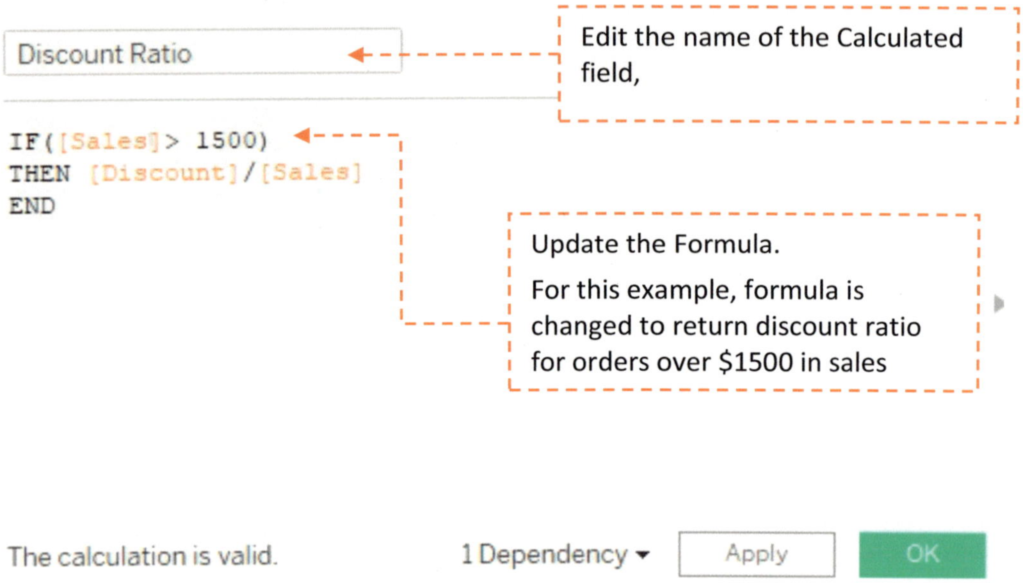

- Click OK. The view automatically updates to reflect the changes. The updated calculated field discount ratio does not need to be re-added to the view.

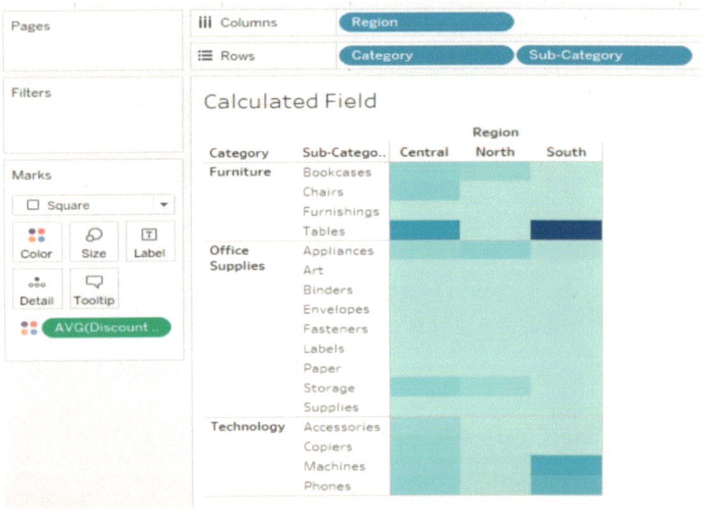

Observation: In the revised view, North seems to have low discount ratio when compared to the rest of the two regions. Tables in the South region is heavily discounted.

10.2Table Calculations

- A table calculation is a transformation applied to values in a visualization.
- Table calculations are calculated field computed on data available in the visualization and do not consider the measures or dimensions which are not part of the view.
- To create a table calculation of Percent of Total Sales. From the Data pane, drag Order Date to the Columns Shelf. From the Data pane, once more drag Order Date to Rows shelf. Change YEAR(Order Date) to Quarter - right-click YEAR(Order Date) and select Quarter. On the Rows shelf, click the + icon on QUARTER(Order Date) and MONTH(Order Date) is added to the shelf. From the Data pane drag **Sales** measure to Text shelf on Marks card. The view created is as seen below.

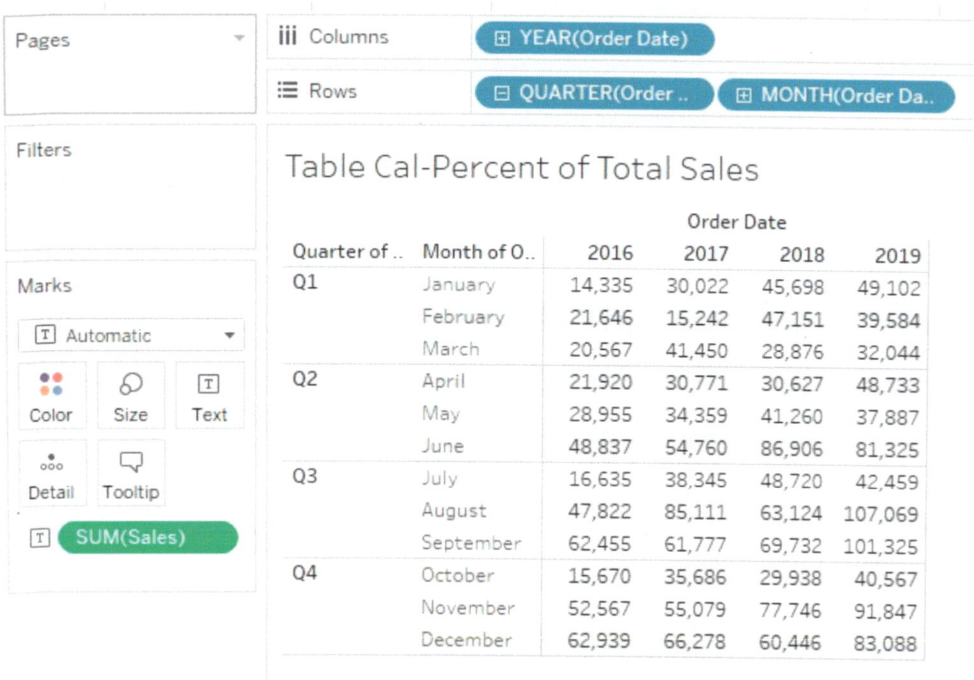

		Order Date			
Quarter of ..	Month of O..	2016	2017	2018	2019
Q1	January	14,335	30,022	45,698	49,102
	February	21,646	15,242	47,151	39,584
	March	20,567	41,450	28,876	32,044
Q2	April	21,920	30,771	30,627	48,733
	May	28,955	34,359	41,260	37,887
	June	48,837	54,760	86,906	81,325
Q3	July	16,635	38,345	48,720	42,459
	August	47,822	85,111	63,124	107,069
	September	62,455	61,777	69,732	101,325
Q4	October	15,670	35,686	29,938	40,567
	November	52,567	55,079	77,746	91,847
	December	62,939	66,278	60,446	83,088

PLEASE NOTE

Table calculations are calculated field computed on data available in the visualization and do not consider the measures and dimensions which are not part of the view.

➢ Percent of Total table calculation can be used for the above view to calculate the percentage of total sales each month within a quarter. To do so, on the Marks card, right-click SUM(Sales) and select **Add Table Calculation**.

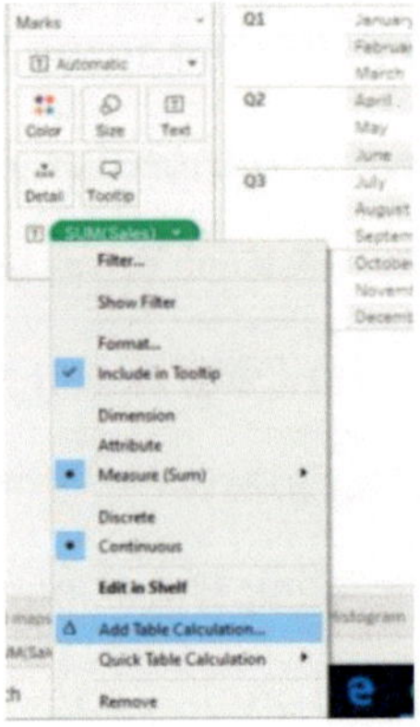

➢ The Table Calculation dialog box opens as seen below.

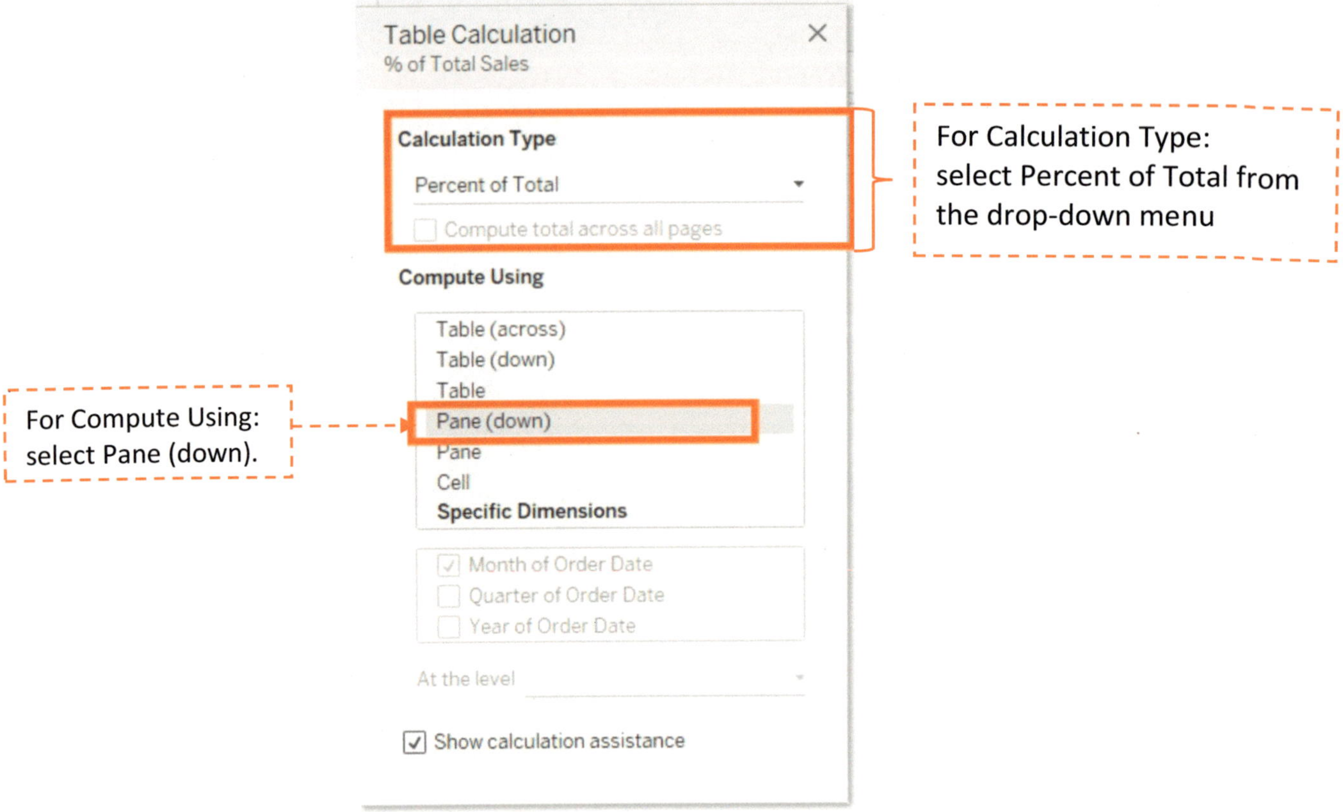

➢ Once finished, click the X in the top corner of the Table Calculation dialog box. The calculation is applied to the values in the visualization. The updated view as seen below.

Table Cal-Percent of Total Sales

Quarter of ..	Month of O..	Order Date 2016	2017	2018	2019
Q1	January	25.35%	34.62%	37.54%	40.67%
	February	38.28%	17.58%	38.74%	32.79%
	March	36.37%	47.80%	23.72%	26.54%
Q2	April	21.98%	25.67%	19.29%	29.02%
	May	29.04%	28.66%	25.98%	22.56%
	June	48.98%	45.68%	54.73%	48.42%
Q3	July	13.11%	20.70%	26.83%	16.93%
	August	37.68%	45.95%	34.76%	42.68%
	September	49.21%	33.35%	38.40%	40.39%
Q4	October	11.95%	22.72%	17.81%	18.82%
	November	40.07%	35.07%	46.24%	42.62%
	December	47.98%	42.20%	35.95%	38.56%

Observation: January, 2016 makes up 25.35% of sales made in Q1.

10.2.1 Edit Table Calculation

➢ Edit Table calculation to calculate the percentage of total sales each month makes within a year.

➢ On the Marks card, right-click SUM(Sales) and select Edit Table Calculation.

➢ Make changes to the Table Calculation dialog box that appears as shown below (Compute using: Table (down)). Once done, click the X in the top corner of the Table Calculation dialog box. The calculation is applied to the values in the visualization.

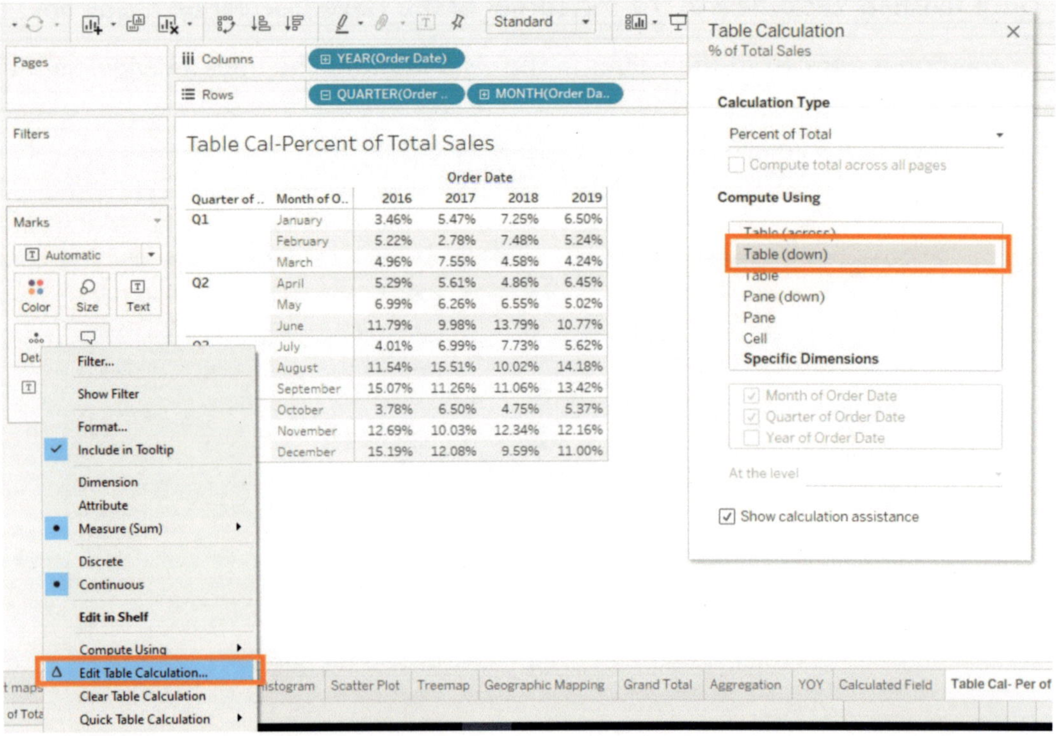

Observation: January, 2016 makes up 3.46% of sales made in 2016.

10.2.2 Remove Table Calculation

- Right-click the measure, SUM(Sales) in the view with the table calculation applied to it and select Clear Table Calculation.

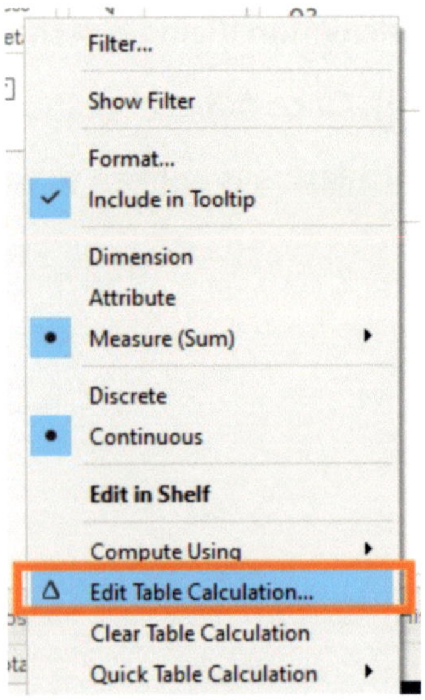

➤ The table calculation is removed from the measure, and the visualization updates with the original values.

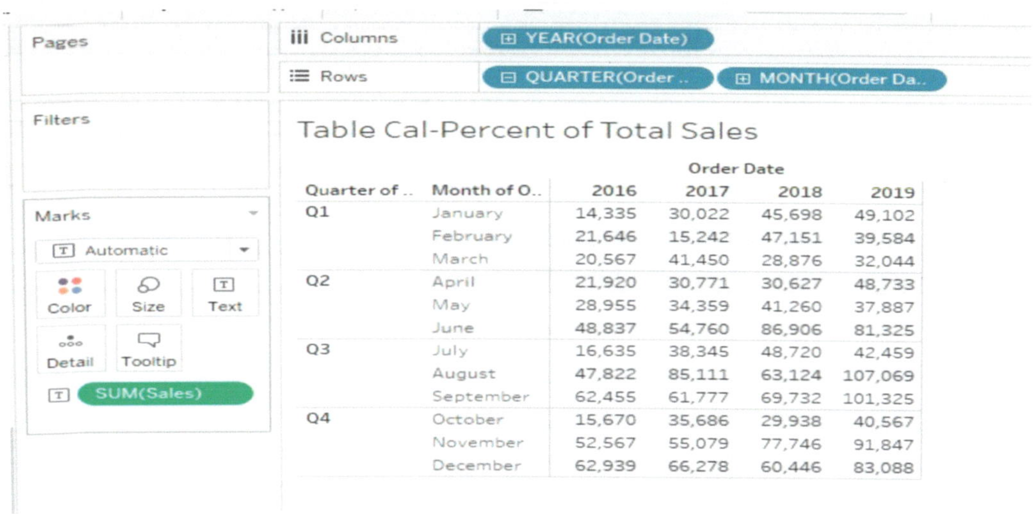

		Order Date			
Quarter of ..	Month of O..	2016	2017	2018	2019
Q1	January	14,335	30,022	45,698	49,102
	February	21,646	15,242	47,151	39,584
	March	20,567	41,450	28,876	32,044
Q2	April	21,920	30,771	30,627	48,733
	May	28,955	34,359	41,260	37,887
	June	48,837	54,760	86,906	81,325
Q3	July	16,635	38,345	48,720	42,459
	August	47,822	85,111	63,124	107,069
	September	62,455	61,777	69,732	101,325
Q4	October	15,670	35,686	29,938	40,567
	November	52,567	55,079	77,746	91,847
	December	62,939	66,278	60,446	83,088

10.3Quick Table Calculation

➤ Quick table calculation allows to perform common table calculation in the visualization work. Quick table contains a set of pre-computed table calculations that can be applied without writing any code.

➤ Quick table calculations are table calculations that you can apply quickly to your visualization in Tableau. Only difference is that, in Table calculation the default settings in Quick table calculations needs to be applied manually.

➤ As ab example of Quick table calculation, create the view as shown below. From the data pane, under Dimensions drag Order Date to Columns shelf and under Measures, drag Sales to Rows shelf as seen below.

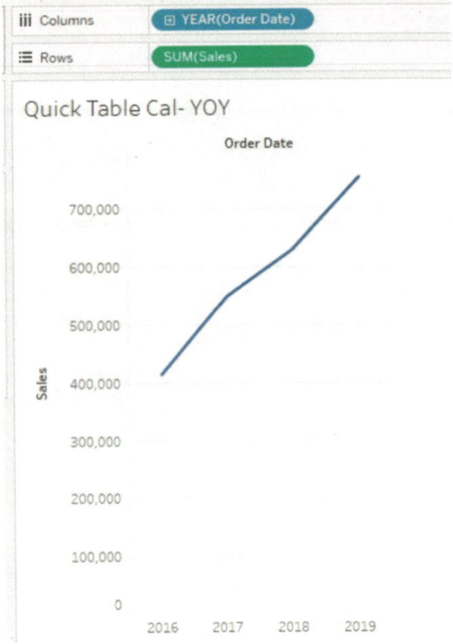

- On the Rows Shelf, click the drop down arrow on SUM(Sales), select Quick Table calculation , and choose **Year over Year Growth**.

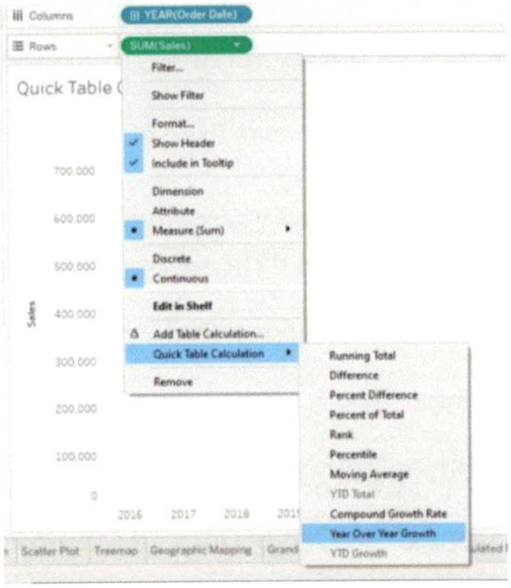

- On the Marks card, change the mark type to **Bar** from the drop down. Press and hold CTRL (command key in mac) and drag SUM(Sales) from Rows shelf to color on Marks card.

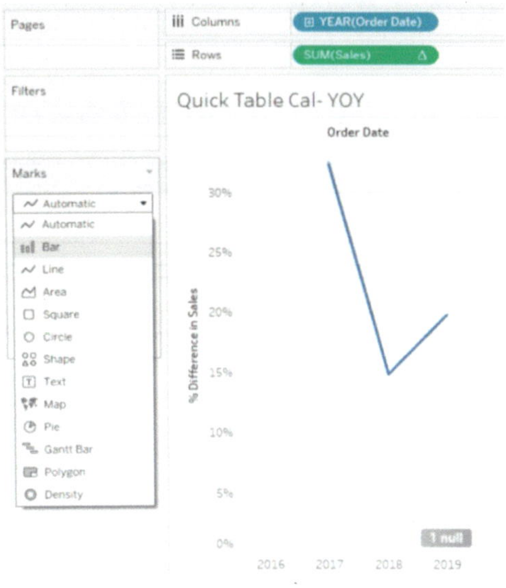

- In the Data pane, under Dimensions, right-click Sub-Category and select Show Filter. In Sub-Category filter choose only Binders.
- Similarly, under Dimensions, right-click Region and select Show Filter. In the Region filter in the view, select South.

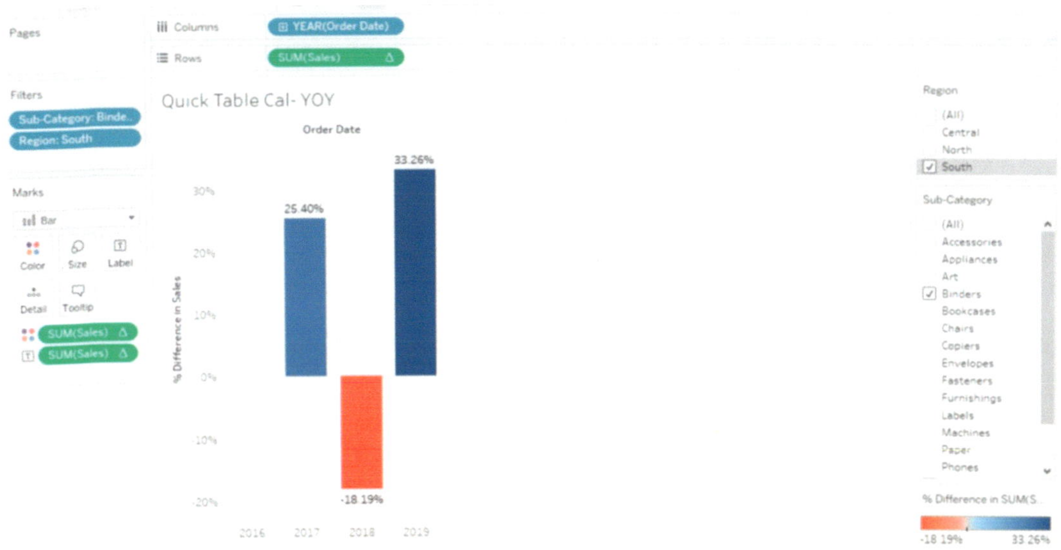

Observation: The percent difference in year over year sales between 2017 and 2018 in South region for Binders is -18.19%. This was the only market with negative percent difference in year over year sales for Binders

10.4Table Calculation types

- Tableau contains a number of table calculations. Some of the types of table calculation are:
  - Running Total Calculation
  - Percent of Total Calculation
  - Year to Year change
  - Moving average
  - Moving calculations, etc.

10.4.1 Running Total Calculation

- Running Total is used to calculate the cumulative total of a measure across a specific dimension or table structure.
- For a Running total, Tableau calculates cumulative value by summing, averaging or replacing all values with either the lowest or highest actual values.
- For the example, of Running Total calculation, create the below view. From the Data pane, drag Order Date to the Columns Shelf. From the Data pane, once more drag Order Date to Rows shelf. Change Year(Order Date) to quarter,right-click YEAR(Order Date) and select Quarter. On the Rows shelf, click the + icon on QUARTER(Order Date) and MONTH(Order Date) is added to the shelf. From the Data pane drag Sales measure to Text shelf on Marks card. The view created is as seen below.

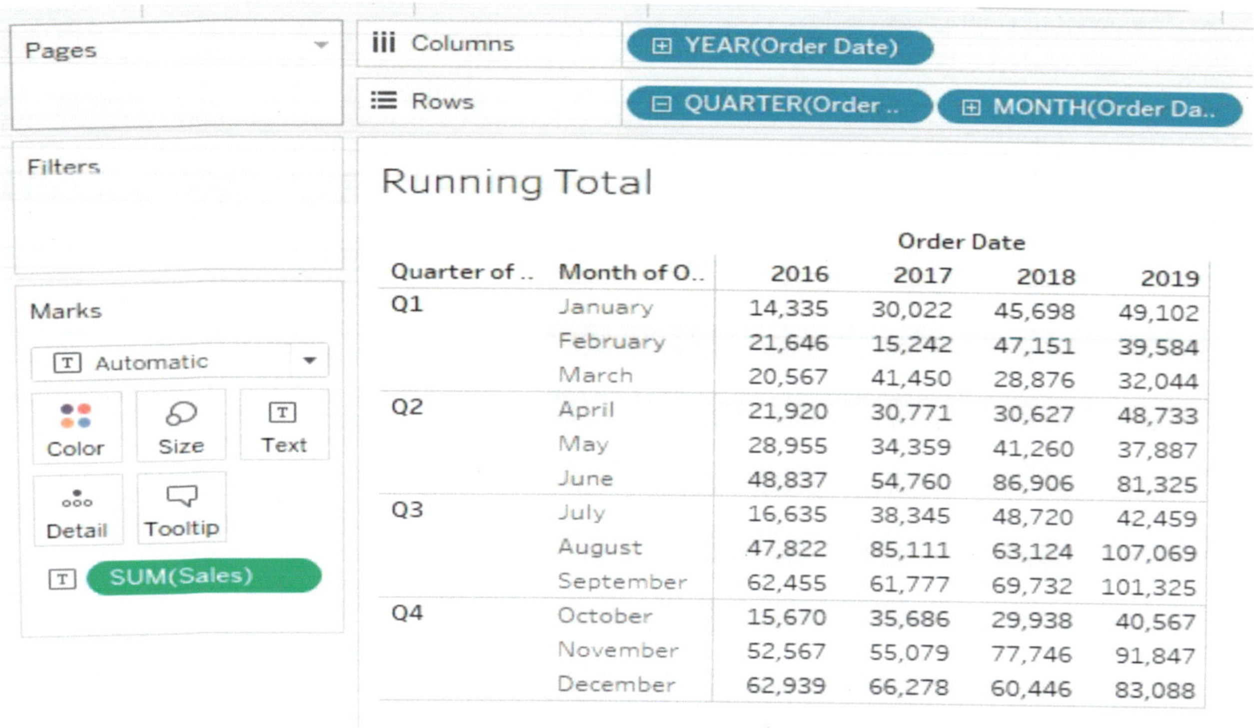

		Order Date			
Quarter of ..	Month of O..	2016	2017	2018	2019
Q1	January	14,335	30,022	45,698	49,102
	February	21,646	15,242	47,151	39,584
	March	20,567	41,450	28,876	32,044
Q2	April	21,920	30,771	30,627	48,733
	May	28,955	34,359	41,260	37,887
	June	48,837	54,760	86,906	81,325
Q3	July	16,635	38,345	48,720	42,459
	August	47,822	85,111	63,124	107,069
	September	62,455	61,777	69,732	101,325
Q4	October	15,670	35,686	29,938	40,567
	November	52,567	55,079	77,746	91,847
	December	62,939	66,278	60,446	83,088

➢ On the Marks card, right click the SUM(Sales) field, select Quick Table Calculation and click Running Total.

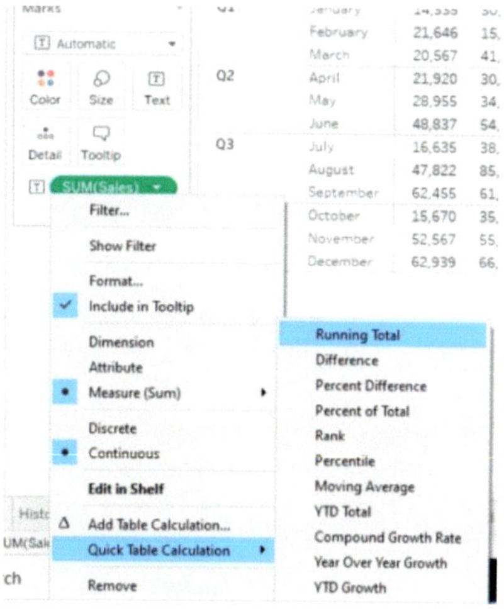

➤ The updated view as seen below.

Running Total

Quarter of ..	Month of O..	Order Date 2016	2017	2018	2019
Q1	January	14,335	44,357	90,055	139,157
	February	21,646	36,888	84,039	123,623
	March	20,567	62,017	90,893	122,937
Q2	April	21,920	52,691	83,318	132,051
	May	28,955	63,314	104,574	142,461
	June	48,837	103,597	190,503	271,828
Q3	July	16,635	54,980	103,700	146,159
	August	47,822	132,933	196,057	303,126
	September	62,455	124,232	193,964	295,289
Q4	October	15,670	51,356	81,294	121,861
	November	52,567	107,646	185,392	277,239
	December	62,939	129,217	189,663	272,751

Observation: Comparing with values with the original view, the cumulation of sum is done across the table

➤ To edit the above view to find the average running total down the table, on the marks card right click the measure, SUM(Sales) and choose Edit Table Calculation.

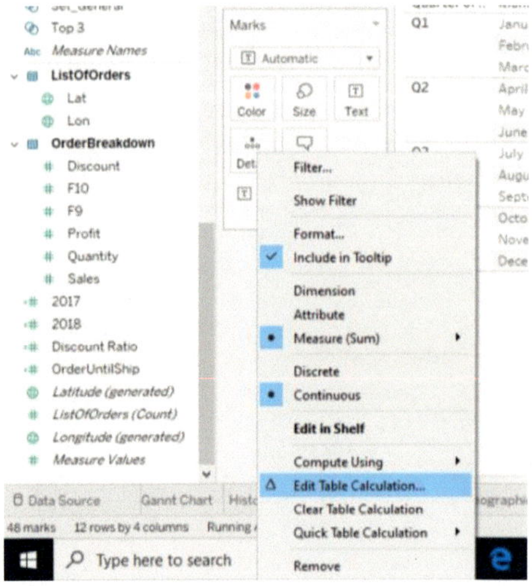

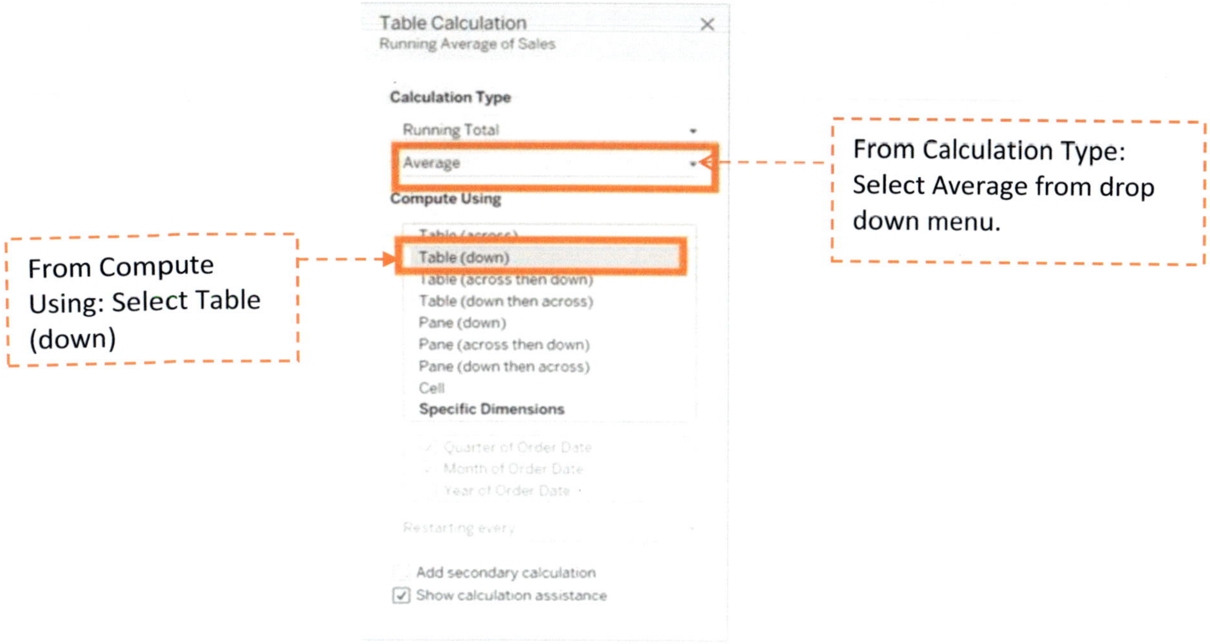

➢ Once finished, click x and the updated view is as seen.

Running Total

		Order Date			
Quarter of ..	Month of O..	2016	2017	2018	2019
Q1	January	14,335	30,022	45,698	49,102
	February	17,991	22,632	46,425	44,343
	March	18,849	28,905	40,575	40,243
Q2	April	19,617	29,371	38,088	42,366
	May	21,485	30,369	38,722	41,470
	June	26,043	34,434	46,753	48,113
Q3	July	24,699	34,993	47,034	47,305
	August	27,590	41,258	49,045	54,775
	September	31,464	43,537	51,344	59,948
Q4	October	29,884	42,752	49,203	58,010
	November	31,946	43,873	51,798	61,086
	December	34,529	45,740	52,519	62,919

Observation: The running average for 2016 in Q4 for October is $29,884. We observe there is a dip in the average when compared to September of the same year.

10.5 Reference Line

- Reference lines are horizontal or vertical lines that act as a reference or baseline for a particular measure against which they are compared.
- For example, create the view below. From the Data pane, under dimensions, drag Category and Sub-Category field onto the Columns shelf. Drag Sales from measures into the Rows shelf. By default, Tableau generates a bar chart.

- To add reference line, right click on the Measure axis in the view and select add Reference Line as seen below.

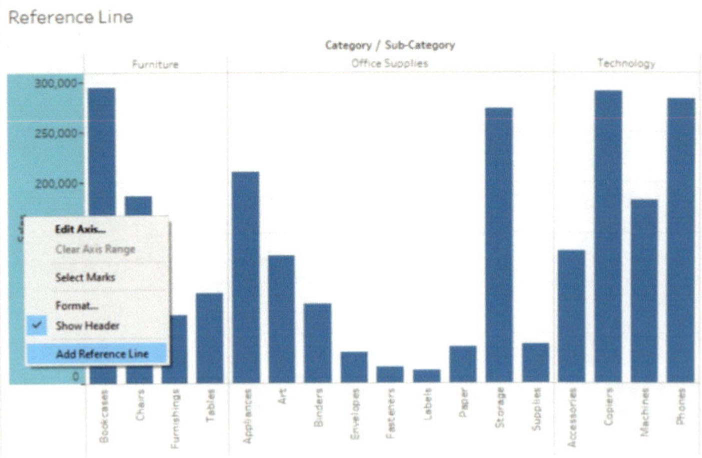

➢ Alternative Method: Click on the Analytics pane of the Tableau desktop, under Custom tab, select and drag the reference line to the view to add it to the chart as shown below.

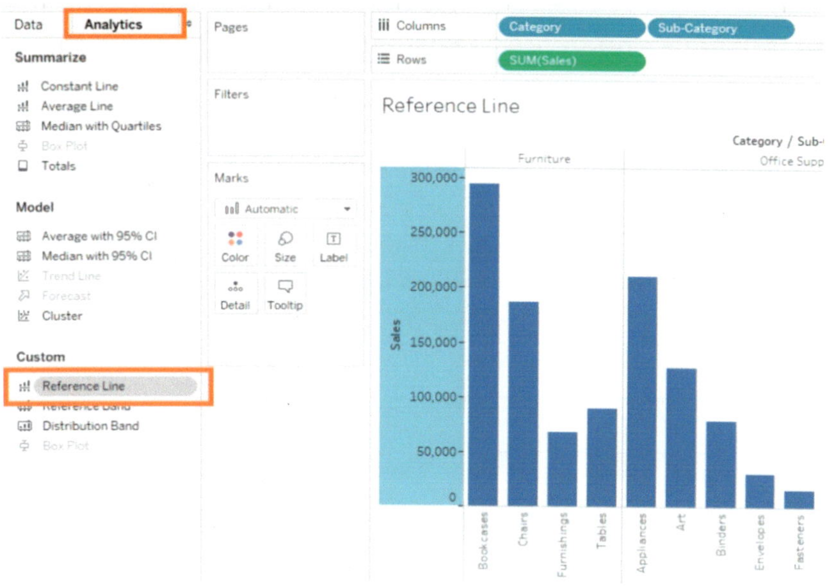

➢ In both methods, a pop-up window, Add Reference Line, Band, or Box is generated that contains:

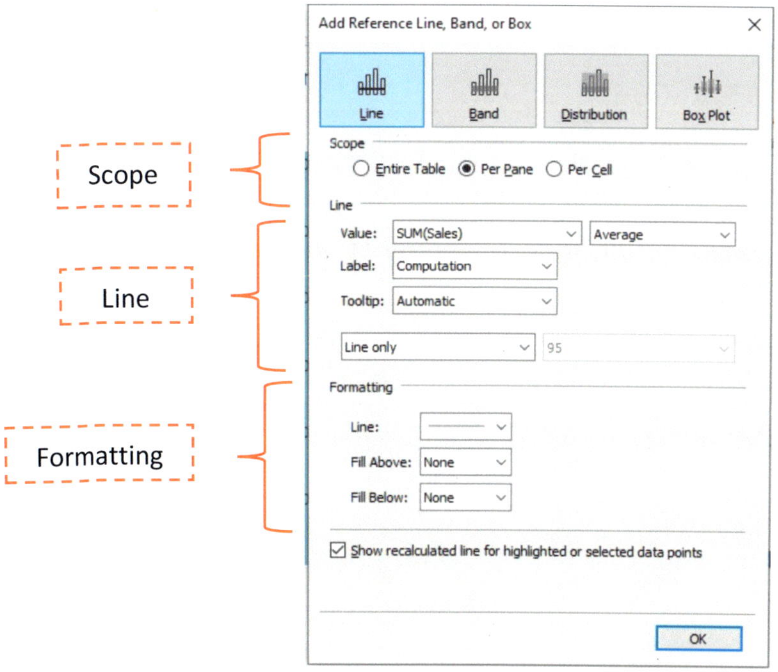

➢ Scope contains options for the reference line as seen below. The three options are:

- Entire Table: Adds reference line to the entire table across all panes. This means Tableau calculates the aggregation for the whole table.
- Per Pane: Adds a reference line on a per pane basis. The computed reference lines are recalculated for each pane in the view.
- Per cell: Adds a reference line within each cell. The computed reference lines are recalculated for each cell in the view.

➢ Select the scope as Entire table as shown below.

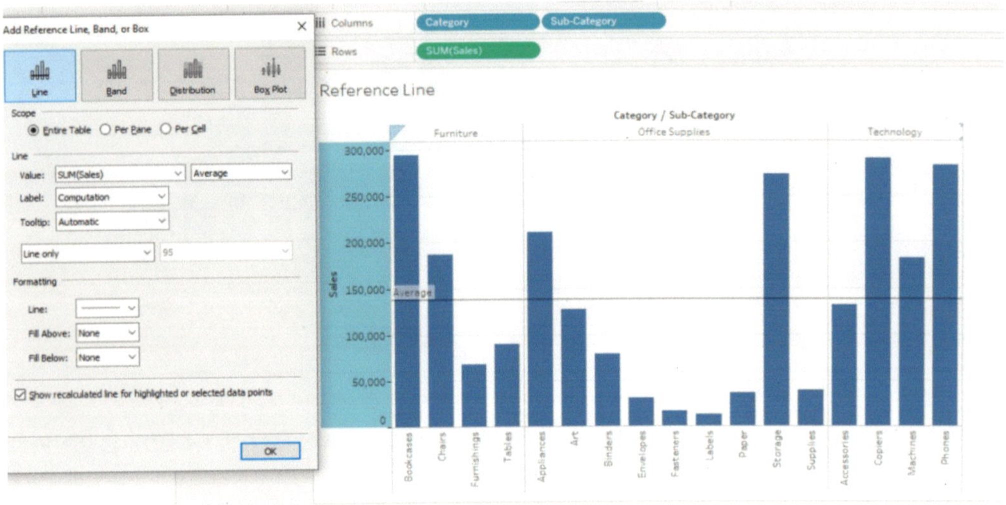

Observation: The reference line is computed for the entire chart and looks incorrect for the above view.

➢ Select Per pane option, which results in three reference lines for each category.

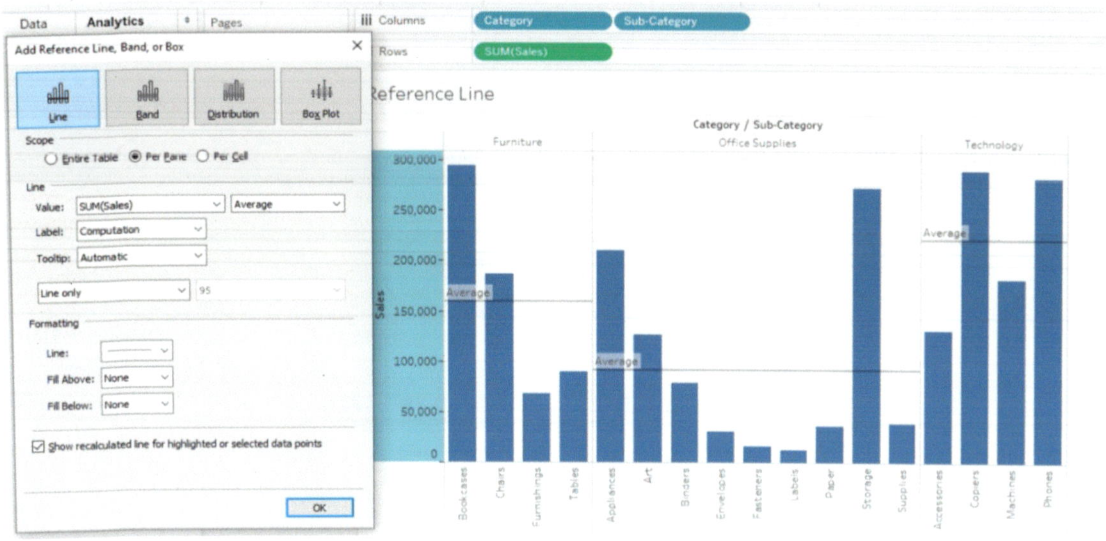

- Line Value: The value option decides the data used by reference line. Select the Measure value used to create the reference line. For this example, select SUM(Sales).
- Next tab displays the default aggregation Average. Select the type of aggregation depending on the aggregation needed to display the reference line. For this example, select the default option: Average.
- The next option is Label, which denotes the label of the reference line. There are four options:

- None: No label will be displayed.
- Value: This option displays the value of the selected aggregation.
- Computation: This option displays the computation being performed.
- Custom: Selecting the custom option, displays another box with the option to add a field value, name, computation etc. Select either one or multiple options as seen below.

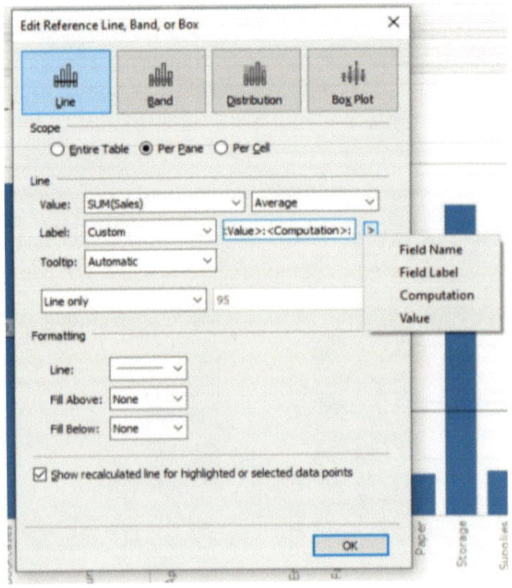

- For this example, select <Value>: <Computation>
- Next tab provides option to choose to display the Reference Line, or Reference Line and Confidence interval, or Confidence interval Only. For the current example, select Line Only option.
- The formatting region formats the Reference Line Type, Color, Width, and Background color of the above area and below area. The below Bar Chart shows how the reference lines can be formatted.

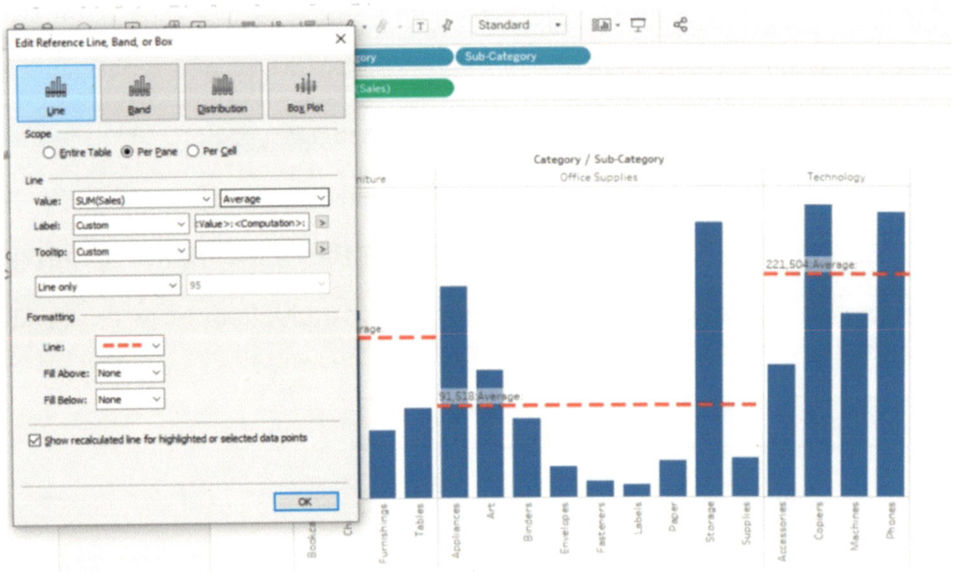

➢ Once done click OK. The updated view as seen below.

Observation: For the above view, reference line is computed across each pane. The reference is calculated as the average of the SUM(Sales) data as seen in the label on the reference line. The reference line is formatted to pink dash lines.

10.5.1 Edit Reference Line

➢ If you want to edit the existing reference line, right click on the Sales measures axis and click Edit reference line as seen in the screenshot below.

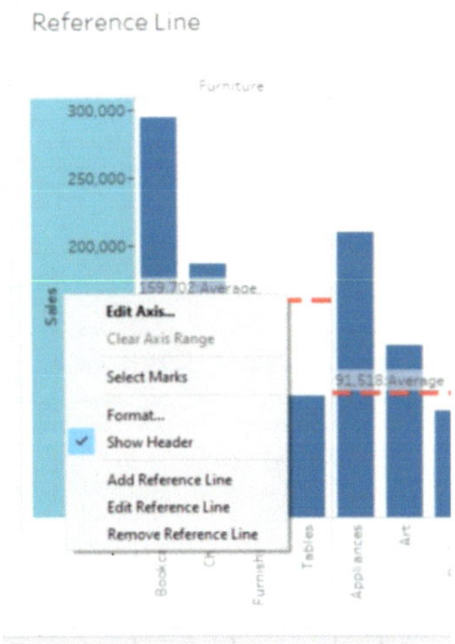

➢ The Edit Reference Line, Band, or Box dialog box appears. Make the required changes. In the current example, add Light Beige color to fill the space below the reference line as seen below. Click Ok to get the updated view.

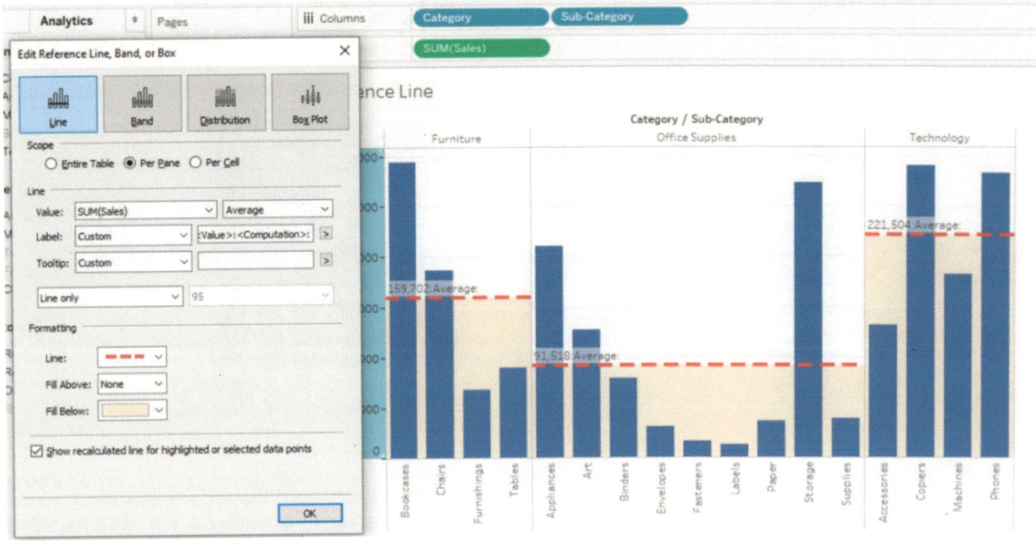

10.5.2 Remove Reference Line

➢ To remove Reference Lines, right click on the Sales Axis and select Remove Reference Line.

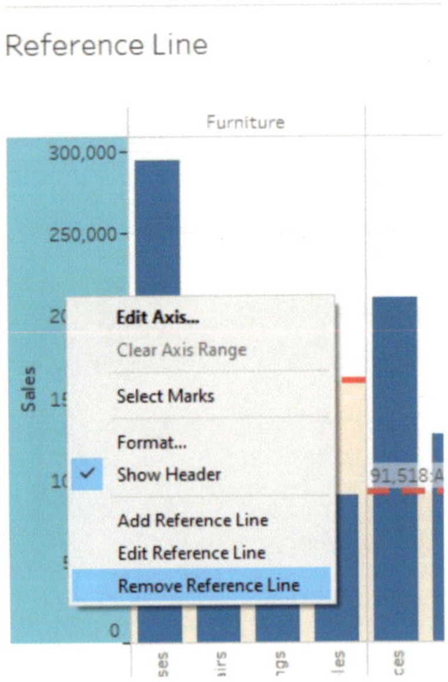

11 Infographics

- Infographics helps to present information clear by graphical visual representations of information, data and knowledge.
- There are two ways of adding objects in Tableau:
- Adding images to Worksheet
- Adding image to Dashboard

11.1Adding images to Worksheet

- Images are added to the Tableau worksheets using Shape marks. The images loaded can be used as filters. For larger number of images this method might be difficult, each shape needs to be manually assigned to a data value, one at a time (assigning can be done automatically if the image and data are ordered the same).
- For the example of adding images to Tableau worksheet, create the simple view of sales of each category across the years. To do so, from the Data pane drag Order Date to Columns shelf and Sales under measures to Rows shelf. In the Marks card, select mark type as shapes as seen below.

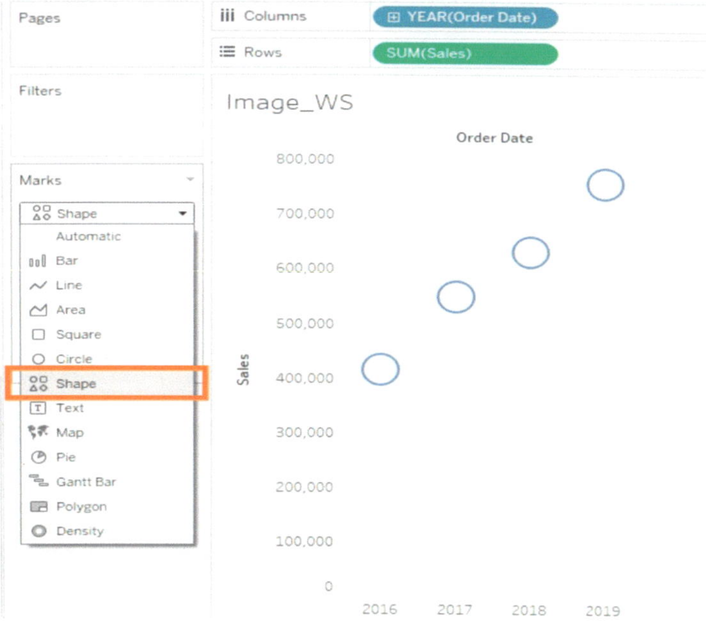

➢ From the Data pane, drag Category to the Shape Shelf on the Marks card.

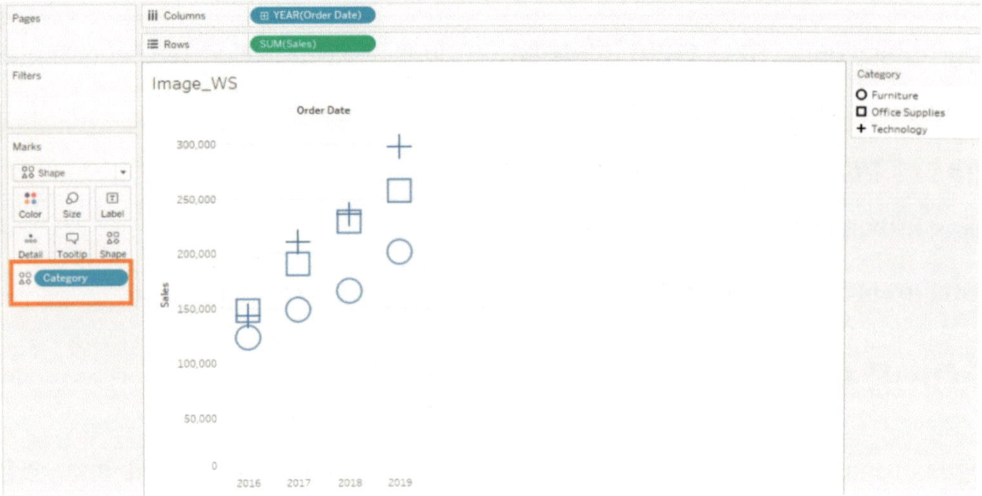

➢ In this example to assign icons for each category, copy the images to be loaded onto the worksheet and browse to the location: C:\Users\<username>\My Documents\My Tableau Repository\Shapes. (On a Mac computer, the default location is Users\<username>\Documents\My Tableau Repository\Shapes.)

PLEASE NOTE

Location of Repository vary depending on User's installation of Tableau and Operating System.

➢ Under the Shapes folder create a new folder, **Category** to store the images.

➢ Return to the Tableau desktop, click on the Data Source tab at the bottom left corner of the page. In the Data Source page click on the icon Refresh Data at the top left of the screen to refresh and load the new shapes.

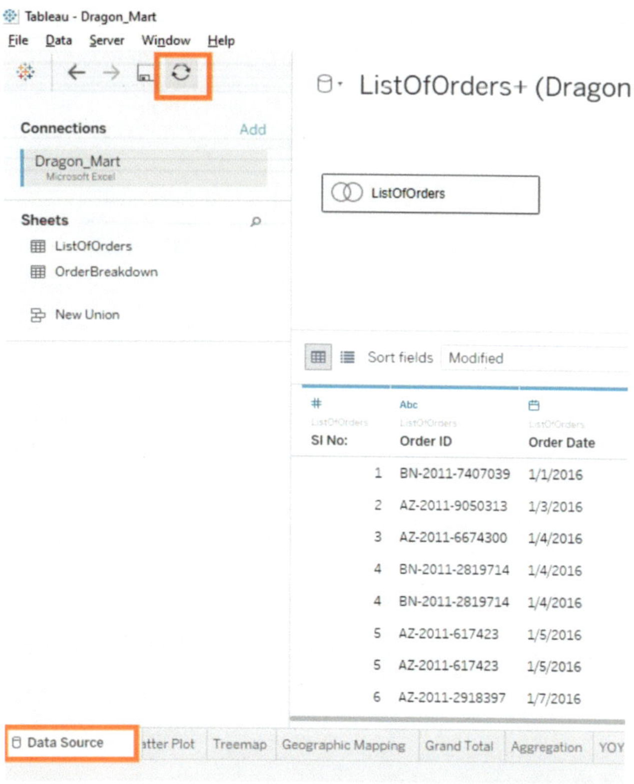

- Return to worksheet. Go to the Marks Shelf and click on the Shape Marks. The dialog box below will appear. From the drop down of Select Shape Palette, select Category.

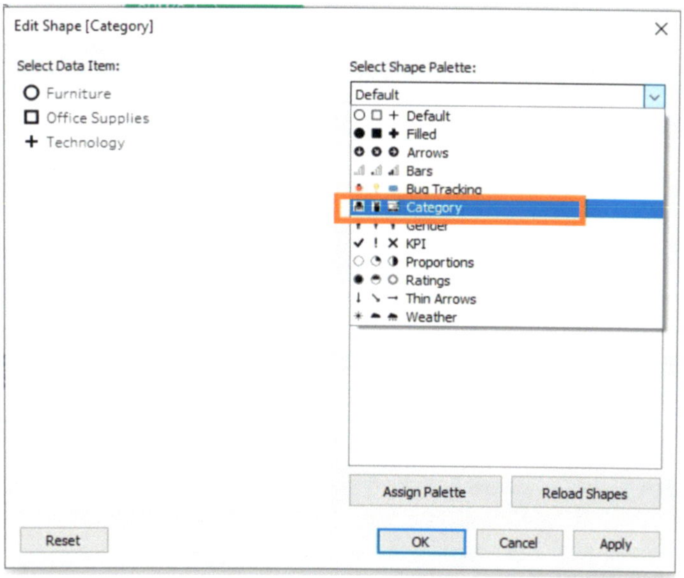

➢ Select Assign Palette as shown below or Manually assign by selecting the Category and selecting the image one by one.

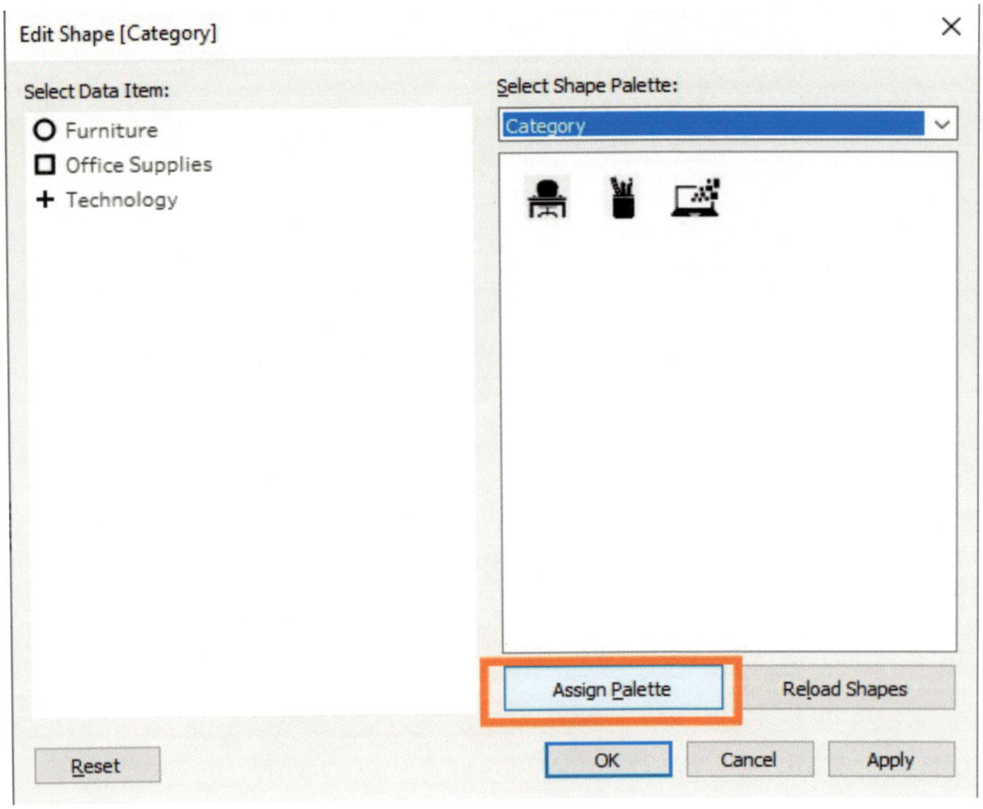

➢ Click OK. The Shapes in the graph are replace by the custom images as seen below. The size of the images can be adjusted using the Size shelf in Marks card.

11.2 Adding images to Dashboard

- To create Dashboard, refer Section 12.
- To add image to the Dashboard, from the Dashboard pane in the left hand-side, drag image from Objects as shown below.

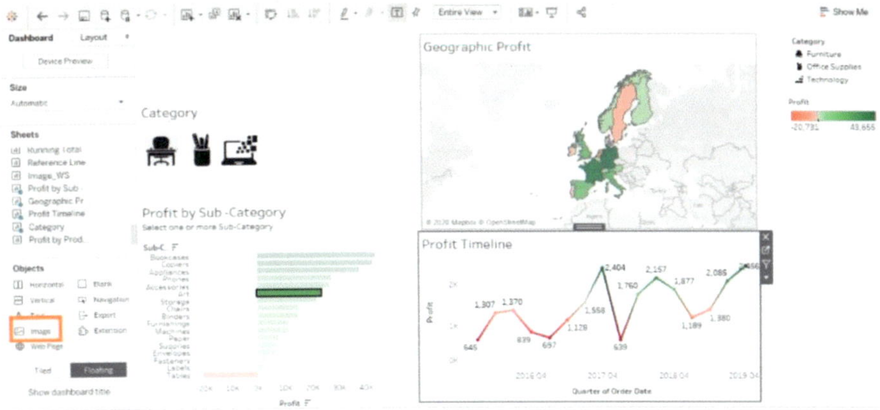

- A box appears with an Edit image object dialog box. Choose image either from local disk or enter URL to download from web.

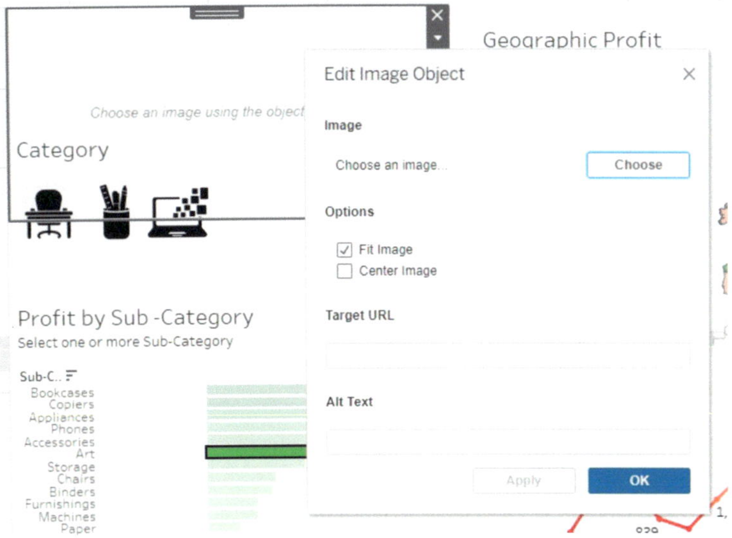

➤ Load the image of Dragon to represent the current Data source Dragon_Mart. Choose the image from local disk and Click Ok.

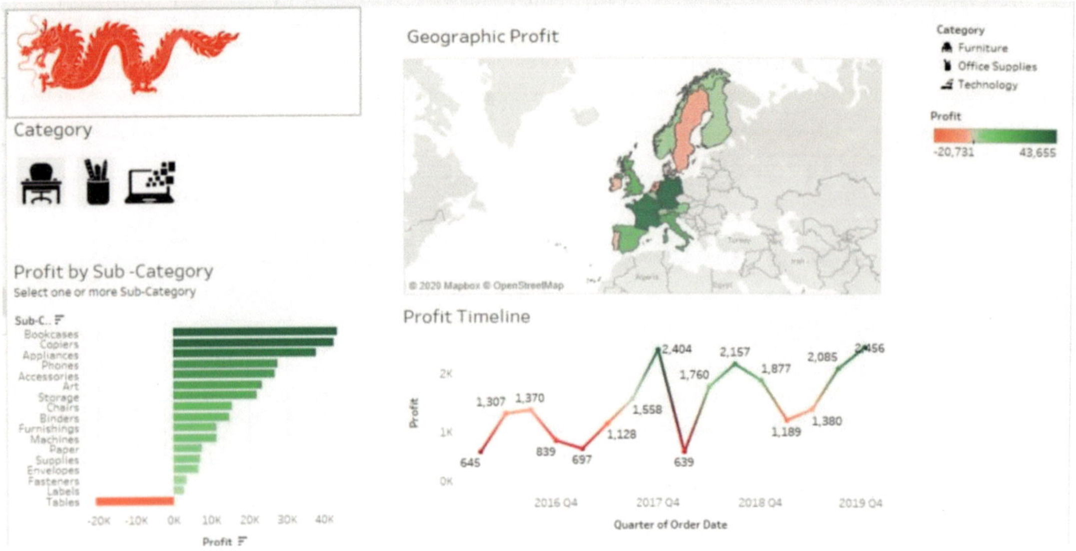

12 Creating Dashboards

- A dashboard is a collection of several views that allows a variety of data to be compared at once. Data in sheets and dashboards are linked in a dashboard. Therefore, any changes made in sheets are reflected in all the dashboard containing the sheets and vice versa.
- Dashboards are created to visually represent business objectives. Tableau dashboards are interactive and can be used to drill down to details based on user's objectives.
- Dashboards are created similar to a worksheet. At the bottom of the Workbook, click the New Dashboard icon .

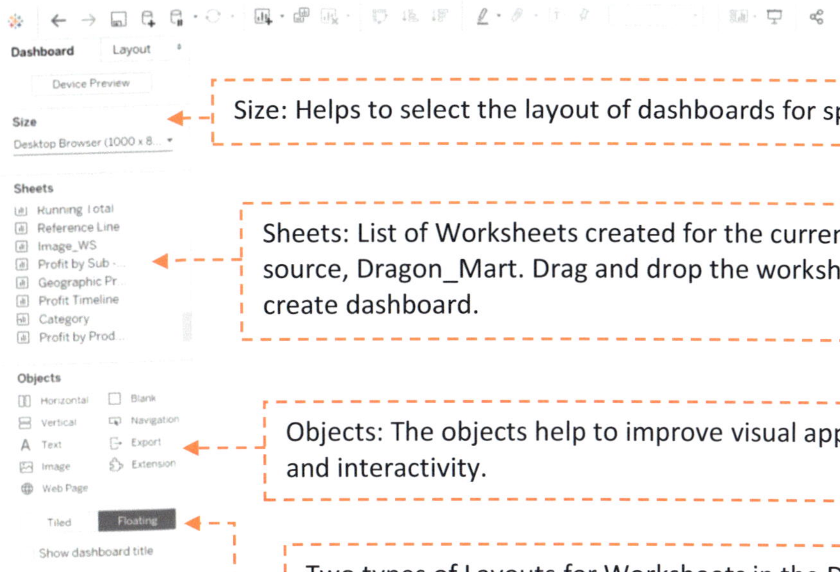

Size: Helps to select the layout of dashboards for specific devices.

Sheets: List of Worksheets created for the current data source, Dragon_Mart. Drag and drop the worksheet to create dashboard.

Objects: The objects help to improve visual appeal and interactivity.

Two types of Layouts for Worksheets in the Dashboards:

- Tiled: Tiled objects are arranged in a single layer grid that adjust in size based on the total dashboard size and the objects around it.
- Floating: Floating objects can be layered on top of other objects and can have a fixed size and position.

- For the Dashboard example: Create the below four worksheets

- Profit by Sub-Category: SUM(Profit) in Columns, Sub-Category in Rows, and SUM(Profit) in Color Marks. Sort if preferred.

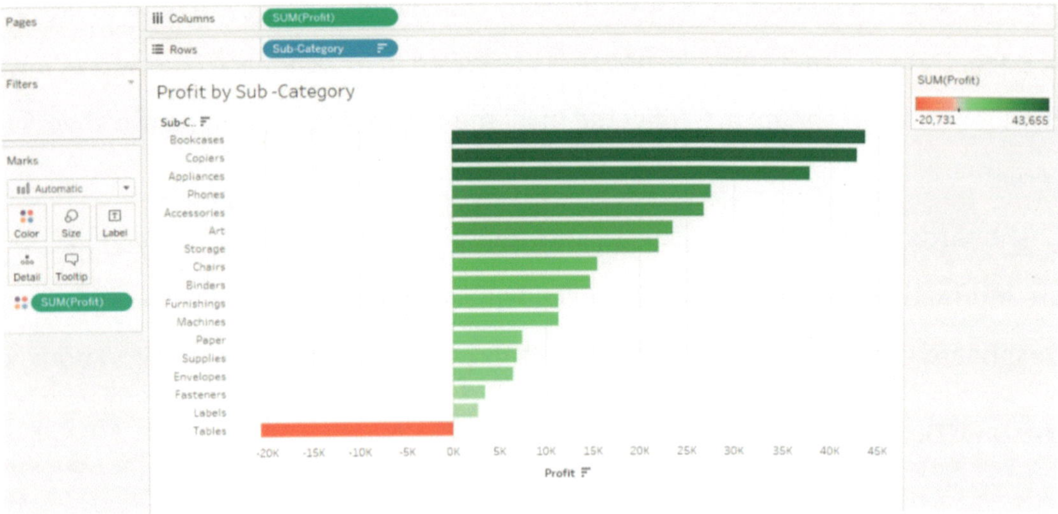

- Profit of bottom 10 least profitable product: SUM(Profit) in Columns, Product Name in Rows, SUM(Profit) in Color Marks, and Filter Product Name (Top Tab: By field, Bottom 10 by Profit Sum). Sort if preferred.

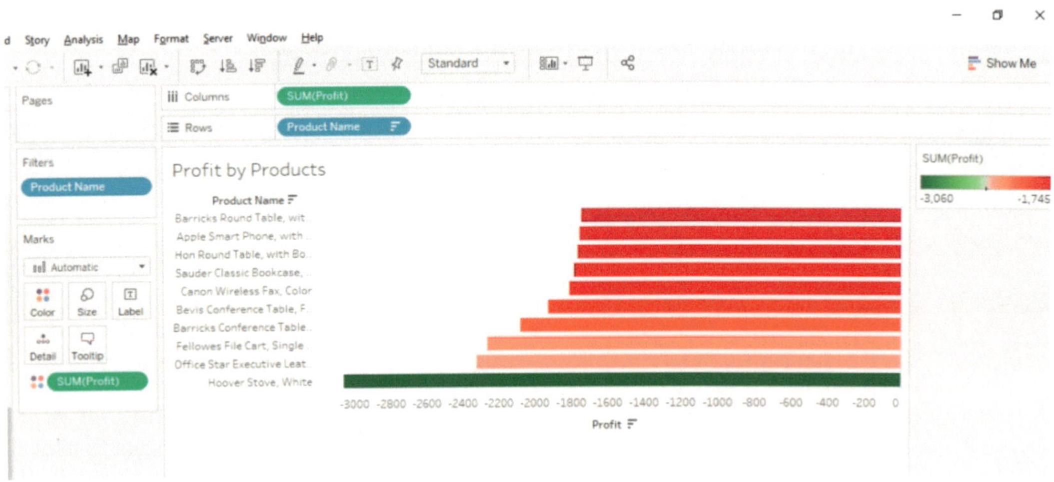

- Geography by Profit: Longitude in Columns, Latitude in Rows, SUM(Profit) in Color marks, and Country in Label.

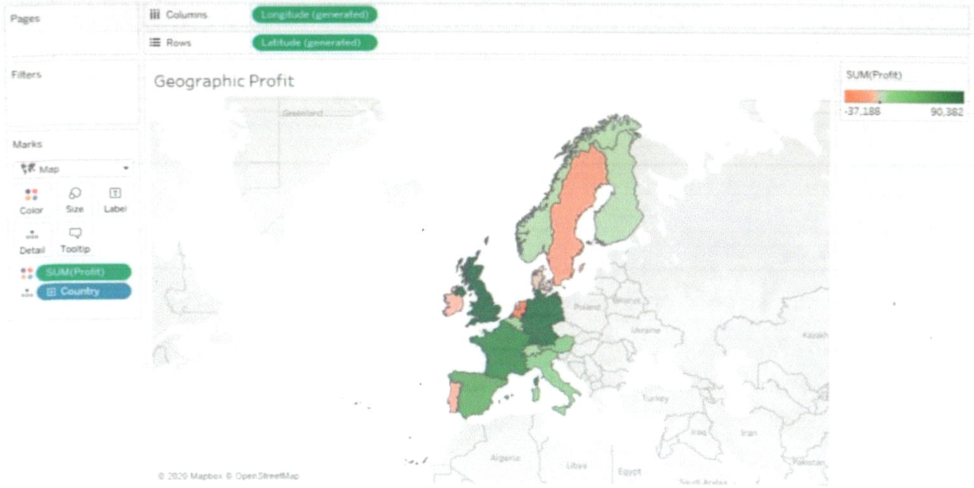

- Profit Timeline: QUARTER(Order Date) in Columns, SUM(Profit) in Rows, and SUM(Profit) in Color marks.

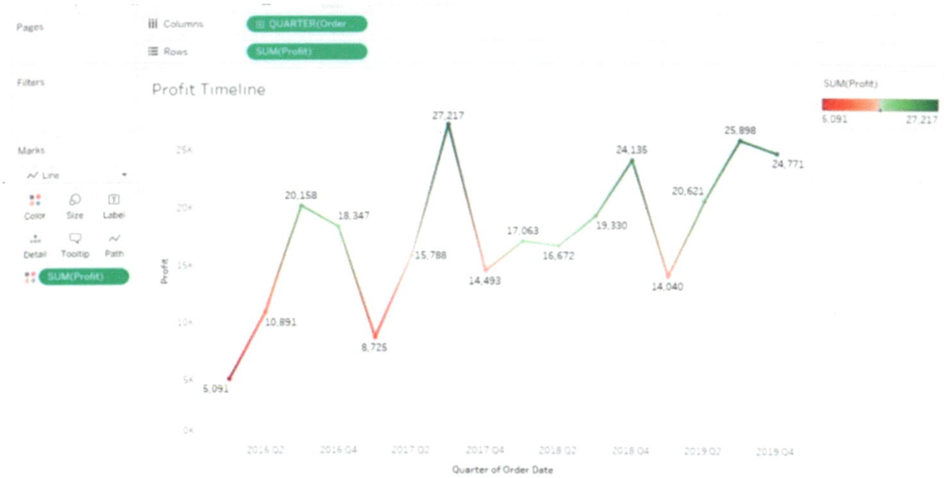

➢ To create a dashboard, Profitability analysis with the above four pages. Click on the New Dashboard icon. Drag and drop or double click on the four worksheets under Sheets in the Dashboard pane onto the workspace as shown below.

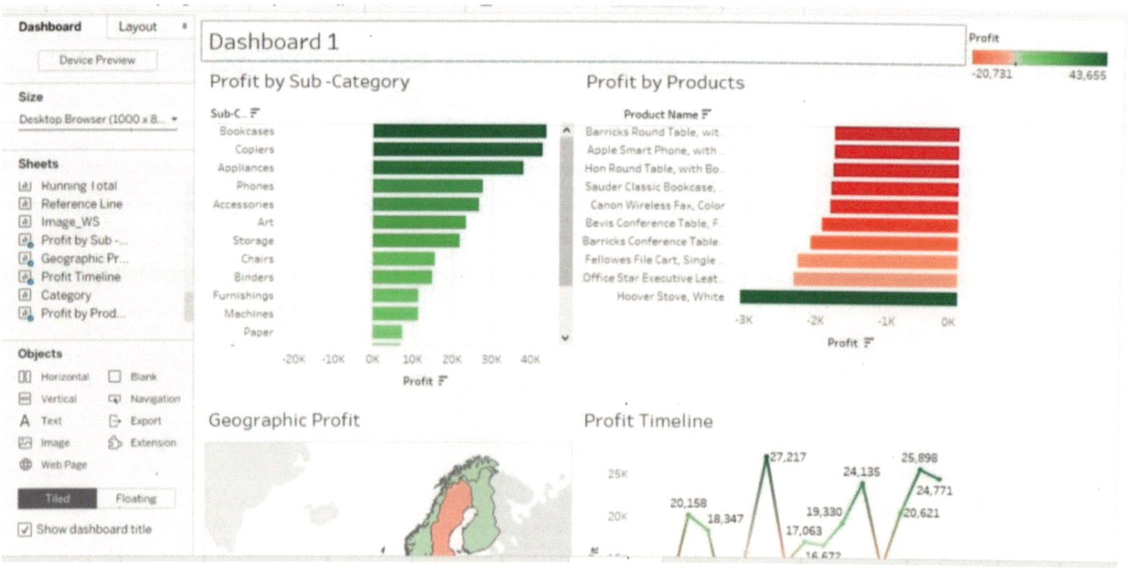

- The visualization does not fit the entire screen. Change Size to **Automatic.**
- Tableau automatically changes the overall dimensions of the visualization based on screen size.

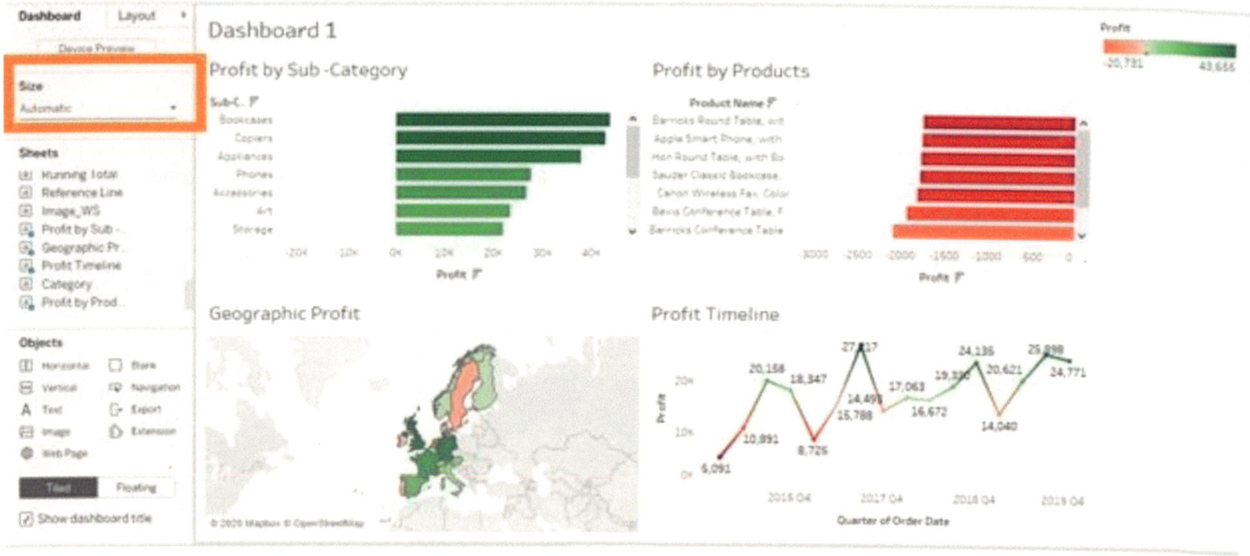

- **Add Title to the Dashboard:** On the top menu bar select Dashboard and select Show Title. Enter the Title as shown below.

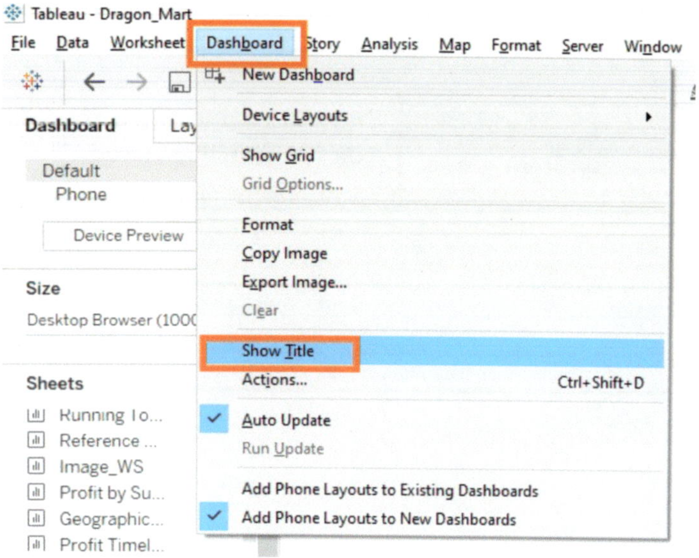

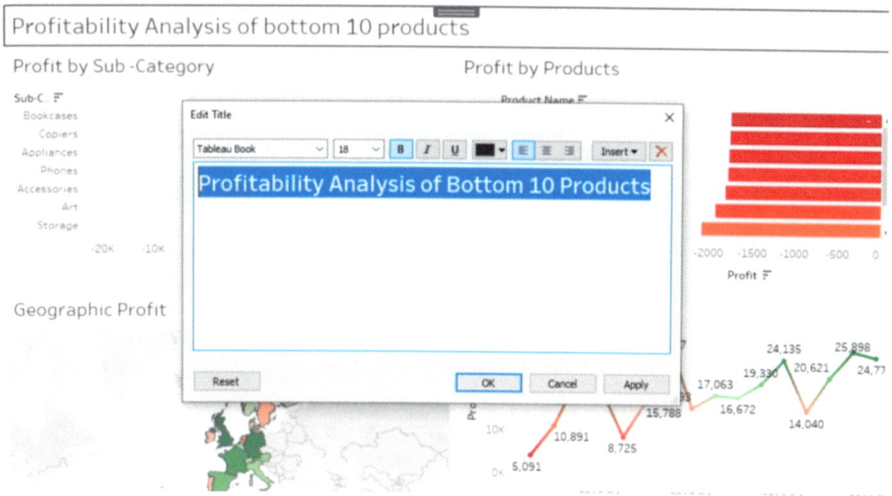

➢ Adding Title to the views helps to explain the purpose of the visualization. Click on the Title of the object, Edit Title dialog box appears. In the box Enter the Title and description if required.

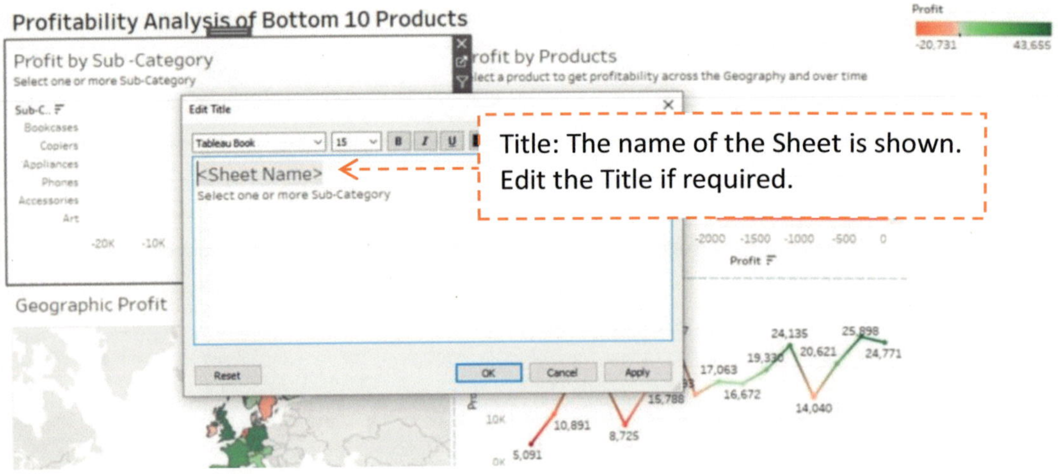

➢ To remove an object from the dashboard, select the view, Profit by Products and click on the X in top right corner as shown below.

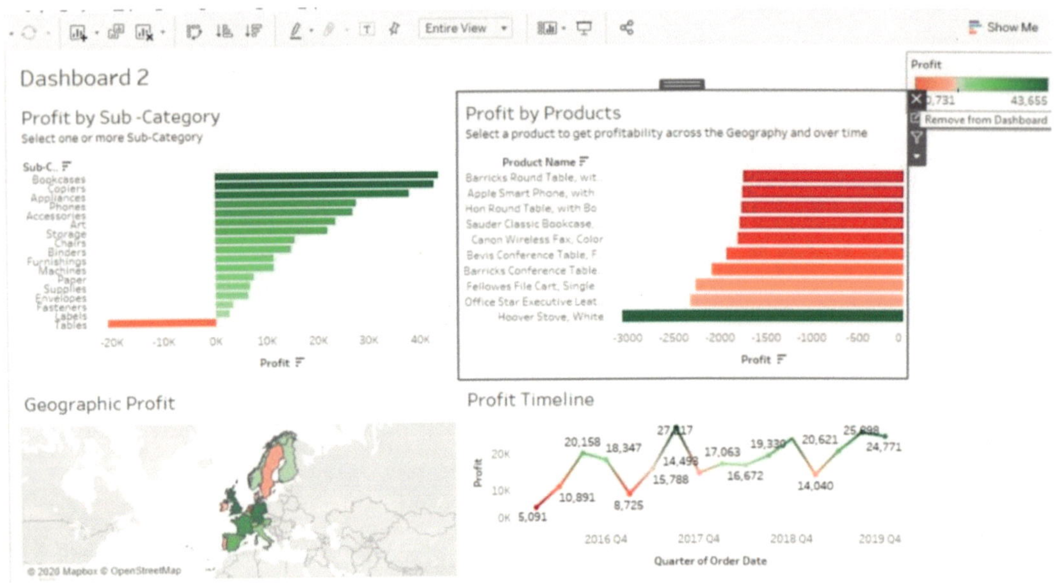

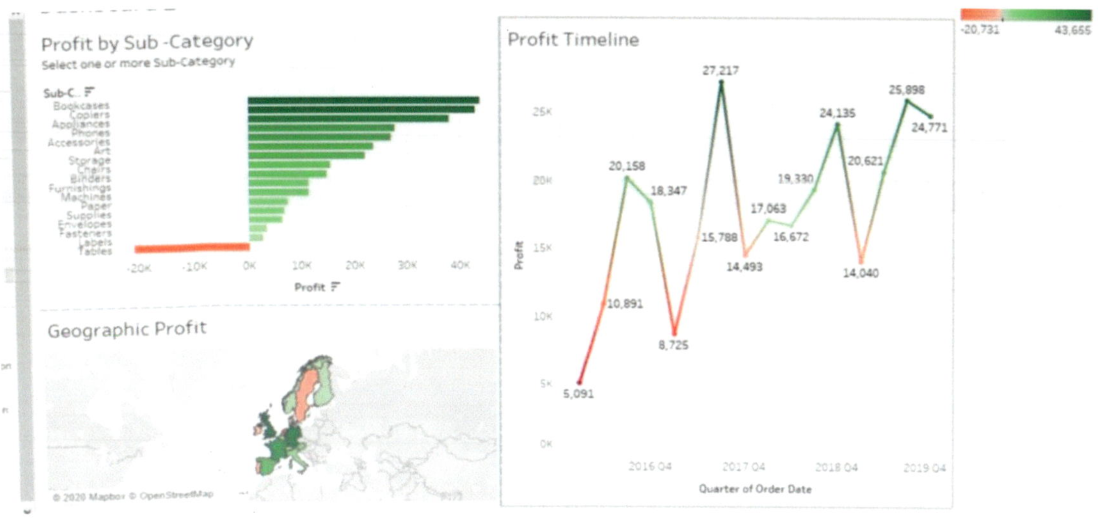

Note: The application of the icons displayed on the top right corner of the highlighted box

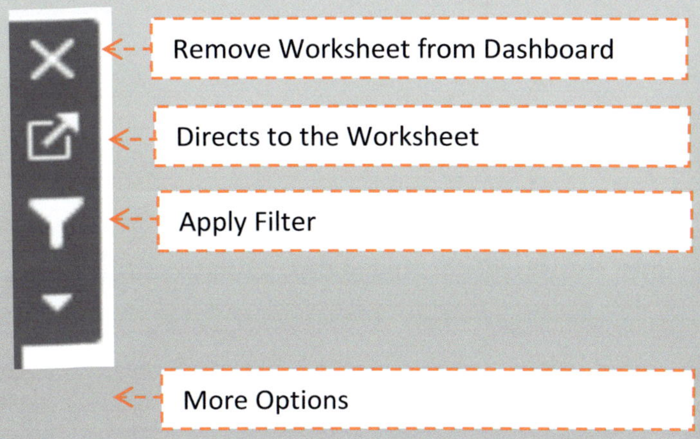

12.1 Filters

- Filters can be dynamically applied using different options. Some examples include:
  - Infographics
  - URL actions
  - Highlight actions

12.1.1 Using infographics as Filters

- Images can be used as filters in dashboards.

- For the example, Category field images are used as filters in the Dashboard. Select a new worksheet. In the Marks card, select Shape and from the Data pane drag Category onto the Shapes Shelf as show below. To assign images to Categories, refer 11.1.
- Adjust the size of the images using the size shelf on the Marks card.

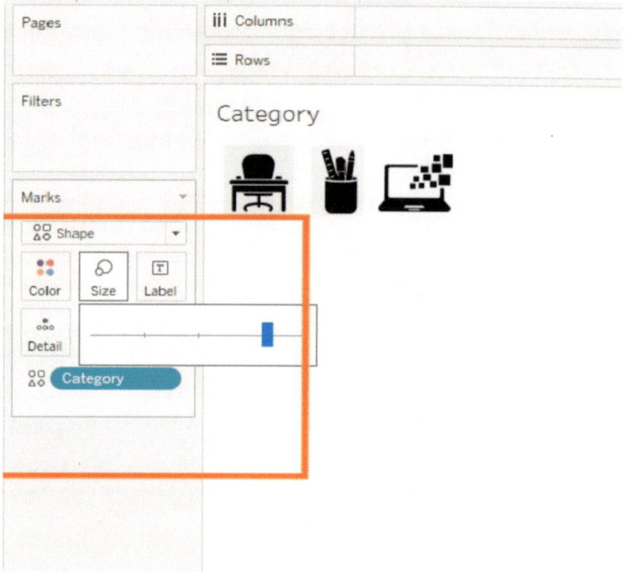

- Return to the Dashboard and drag the newly created sheet, category onto the Dashboard as seen below.

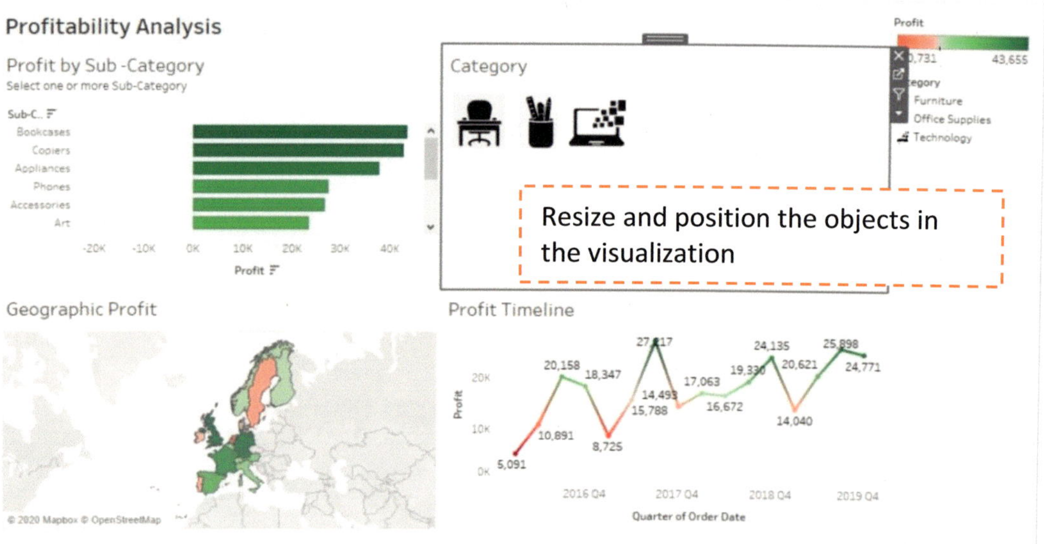

➢ To select infographics as filter, select the object in the dashboard, Category. Category gets highlighted with grey box. On top right corner of the selected object, click the dropdown arrow (below the funnel icon) and select **Use as Filter**. Filter gets applied to all the object in the Dashboard.

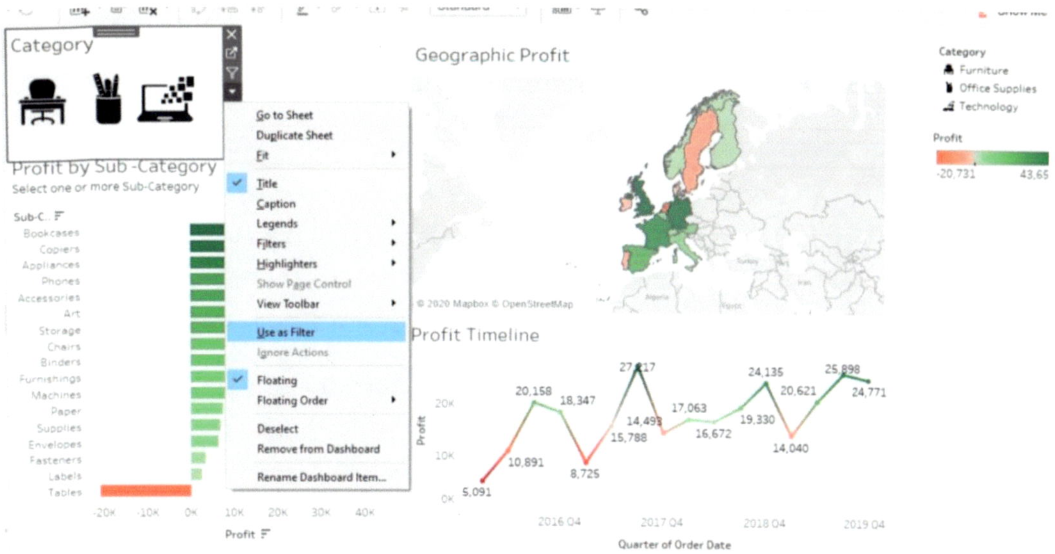

Alternative method to use Category as Filter: Select Category >Click on the Filter icon which appears on the top right corner of the highlighted object.

➢ Filter the data for Office supplies by clicking on the office supply icon.

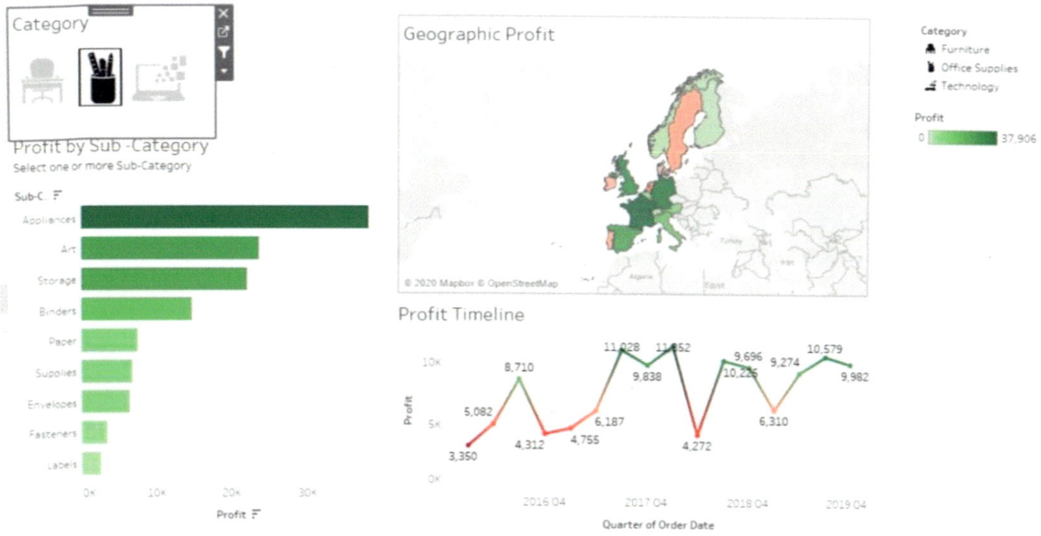

Observation: When office supply is selected to filter data, the data shown in all the other views reflects data under office supply.

- To remove the applied filter, click on the Filter icon on the top right corner of the Category sheet.

12.1.2 Applying filters on Objects in Dashboard

- Select the object, Product Sub-Category and click on the Filter icon to apply.
- Select Tables bar in the Sub-Category and observe the changes reflected in the rest of the objects.

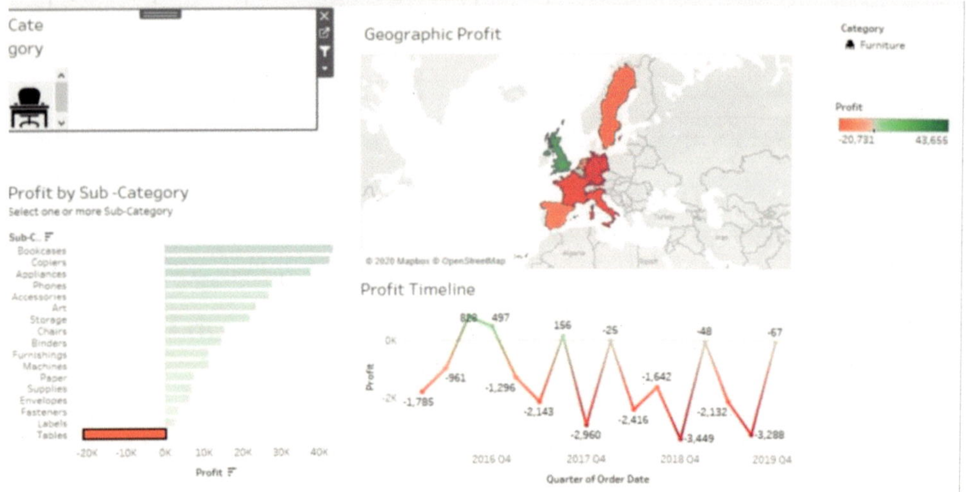

Observation: If Table is selected from the Profit by Sub-Category

In Category object: Only the Furniture Category is Displayed

In Geographic map: Profit of Tables across the country is displayed. From the map we can infer tables are profitable only in the UK and rest of Europe it is a loss.

12.2Actions

- Dashboard actions add context and interactivity to the data. The actions are filtering, highlighting, URL etc.

12.2.1 Filter Action

- Data from one view is used to filter data in another view.
- To apply Filter Action, use the view used in Section 12.1.2 and remove all the filter applied.

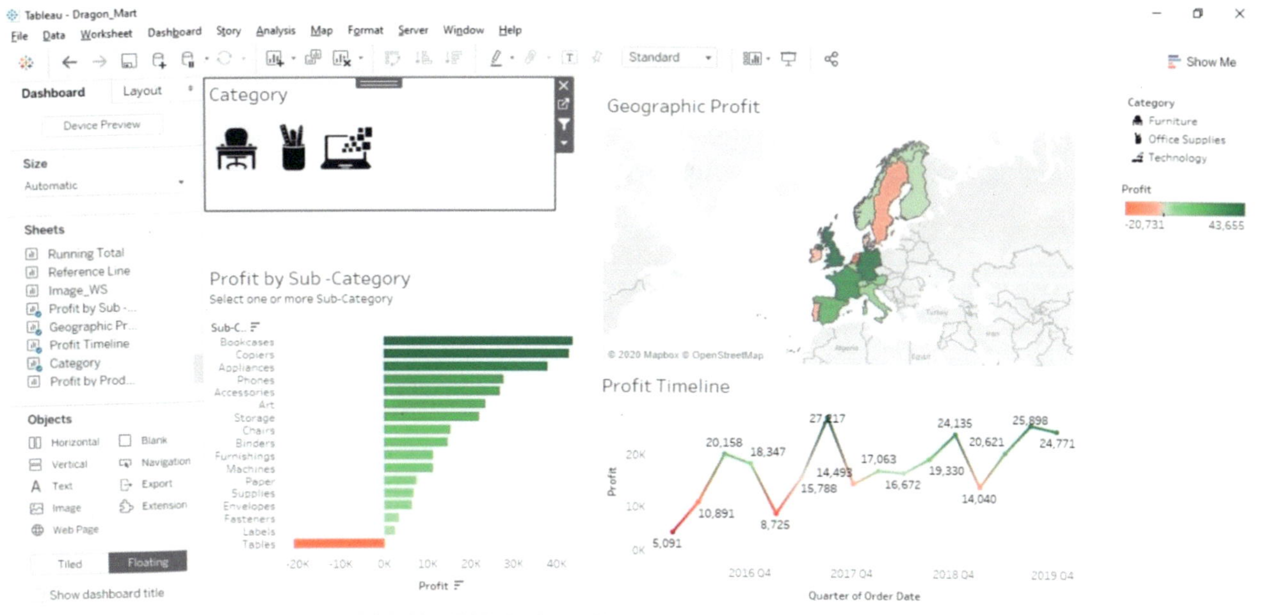

- On top menu, select Dashboard, from the drop-down menu click Actions as shown below.

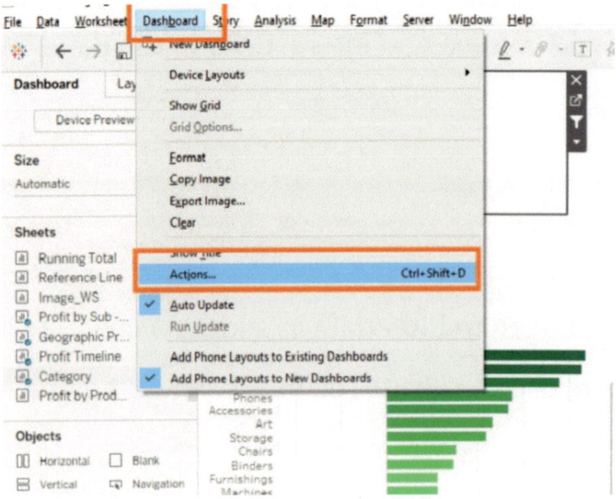

- Actions dialog box appears. In the Actions dialog box, click Add Action, select Filter

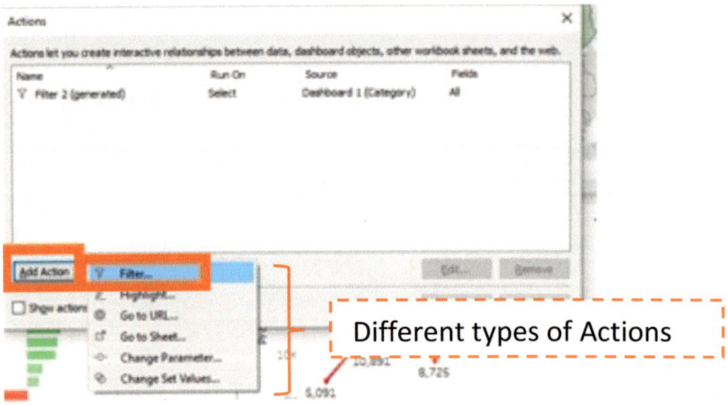

➢ Add Filter Action dialog box appears. Select the following options as shown below.

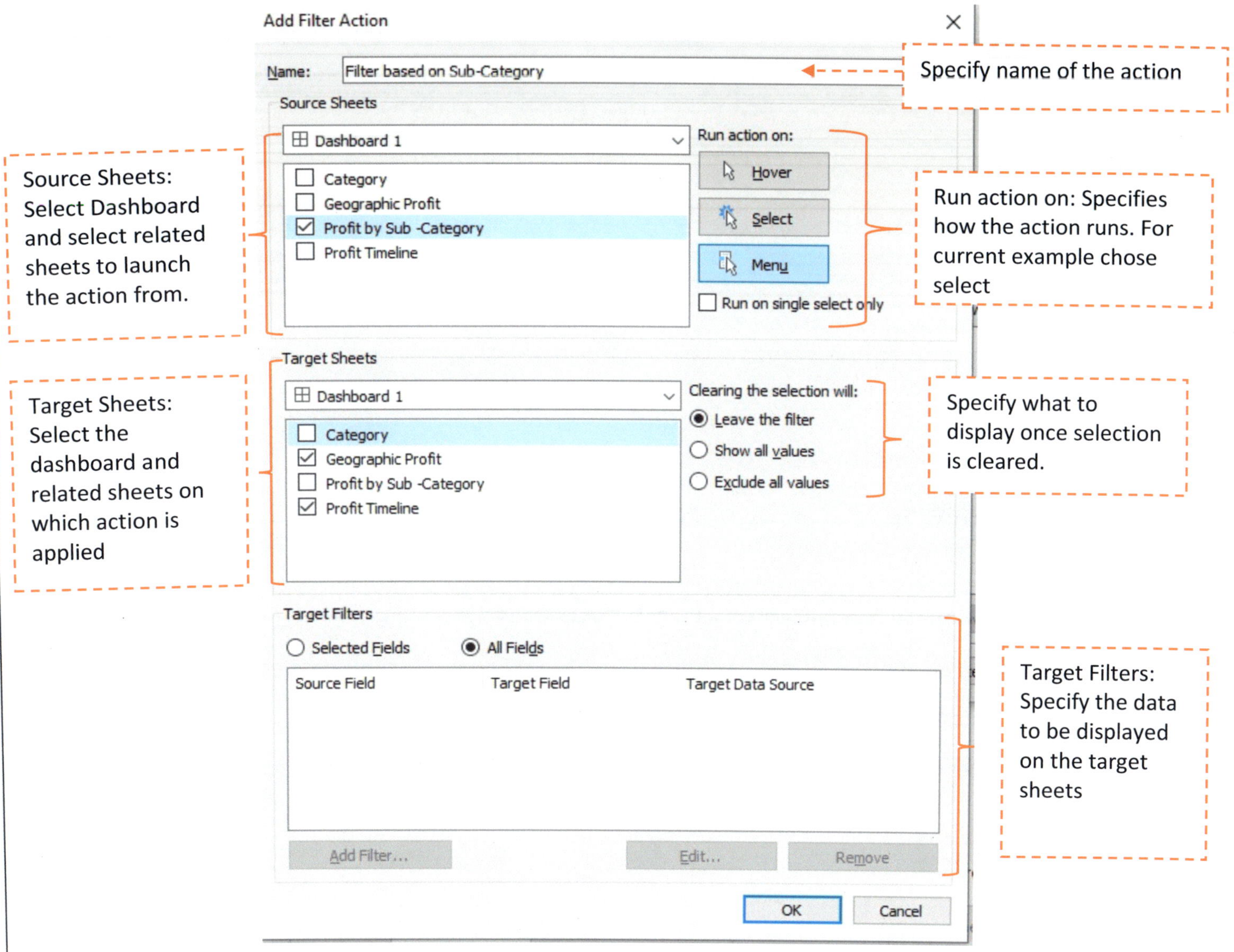

- Click Ok and the newly created filter, Filter by Sub-Category is displayed in Actions dialog box as seen below.

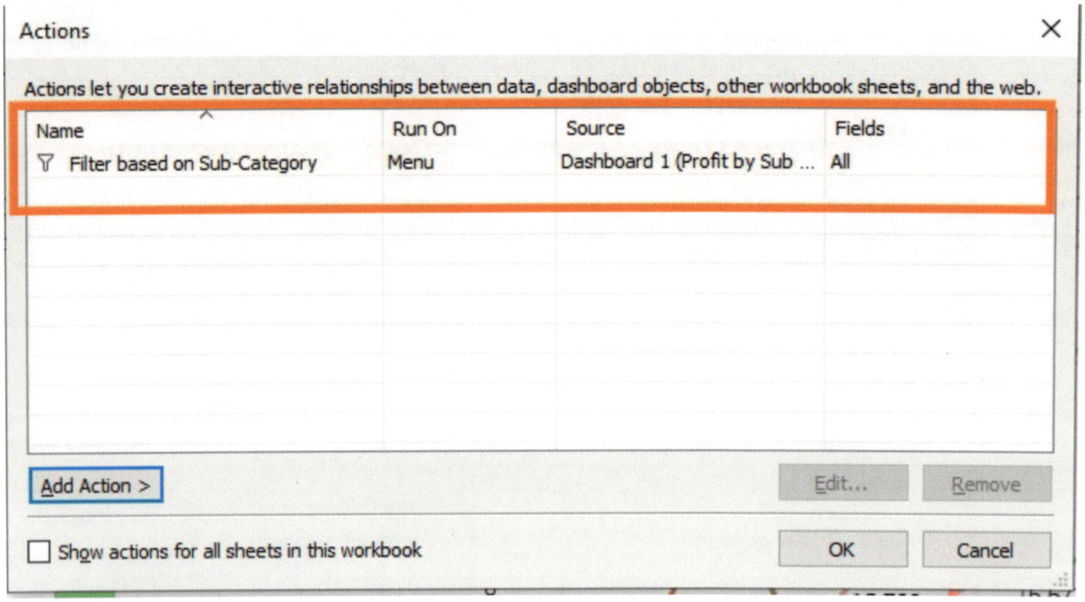

- Click Ok. On the Dashboard, select a Sub-Category (Source Sheet), Bookcase, the action is applied on geography and profit timeline (Target Sheets) to filter data corresponding to bookcase.

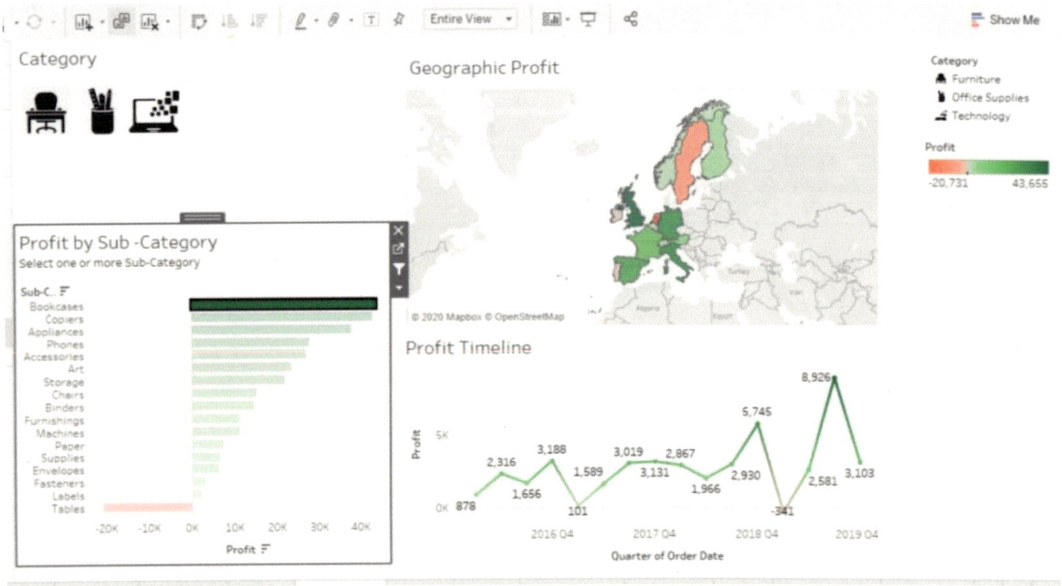

➢ To edit the Filter: Select Dashboard on the top menu bar, Select Actions. In the Actions dialog box select the Filter and click on Edit. The Edit Filter action dialog box appears were the necessary changes can be made.

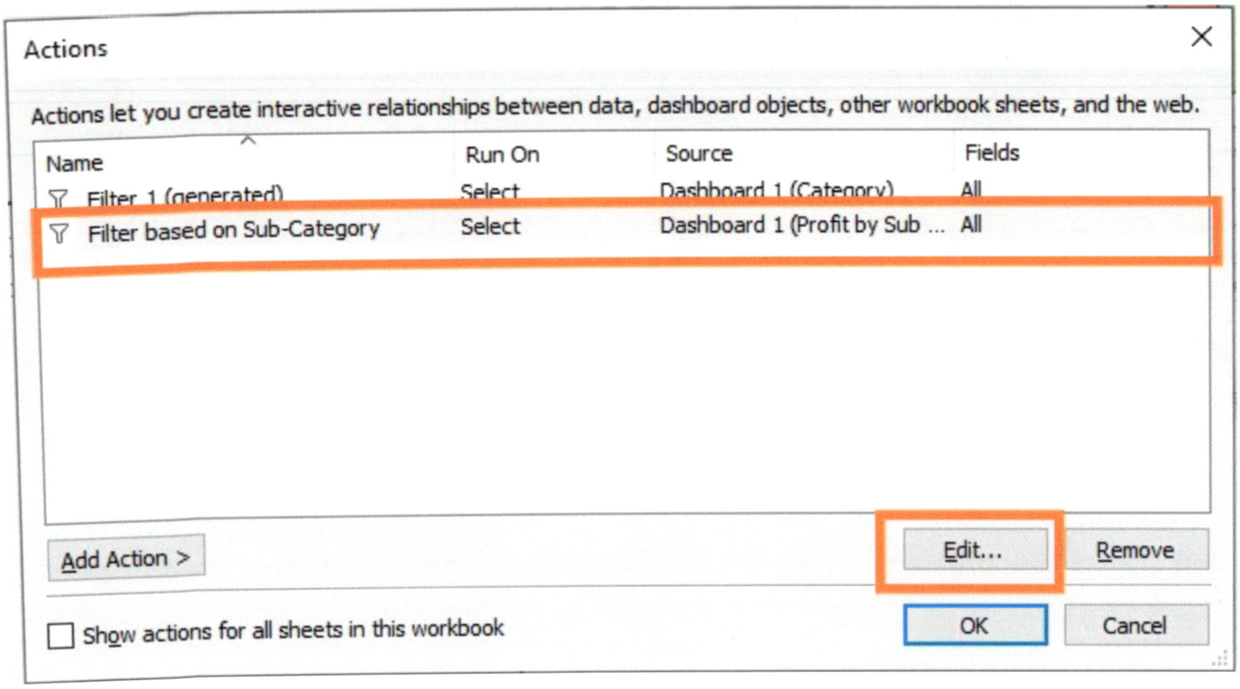

➢ For Quick Access Filter application refer 12.1. The Filters applied using quick access is also displayed in the Actions dialog box.

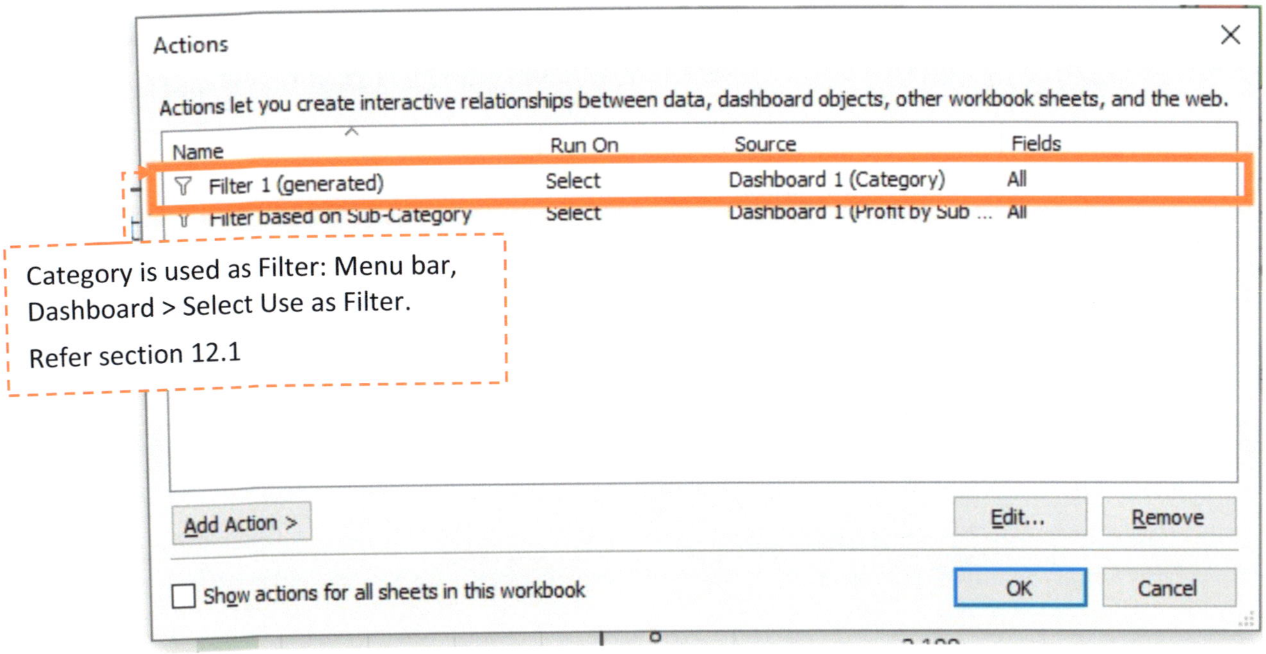

➢ Observe the data displayed in Dashboard when you select Furniture in Category, from the subcategory select Tables and observe the changes reflected in the rest of the two views.

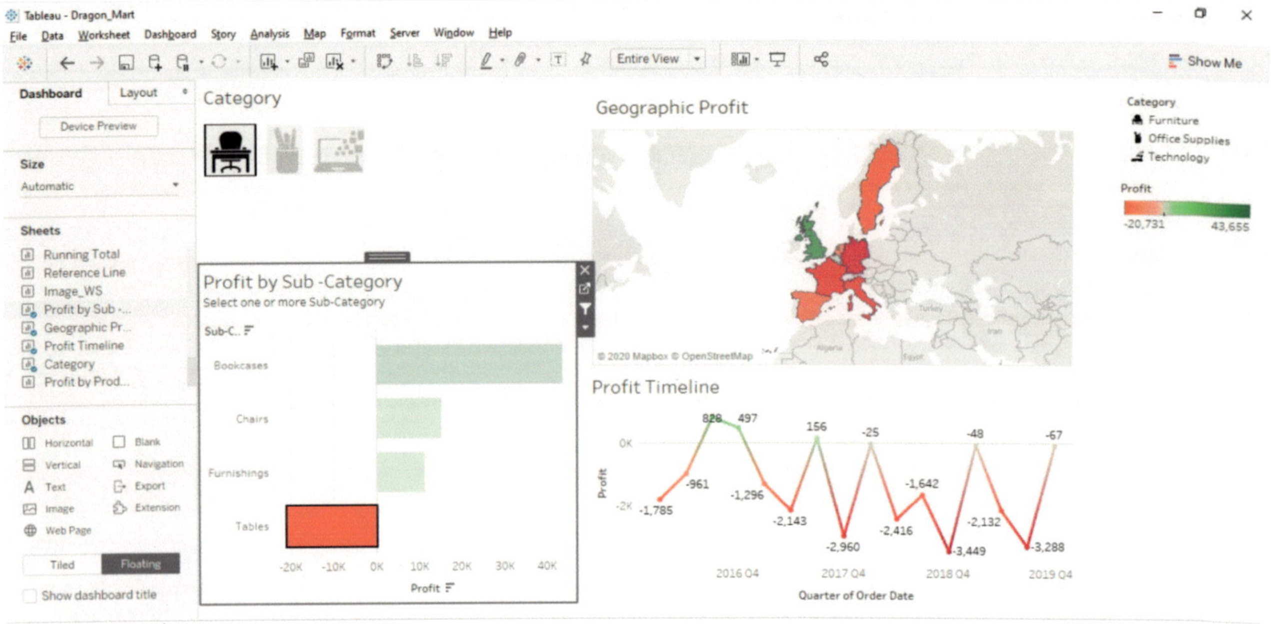

12.2.2 URL Action

➢ URL action is a hyperlink that points to a web page, file, or other web-based resource outside of Tableau.URL actions can be used to create an email or link to additional information the data.

➢ To open web page with URL action, from the Top menu bar select **Dashboard** and select **Actions**. In the **Actions** dialog box, click **Add Action** and select **Go to URL...**.

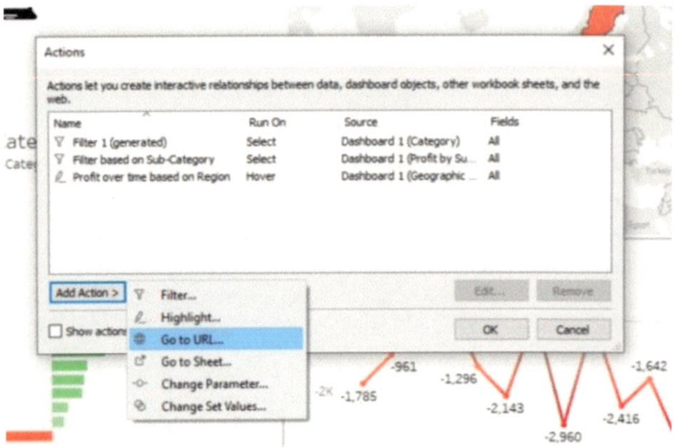

➢ Add URL action dialog box appears.

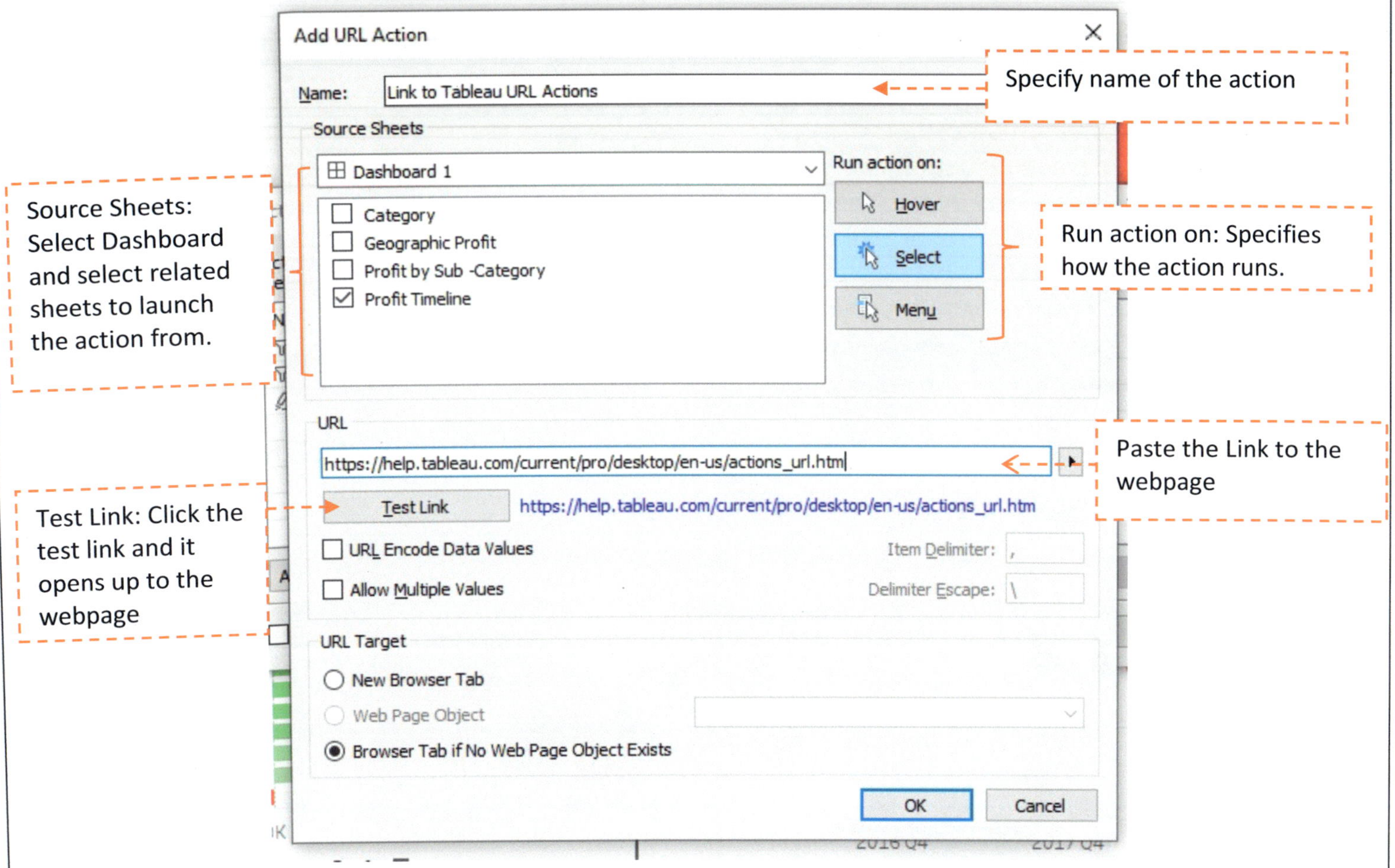

➢ Click Ok. The newly created actions, Link to Tableau URL Actions is displayed in Actions dialog box.

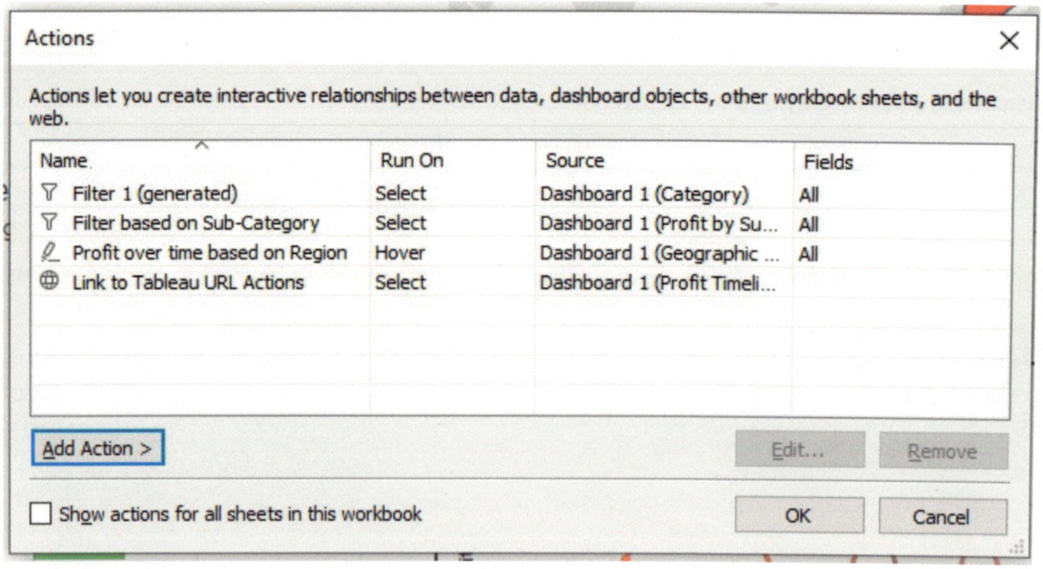

➢ In the dashboard, in Profit Timeline, click on one of the profit points, the Tableau URL Actions page opens up as seen below.

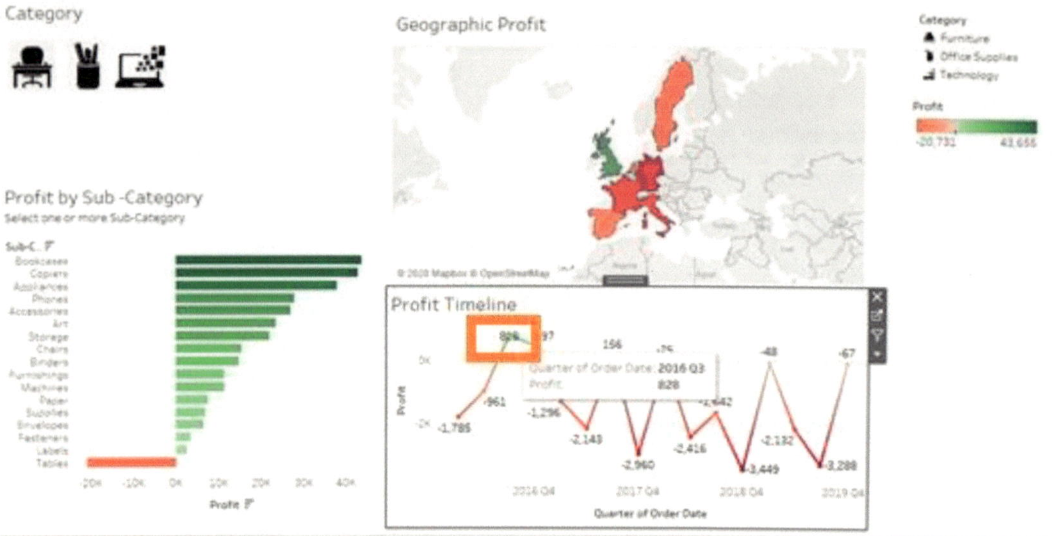

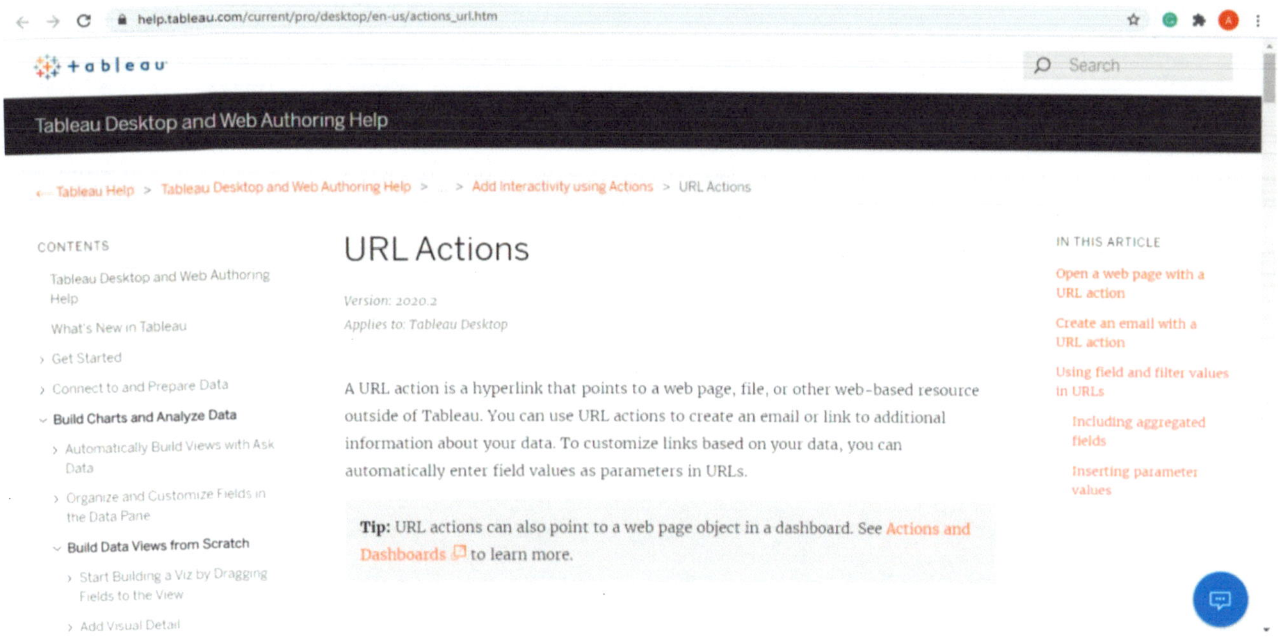

- To edit the URL action: Select Dashboard on the top menu bar, Select Actions. In the Actions dialog box select the URL and click on Edit. The Edit URL action dialog box appears were the necessary changes can be made.

12.2.3 Highlight Action

- Highlight actions calls to attention specific marks of interest by coloring the specific marks and dimming all others.
- For an example of highlight action, create the dashboard below. The Discount Dashboard contains sheets from Section 8.9 (scatter plot to compare the Sales to profit across different categories and Regions; S8.9-ScatterPlot in the Tableau Solution file) and Section 13 (Avg discount based on Category and Sub-Category across 4 years; S13-AvgDiscount in the Tableau Solution file) as shown below.

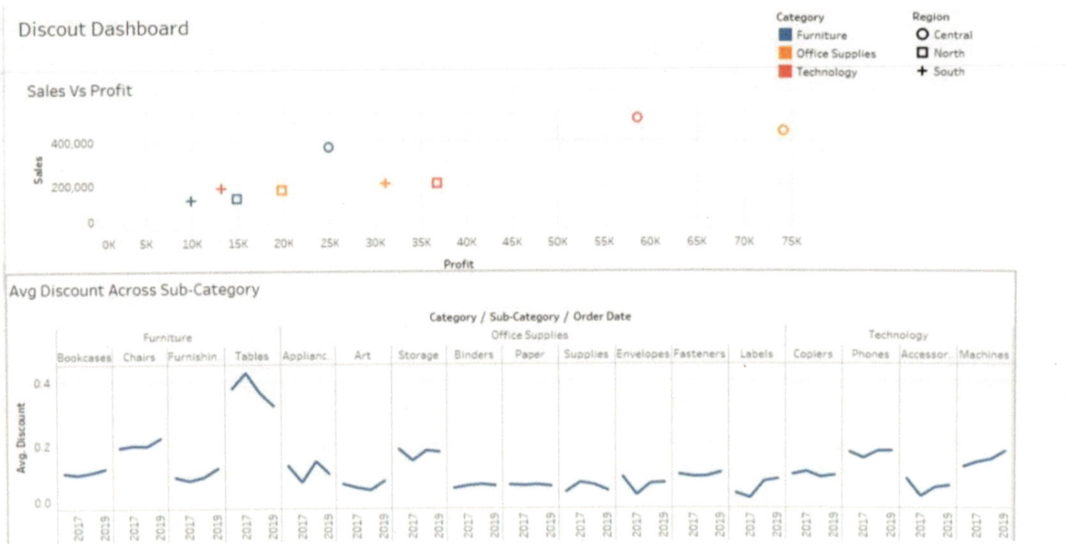

➢ To apply highlight action to Dashboard, On the top menu bar select **Dashboard** > **Actions**. In the Actions dialog box, select Add **Action** > **Highlight**.

➢ In the Actions dialog box, click Add Action and select Highlight.

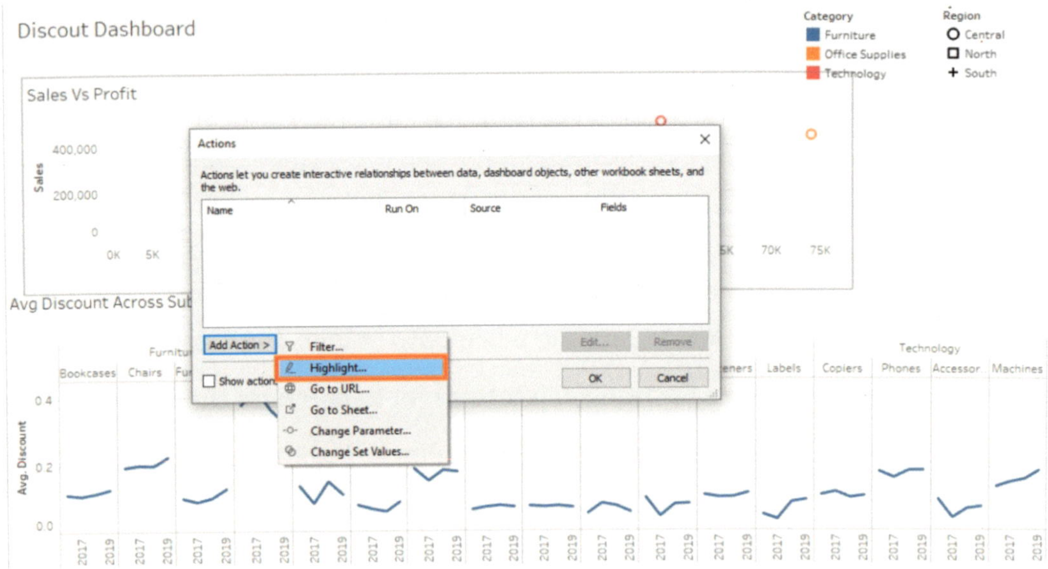

➢ Add Highlight Action dialog box appears. Select the options as shown below

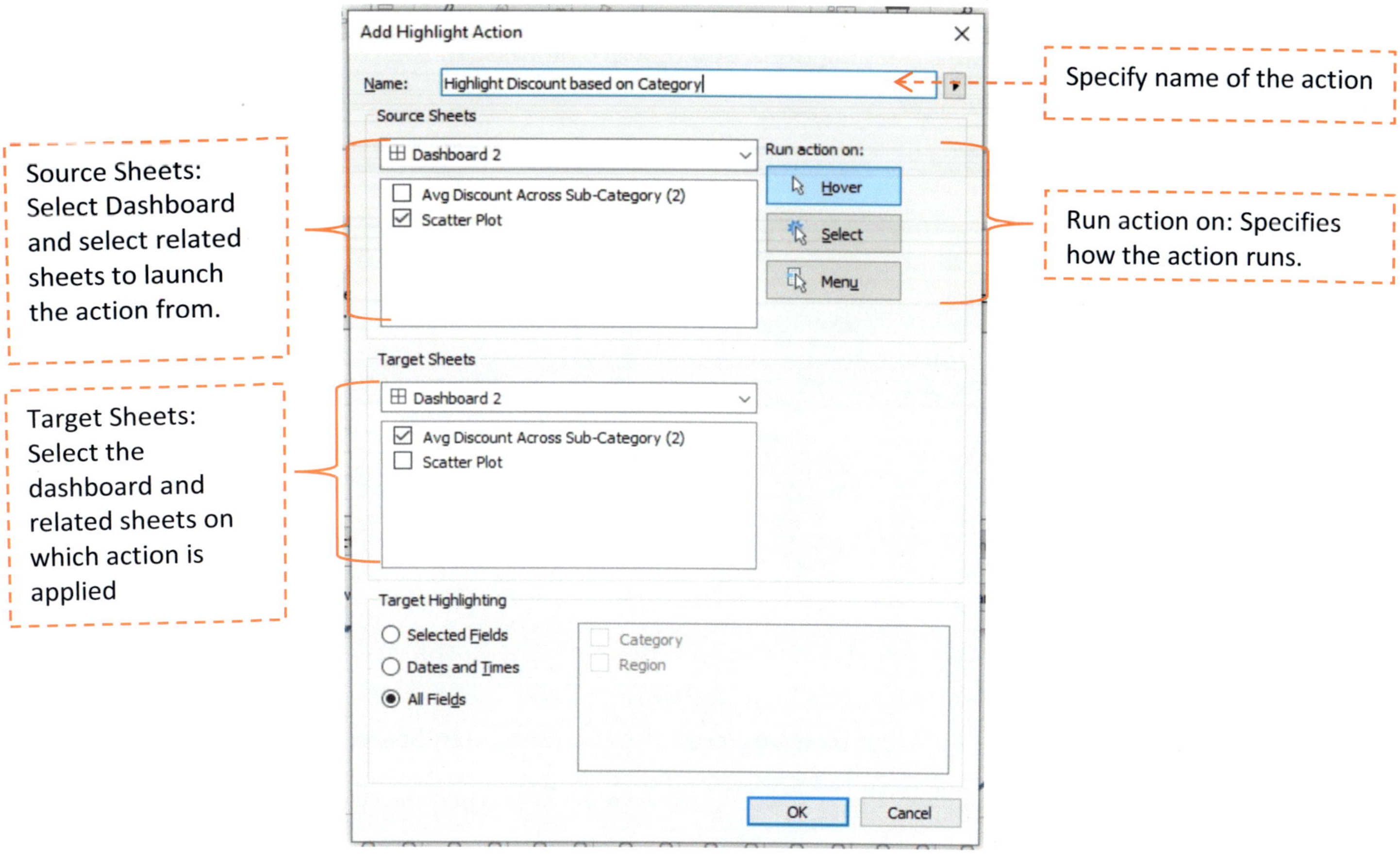

➢ In the Actions dialog box, the newly created highlight is visible as seen below.

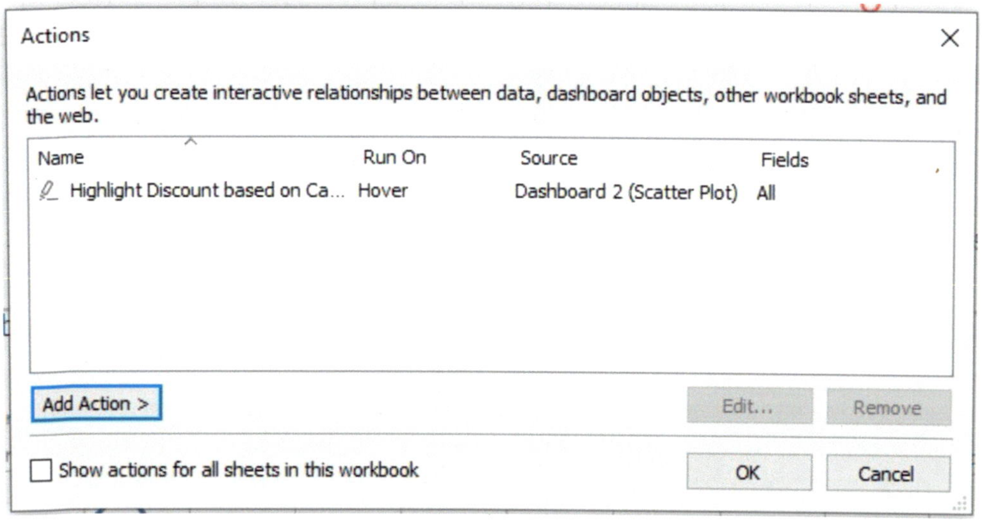

- Click Ok. In the Dashboard, in the Sales Vs Profit view, hover over Furniture, the Avg Discount for Furniture is highlighted, and rest are dimmed in the Discount view as seen below.

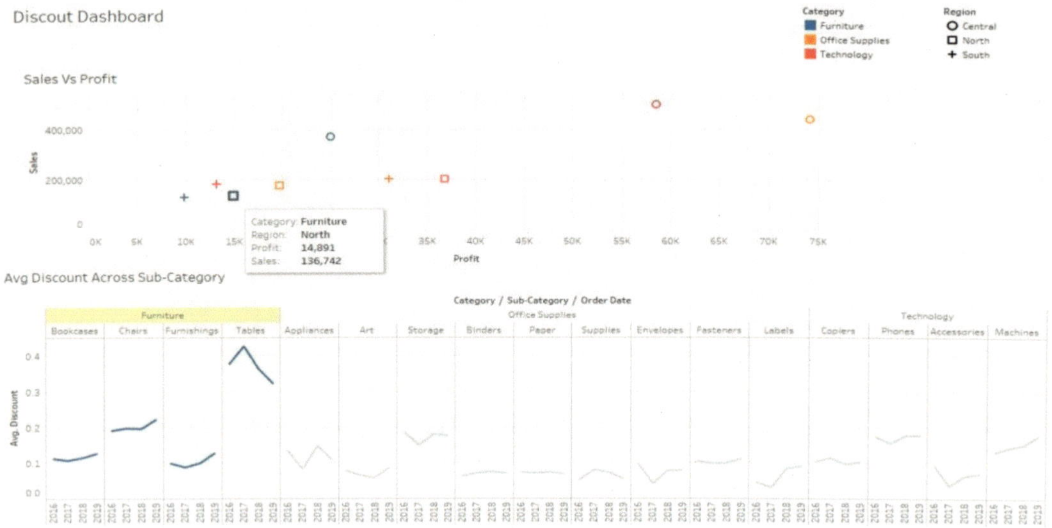

- To edit the Highlight: Select **Dashboard** on the top menu bar, Select **Actions**. In the Actions dialog box select the **Highlight** and click on **Edit**. The Edit Highlight action dialog box appears were the necessary changes can be made.

13 Creating Stories

- A story in Tableau is a sequence of visualizations, Worksheets or Dashboard that work together to provide context and better enable decisions making based.
- For example, create a story analyzing the negative profit of Tables (a Sub-Category of Furniture). To create the story based on the global performance of Dragon Mart, create the below four sheets.
  - Profit based on Category and Sub-category: SUM(Profits) in Columns, Category and Sub-Category in Rows, SUM(Profit) in Color marks, and SUM(Profit) in Filters (with 'Range of values' selected and Show: Only Relevant Values).
    - Sheet S13-Profits in the solution file.

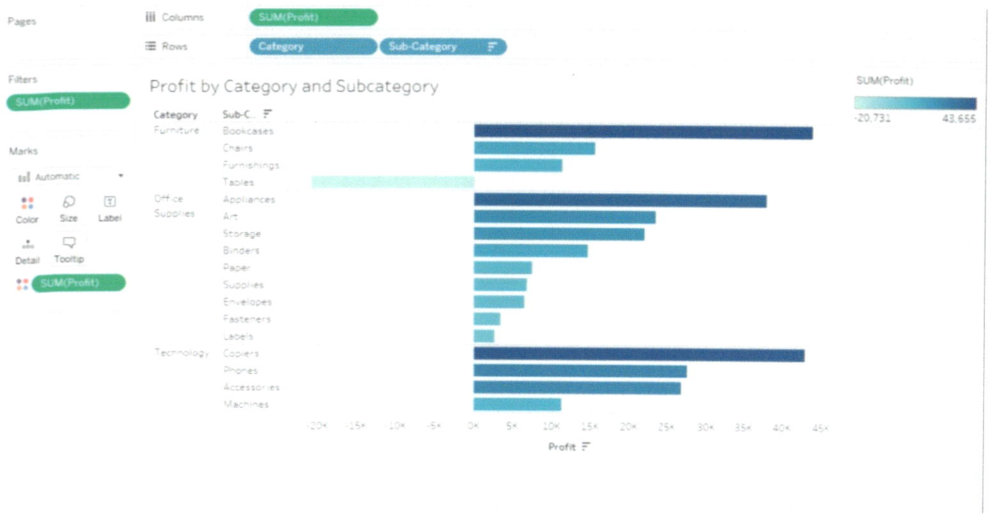

  - Profit and Sales based on Category and Sub-Category: SUM(Profit) and SUM(Sales in Columns, Category and Sub-Category in Rows, SUM(Profit) added to Color marks, and SUM(Sales) added to Color marks.
    - Sheet S13-PandSC in the solution file.

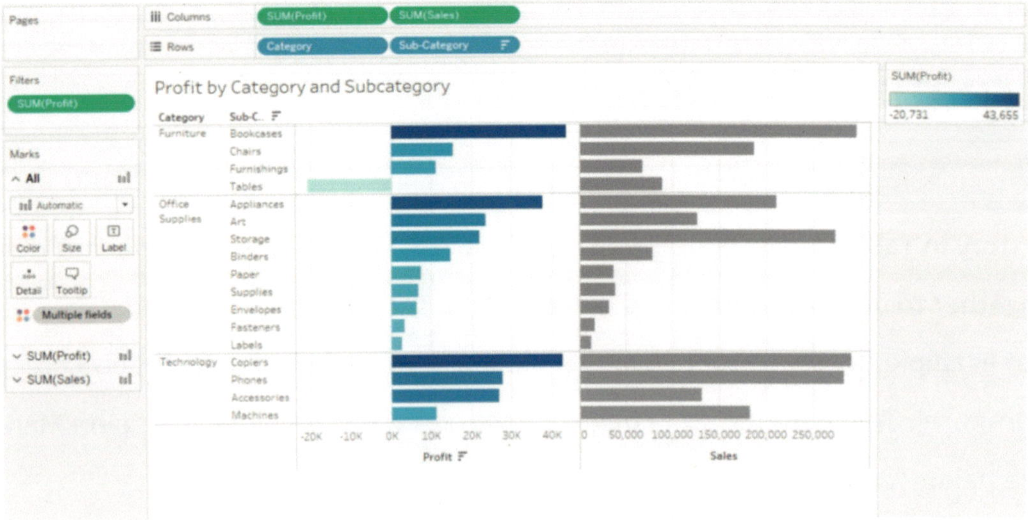

- Avg discount based on Category and Sub-Category across 4 years: Category, Sub-Category, and Year(Order Date) added to Columns, and AVG(Discount) added to Rows.
  - Sheet S13-AvgDiscount in the solution file.

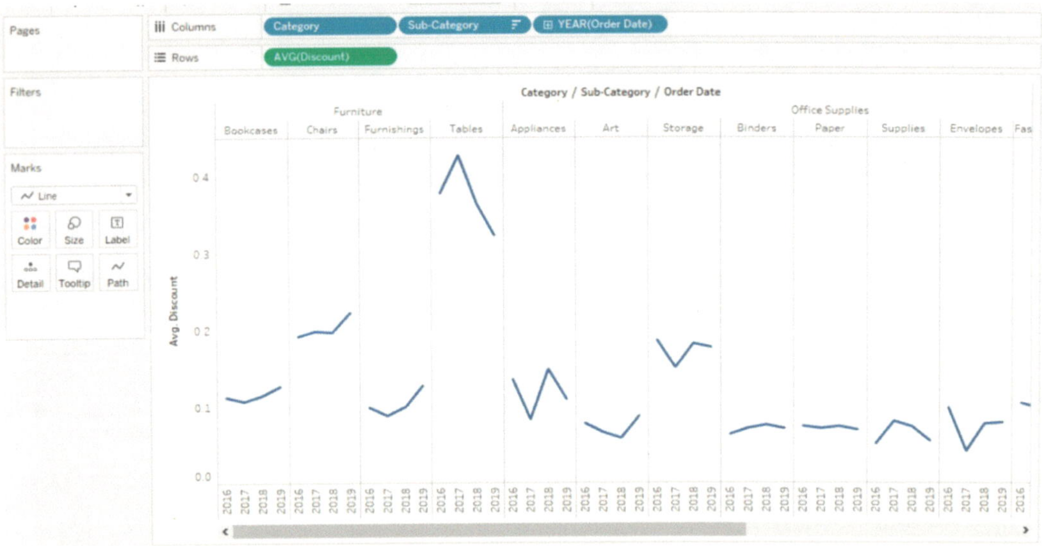

- View of Profit, Sales and Discount for each Sub-category: SUM(Profit), SUM(Sales), and AVG(Discount) added to Columns, and Category and Sub-Category added to rows. Mark colors are added to all dimensions in Columns.
  - Sheet S13-PSDSubCat in the solution file.

- Click on the New Story button at the bottom right corner.

- Tableau Storyboard opens up as seen below.

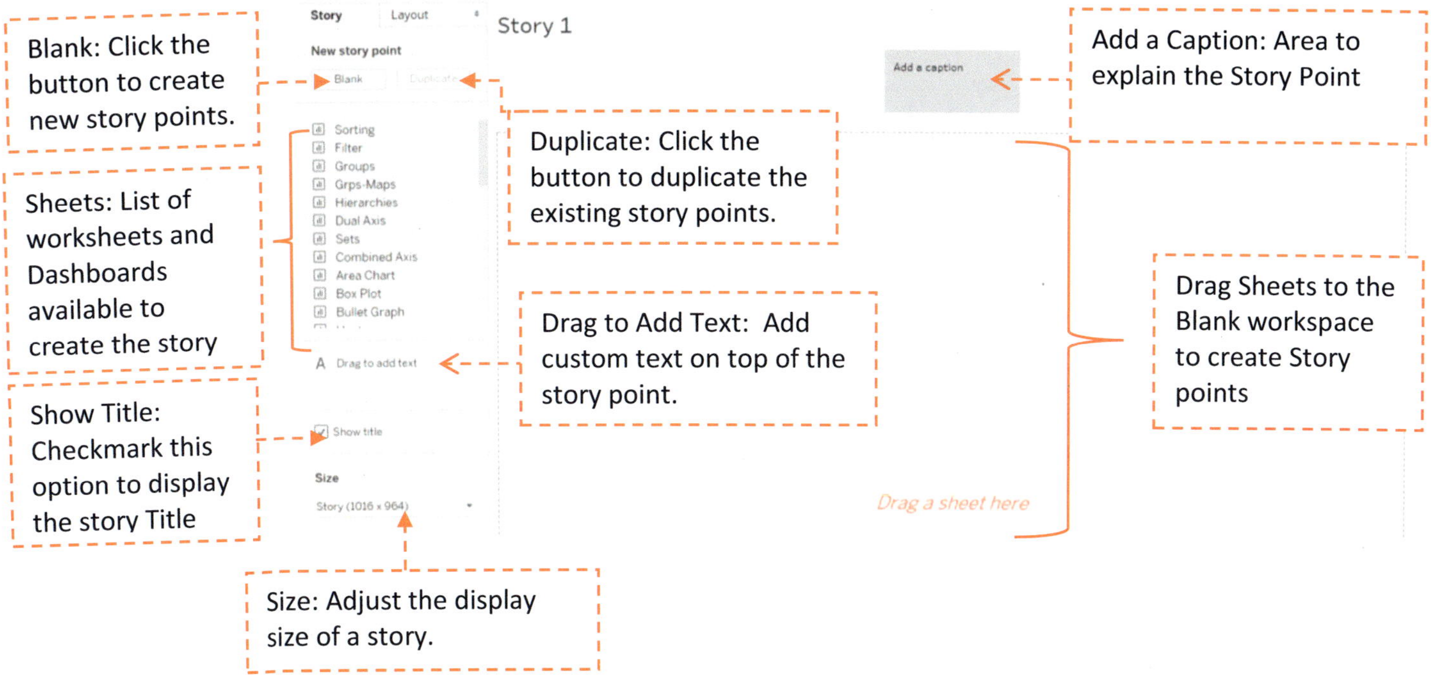

- Story title by default is the sheet name. To edit it, right click the sheet tab and choose Rename Sheet or double click on the title and enter **Dragon Mart Global Performance**.

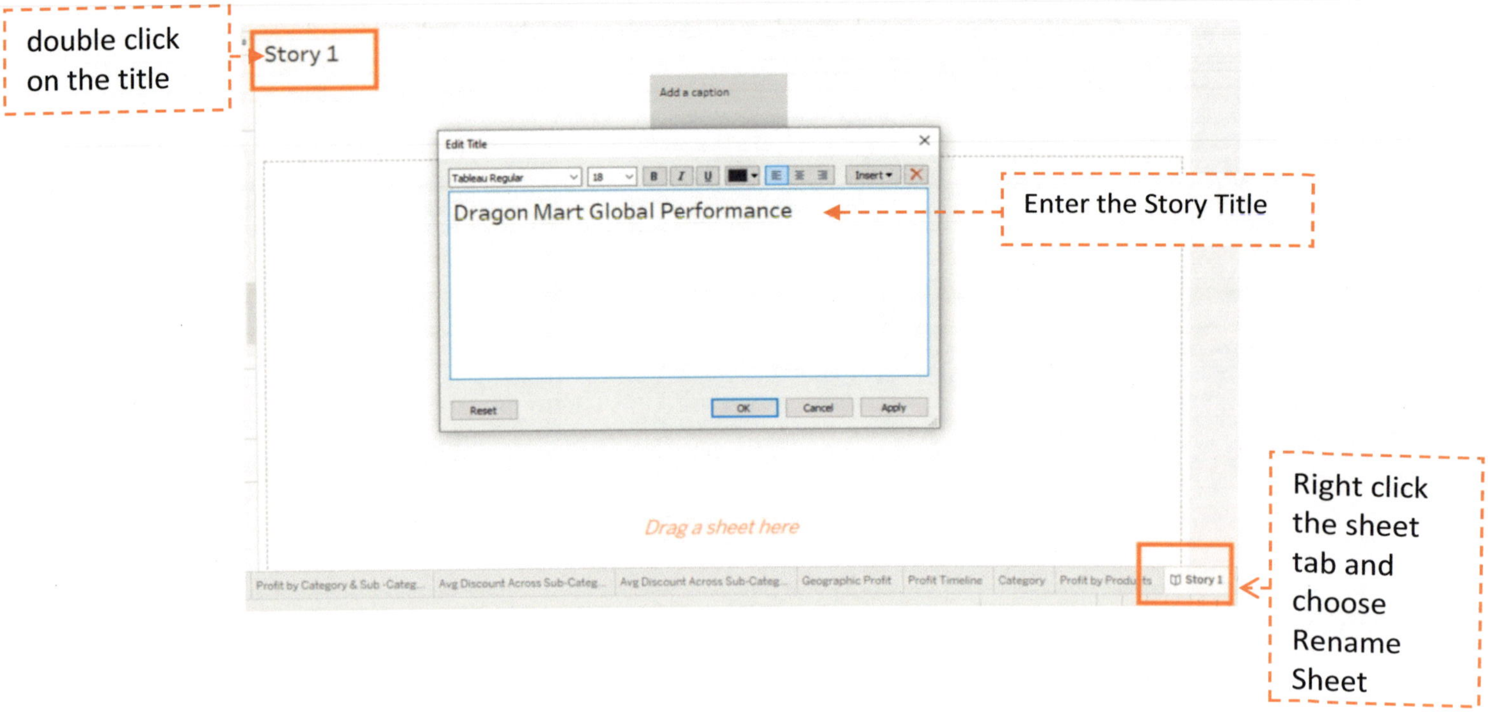

- To build the story, double click on the sheet Profit by Category (Sheet S13-Profits in the solution file) on the left or drag the sheet onto the story point as shown below.

Note: Sheets added to the story point remains connected to original sheet. The changes made in the original sheet is reflected on the story points.

- Summarize the story point by clicking Add a caption as shown below.

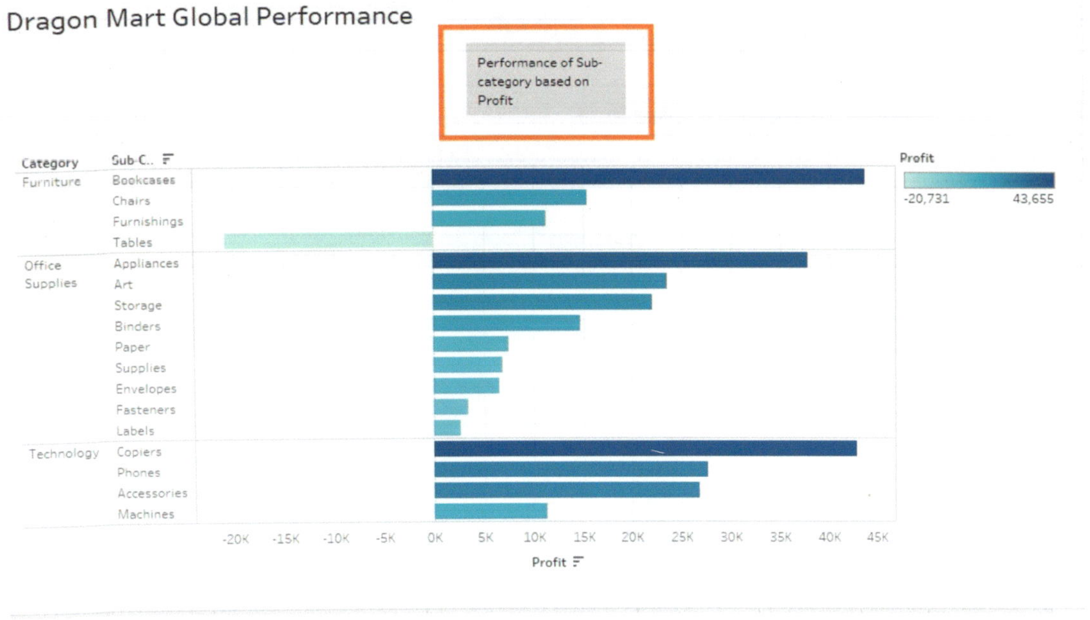

➢ When mouse hovers over the caption box, 4 buttons are displayed on top of the caption box as seen in the below screenshot.

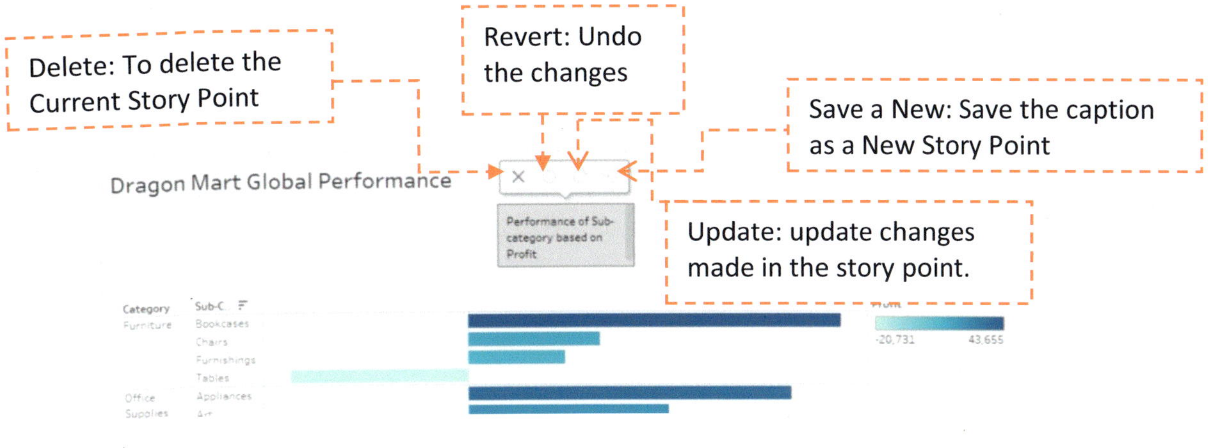

➢ Another Story point is added by clicking on the blank button in the story pane on the left-hand side. Double click or drag sheet Profit and sales of Sub-Category from the Sheets tab (Sheet S13-PandSc in the solution file) in the Story pane on to the newly created story point as shown below.

Add caption to newly created story point

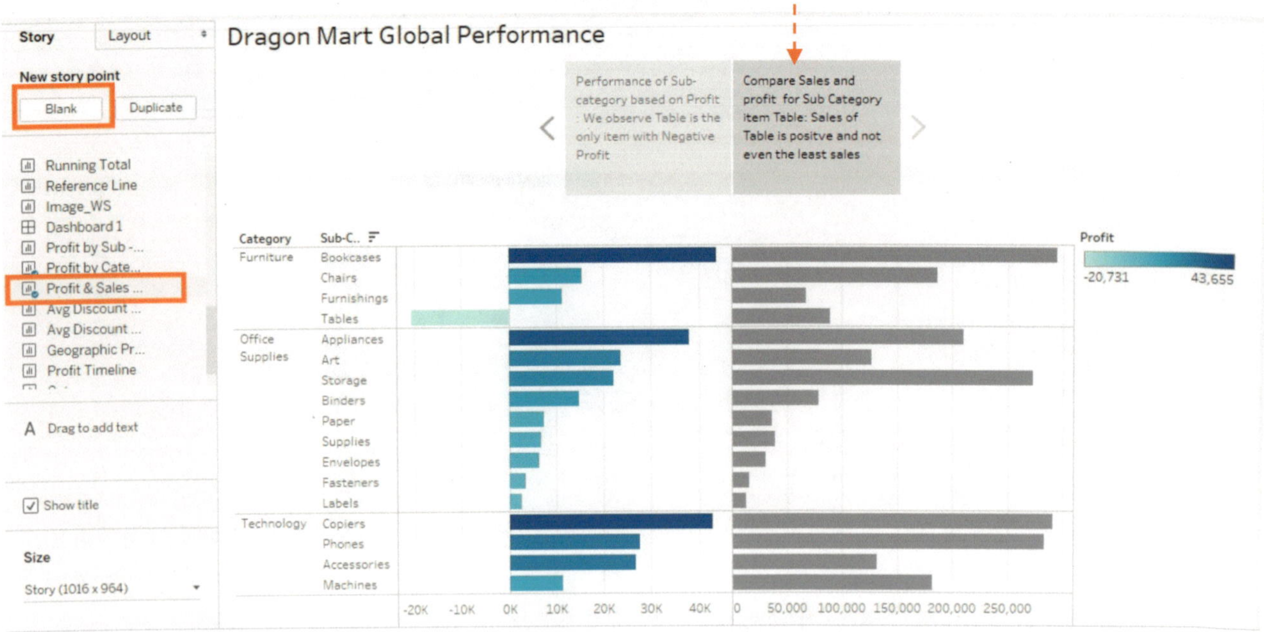

- Highlight Profit and sales of Tables, by clicking on the Profit bar and selecting the update button as shown.

Update the selection by clicking on update button

Highlight Profit and Sales of Filter

- Add the remaining two sheets as story points (sheets S13-AvgDiscount and S13-PSDSubCat in the solution file) in a similar manner with the captions as shown below.

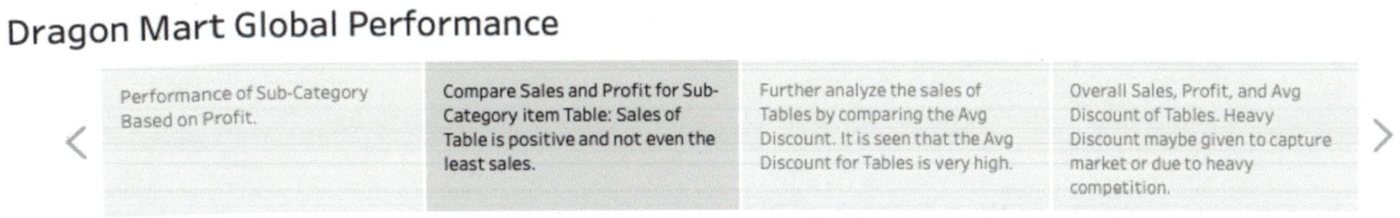

- Resize caption: As seen in the example, sometimes text in the caption may not fit in the navigator. In this case, in the navigator, select a caption and resize the captions. All captions in the Navigator update to the new size.

PLEASE NOTE

The arrow key on either side of the captions act as a navigator to move from one Story Point to the next or back.

Present the story by clicking on the Presentation mode button  on the toolbar.

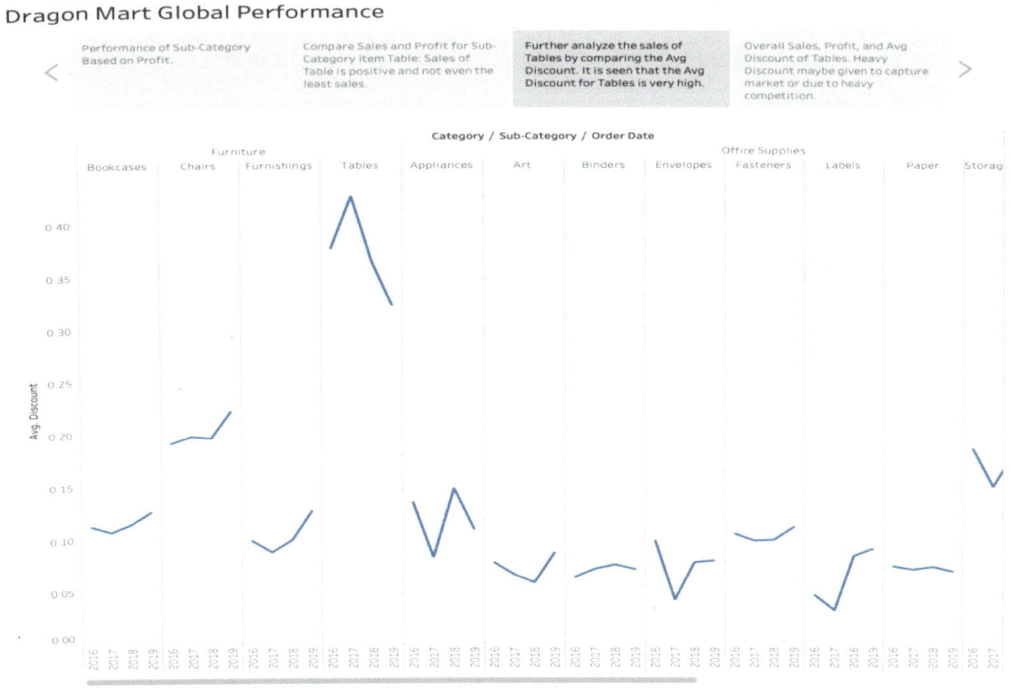

PLEASE NOTE

To step through the story, click the arrow to the right of the story points.

To exit Presentation or Full Screen mode, press Esc.

14 References

- Tableau Desktop and Web Authoring help
  https://help.tableau.com/current/pro/desktop/en-us/gettingstarted_overview.htm
- Tableau Resources
  https://public.tableau.com/en-us/s/resources
- Tutorial Gateway
  https://www.tutorialgateway.org/
- Mind Majix
  https://mindmajix.com/tableau
- Data Flair
  https://data-flair.training/blogs/tableau-tutorial/
- EDUCBA
  https://www.educba.com/data-science/data-science-tutorials/tableau-tutorial/
- Tutorials point
  https://www.tutorialspoint.com/tableau/index.htm
- Evolytics Analytics
  https://evolytics.com/blog/tableau
- General Assembly blog
  https://generalassemb.ly/blog/designing-dashboard-tableau-business-intelligence/
- Tableau Actions overview
  https://vizualintelligenceconsulting.com/blog-tableau-actions-overview/
- Pluralsight
  https://www.pluralsight.com/guides
- Interworks
  https://interworks.com/blog

ISBN: 978-0-6489304-1-9

Made in the USA
Las Vegas, NV
03 November 2026

57423042R00109